REVISED A̶N̶D̶ ̶E̶X̶P̶A̶N̶D̶E̶D̶

New: Group discussion questions at the end of each chapter

Every chapter revised and expanded

Brand new chapter on the War in Heaven

Brand new chapter on Theodicy (*Why does God allow suffering?*)

New: Martin's simple, effective CWP Bible Marking System

Bonus preview chapter from upcoming prequel

Recipe: World's Best Tamale Pie (you'll see why!)

"Carl flavors his writing with a unique emphasis on the warm interactions and relationships of people, real people, in heaven who will make it a place of eternal warmth and security. He provides the reader with a literary mental ladder to climb into the lofty courts of that bright land above that is engaging and transforming."

-DELBERT W. BAKER, PhD

What will it be like to "behold" the entire planet being rebuilt before your eyes? (Rev. 21:1-5)

Will we really be able to travel at the speed of a thought? (Acts 8:39-40)

Why does Christ invite you to sit with Him on His throne? (Rev. 3:21)

Explore the dazzling expanses and multiple levels of a giant city larger than Oregon, built by Christ Himself. (Rev. 21:16)

Will we really mount up with wings as eagles? (Isa. 40:31) (and fly with giant bats!)

What will it be like to finally meet and talk with your guardian angel? (Psalm 91:11)

What happens when God — whose very words have creative power — "sings" over you with joy? (Zeph. 3:17)

Hey! Who is that active college kid there? It's YOU, in your eternal youth. (Philip. 3:21)

Join a multi-billion-member choir every week before God's throne (and sound great doing it!). (Isaiah 66:22-23)

Plunge into the refreshing, crystal-clear River of Life, which flows right through the Tree of Life. (Rev. 22:1-2)

Travel to distant worlds with your old friends... and constantly make new ones. (Heb. 1:1-2; Is. 45:18)

Satisfy the cravings of your heart with something God invented: Pleasure forever. (Psalm 16:11)

"Carl Martin is a wordsmith. An artist, really... As I settled back into my seat, I wondered half aloud **Can an aspiring Hollywood writer avoid the slick stuff? Will this have the glitzy glitter of sleazy Tinseltown? Or speak to my heart?...** Carl's words began to work on me. I was in for a pleasant journey full of spiritual surprises...

"Carefully and painstakingly researched and backed up with solid Scripture. Its pages read almost like a modern prophet."

-E. LONNIE MELASHENKO,
CHRISTIAN RADIO BROADCASTER

"I found the combination of Biblical statements and facts and Martin's vivid imagination of Heaven delightful... I highly recommend it to anyone who thinks about Heaven as a real place."

-DR. WILLIAM DYSINGER, SPEAKER: SafeTV,
AUTHOR, *HEAVEN'S LIFESTYLE TODAY*

HEAVEN

HEAVEN

Think On These Things

CARL MARTIN

G4G Press
Chattanooga, Tennessee
U.S.A.

G4G Press produces exceptional nonfiction books that inform and inspire.
Sold in quality bookstores everywhere.

ISBN-13: 9780615608280
ISBN-10: 0615608280

All texts taken from the
Authorized King James Version

G4G Press
6103 Lee Highway #302
Chattanooga, TN 37421
G4Gpress.com

For Coleen:
My girlfriend, best
friend and wife.
Still making my world
a little bit of heaven.

In loving memory:

Piper Marie Ivins
1964 - 2011
Who insisted her husband, Stanley read portions
of this book to her over and over

Brenda Lee Crawford
1963 - 2016
Who told her mother,
Judith this was her very favorite book

AUTHOR'S NOTE

The events described in this book pertain to both heaven and the new earth, and the terms are used interchangeably. Chronologically speaking, they all take place after the great Resurrection at the Second Coming. Christians have long debated what happens on earth during the "one thousand years" spoken of in Revelation 20 (commonly referred to as "the Millennium"). Although the Bible explains itself and will make the truth known to all who study prayerfully and with a teachable spirit (John 7:17; 16:13; 8:32), we do not address the issue in this writing. The chapters entitled "Strange Fire" and "Behold All Things New" cover events occurring just after the Millennium, when the New Jerusalem (heaven) comes down to earth (Rev. 21:1-2), but otherwise, little mention is given to the subject. I highly recommend the BibleSchools.com Bible studies for anyone who wishes to learn more about this and other Bible prophecies. That there will be a new earth is confirmed by the writings of Isaiah, Peter, and John (see Isa. 65:17; 66:22; 2 Pet. 3:13; Rev. 21:1).

One area that is not comprehensively clear in the Bible is the extent of our relationships with each other in heaven and the new earth. Jesus said in Matthew 22:30 that "in the resurrection they neither marry, nor are given in marriage." His point was that if a man dies and his wife remarries, she will not necessarily have to choose one to share eternity with while breaking the other's heart. On the other hand, as one pastor put it, we shouldn't deduce that when the Lord returns He will give every happy couple their divorce papers. The fact is, we don't really have a lot of scriptural information on this issue. It is for this reason that all of the redeemed in this writing are portrayed as individuals enjoying various activities as opposed to doing so as married couples. Christ's words are clear, but we still don't know exactly how we will relate to one another in that glorious land. As Christians, we should always trust that whatever God has planned, it will be better than we can imagine. It's an understatement that no one will be disappointed when they get there.

While certain subjects herein are definitely detailed in Scripture (the dimensions of the City, the fact that we will build houses, the truth about hell, etc.) others are merely implied in Scripture. These fall into the category of "eye hath not seen" and "with God all things are possible" (flying like angels, inner space study, exploring the galaxies, etc.). In either case, the main purpose is to get the reader to understand that our God is a God of endless creativity and limitless possibilities. While we should not speculate with definite details of such activities and call them a sure thing, we need to be equally cautious renouncing them simply because "eye hath not seen." Otherwise, the mind will focus solely on earthly things and forget that God does indeed have something better, which is as real as the ground on which you stand.

Although I realize there can be value in quoting various Bible versions, I have opted to use the King James translation, for consistency. Quotes from the King James render pronouns of the Deity in lowercase. All commentary and narration render these in upper case as a gesture of reverence and respect.

I am under no delusion that I have gleaned all there is to say about the home of the redeemed. One of the things I most look forward to is seeing how far short all of my portrayals fall. However big I describe it, think bigger. However bright, think brighter. However glorious, think more glorious. No matter what image comes to mind, remember that it hasn't even entered into your heart what God has prepared for them that love Him.

TABLE OF CONTENTS

FOREWORD TO
REVISED EDITION

THE SUBJECT OF heaven is central to the believer's deepest longing. It is the affectionate core of the Christian's worldview. Yet we seldom hear of its reality and coming glory. It is the ultimate goal of the highest ambitions and loftiest aspirations of the child of God. It is the bright spot at the end of the dominion of sin and suffering. Yet so little time is spent talking of this land that will be filled with happiness and health; so little time is spent imagining and sharing what heaven will be like. This book addresses that need.

Heaven is the grand focus of the plan of redemption. Yet we give it only passing mention and even less time describing its exciting features. Heaven will be the meeting place and eternal rendezvous of the saved of all the ages. Yet members of the body of Christ spend little time talking about the relationships to be made and nurtured in that wonderful land. Heaven is the place where those who love God will finally be reunited with their loved ones who died in Christ. Yet conversations on such subjects are lacking except at funerals and cemeteries. This book addresses that need.

Heaven is fertile ground to bring cheer, inspire the heart, and make the gospel reward concrete and real. Heaven is the place where the grandest enterprises will be realized in a land that is sinless and endless. Yet sadly so often heaven doesn't receive the time and attention it deserves. Too often heaven is not prioritized, and other mundane issues occupy our attention. Thus, we miss the comfort and hope that heavenly perspectives can provide. This book addresses that need.

The author of this fascinating little volume, Carl Martin, helps to facilitate the task of imagining and realizing heaven. With a compelling style of artfully combining Bible insights with the reasonable perspectives of a sanctified imagination, the author provides the reader with a charming and elegant view into the lofty courts above.

Carl flavors his writing with a unique emphasis on the warm interactions and relationships of people, real people, in heaven who will make it a place of eternal warmth and security. He provides the reader with a literary mental ladder to climb into the lofty courts of that bright land above that is engaging and transforming.

You are invited to think on these things, to imagine heaven. You won't be disappointed.

Delbert W. Baker, PhD.,
Vice President, General Conference

FOREWORD TO FIRST EDITION

CARL MARTIN IS a wordsmith. An artist, really. When he sent me his preliminary draft for this book on "Heaven" I was eager to lay eyes on the manuscript. There was a secret reason why I was so intrigued, albeit a somewhat selfish one. I had heard about Carl and his insatiable quest to make it big in Hollywood by writing. Frankly, I couldn't wait to take the document with me aboard my scheduled airline trip en route to a speaking engagement. As I settled back into my seat, I wondered half aloud, How can someone whose life has changed so dramatically from sinner to saint handle a sacred topic like heaven? Can an aspiring Hollywood writer and producer avoid the slick stuff? Will this have the glitzy glitter of sleazy Tinseltown? Or speak to my heart?

Words have a powerful effect on our lives. And I must tell you that before I immersed myself into the third chapter of the transcripts, Carl's words began to work on me. I was in for a pleasant journey full of spiritual surprises. "This stuff reads like biblical fiction," I mused half-aloud. Fascinating. Thrilling insights! Yet carefully and pains-takingly researched and backed up with solid Scripture. Its pages read almost like a modern prophet - although Carl would be the first to vigorously deny any such categorization.

Yet, why not? That is partly what the prophetic gift is all about, isn't it? Prophecy is simply the practical exposition of Scripture in new and dynamic ways. Timely. Other-worldly. Heavenly.

I know you are busy. So was I. But you will be glad to discover that eating blueberry pie à la mode in heaven would be sheer punishment (due to lack of flavor) compared with the main course at the wedding feast which chef Jesus has in mind to serve you. Every believer in Jesus Christ will be challenged and inspired by this powerful, instructive devotional book on the eternal home of the saved.

E. Lonnie Melashenko
Moorpark, California

PREFACE

THE FEEDBACK I'VE received from countless readers of this book's first edition has been an incredible blessing to me. The emails, the letters, the stories, all made its writing worthwhile.

THE STUDY GROUPS, meeting weekly in churches and homes, eagerly discussing the realities of the world to come.

THE UNIVERSITY PRESIDENT, who, after reading it, sought me out to come and speak to two universities during a joint retreat on this fascinating subject.

THE PRISONERS, confined behind bars, sharing that they were able to escape for just a moment and journey into their newly-chosen future each time they opened its pages.

THE MASSAGE THERAPIST TO THE STARS, who eagerly shared copies of the book to various people in Hollywood's entertainment industry.

THE LOVING HUSBAND, who purchased a used copy for his terminally-ill wife, who asked him to read chapter 2 to her over and over again.

THE CAR DEALER, who gave a free copy of the book to each purchasing customer, one of whom went on to become a pastor after reading it.

THE SCHOOLTEACHER, who, after learning the book was out of print, asked for permission to photocopy the original manuscript, eager to share it with his students.

THE LOVING MOM, who had purchased it for her daughter and told me that it had been her daughter's favorite book.

The homeschoolers, homemakers, executives, and working class, the Christians of many denominations, along with the seeking (or at least curious) atheists, and folks from various other religions. These all shared with me what this content meant to them. They picked up the book with radically different backgrounds and finished it with a renewed hope in the future.

Consider this an Acknowledgement of all the people who responded positively and also a big Thank You to those who kept pushing me to get the second edition finished. You know who you are. You're the best.

FROM HOLLYWOOD TO HEAVEN

If you had told me as a young intern, sitting in a Hollywood soundstage enjoying the "dailies," that I would someday write a book on heaven, I wouldn't have believed you. Having journeyed from Tennessee to Hollywood shortly after my graduation, I was determined to make it in acting and screenwriting, but my plans had nothing to do with heaven. I share this to reassure you that if you feel you might be too attached to the world to have any interest in this subject, I can relate. I've been there. I was so determined to succeed, I remember declaring to director Ron Underwood that I would "make it," no matter what. My agent told me to try everything, so I auditioned for any commercials I could, joined acting workshops, interned for film, performed at the Comedy Store on Sunset Blvd., worked as an extra in film and music video, and similar small-time things just to get my feet wet. On the writing front, I took screenwriting courses, skipped other college classes to hang out reading screenplays at the American Film Institute, and even dabbled in writing greeting cards (I actually made some money!).

Entertainment was everything to me. Heaven? A future golden city to think about *someday*. My favorite reading was "Premiere Magazine," and my favorite movies were action films. Although an uncredited intern, I was thrilled when I got to work on the set of Kevin Bacon's hit film *Tremors* (I believe part 6 came out in 2018). Not only did it help me learn about the industry, but it opened doors to have my screenplays read. My Saturdays and Sundays were dedicated to entertainment. I lived for the movies. Studied them, dissected them, crafted them. But mostly, I loved them.

I learned much about the elements that make compelling stories and the impact – good and bad – those stories can have on individuals and society. It was during all of this that God opened my eyes and moved me in a different direction altogether. I have since found the Bible to be much more fascinating than anything Hollywood could ever produce. I haven't been to a movie theater in years, and I can honestly say, I don't miss it. One theme we revisit often in this book is that God knows more about what would make you happy than you do. It certainly proved true in my reading material, and I believe it can prove true for you, as well.

THE DELICATE BALANCE

I'm not a fan of biblical fiction. It's just not my thing. I like the Bible stories just as they read, and the idea of implanting dialogue, motives, characters and major elements of the story structure just to move the plot along is not for me; and it might even change the meaning of God's intended lesson from the story. This is one of the reasons this book takes the unusual approach of "second person" narrative, meaning every chapter unfolds with scenarios asking you to imagine experiencing the events, rather than a traditional story with developed characters and a plot line. I intentionally avoid creating actual conversations or naming characters and places, concerned that such a level of detail would move the narrative from "thinking on these things," to sitting back and watching a sci-fi unfold. This created a very fine line on which to walk: Give just enough detail to make the scenario as interesting as biblical fiction, while at the same time remaining general enough for the reader to prayerfully consider for themselves what such Bible promises might look like in the world to come (the questions at the end of each chapter give the reader a chance to do just that). My prayer is that I accomplished this and that you experience this balance as you take the following journey.

My style also leans away from visions of heaven that are basically modern lifestyles of today, transported to heavenly real estate. This is akin to merely replacing the "Twin Pines Mall" sign with a "Welcome to Heaven" sign. Much of the entertainment we are addicted to in this life would prove boring in heaven, with endless options ever before us. It is my hope that the tiny fraction of those endless options described here will whet your appetite enough to draw you into a deeper study of the treasure house of God's Word. When this happens, the entertaining distractions around us will, by contrast, begin to lose their luster.

GETTING THE MOST OUT OF THE BOOK

Each chapter concludes with five "**Thought Questions**" for individual reflection, group/pair study, or family worship:

1) **Your main takeaway** - what meant the most to you, and why
2) **A brainstorming or experience question** (often several related questions) soliciting further imaginative possibilities on the chapter topic and/or the reader's own experience
3) **Something you learned about God's *character***
4) **Something you learned about God's *promises***
5) **Something you learned about God's *will for you***

Questions 1 & 5 are designed to be answered in writing for easy future reference when reviewing the book later (feel free to write on any, though).

Questions 2-4 are mostly for open discussion or personal reflection. Question 2 is often composed of multiple elements, and for discussion, readers can choose to share just one, some, or all their responses with the group or partner, since not every question may apply to them.

CONSIDER AN ACCOUNTABILITY PARTNER

It's good to read alone, in a quiet place for deep reflection. But don't just stop there. As I've taught many corporate managers: It's always helpful to have an "accountability partner" to share your thoughts (and prayers) with, on a regular basis. This might be someone in your home or a connection via phone or Internet. Whether in pairs or as part of a group, if you want to get the most out of this reading - or *any* learning - consider at least a temporary accountability partner.

LOOK IT UP

I also recommend looking up the plethora of Bible texts referenced in this volume, and cross-reference as much as you can. There are many free online tools and phone apps available for this. The main point is, go right to the source: the Bible. Reading *about* the Bible is *in*formative. It educates you. Reading the Bible *itself* is *trans*formative. It changes you.

MARK IT UP

Have a pen or highlighter handy for underlining or highlighting as you go through this book. It will be easier to go back and find things when you want to share them with others or discuss them with your partner or group. Also, marking the referenced Bible texts will make memorizing them much easier.

ENJOY

Mostly, enjoy yourself. With so many negative things bombarding you every day, let your time in this book be *your* time - a chance to clear your mind and hit the reset button, focusing on the bright, the sunny, the positive. Pray for enlightenment as you take this journey and invite others to take the journey as well. "Taste and see that the Lord is good" (Psalm 34:8).

Your place in heaven will seem to be made for you
and you alone,
because you were made for it — made for it stitch
by stitch
as a glove is made for a hand.

— C.S. Lewis

INTRODUCTION

I ONCE HEARD AN allegory of a man who, upon arriving in heaven, was shocked as he recognized among the residents, some he had previously considered unworthy. His shock, however, soon faded when he noticed that there were others there who appeared to be even more astonished at the sight of *him* in such a holy place.

Perhaps you've never spent much time thinking about heaven because you don't find a place filled with hypocrites very appealing. This book is for you. I remember a disgruntled elderly lady once told me, regarding five other elderly women in her church: **"If they're going to be in heaven, I don't want to be there!"**

What you will find on the following pages is not what you expect. One of the things people have said they appreciate most about the book is that it is not an attempt to prove anyone wrong or cram something down their throats. It is simply an exploration of what the Scriptures tell us heaven will be like. And it pales in comparison to what the reality will be.

"KEEP OUT"?

It reminds me of another allegory where a woman kept trying to attend the local church, but they "knew things" about her and didn't think she was good enough, so they kept her out. Desperate for help, she prayed to God about the situation, to which a voice from above responded, "I understand how you feel. I've been trying to get into that same church for years."

Are you living a lifestyle that others have condemned, and feel sure that God doesn't want someone like *you* in His Kingdom? Nonsense. Of *course*, He wants you there (2 Pet. 3:9; John 3:16). His thoughts about you are too numerous to count (Ps. 139:17-18; Matt. 10:29-31). And nowhere does Scripture teach that you must change your ways *before* coming to God. Come as you are, is His offer (Luke 5:32; Matt. 11:28; Rev. 22:17). He's well aware of everything you're going through and will take you step-by-step where you need to go for healing. He never says, "Get your act together first."

HEAVEN IS FOR YOU

Tired of the **hypocrisy**? Heaven is for you. Hypocrisy won't exist there (Matt. 7:5; 23:15). Tired of all the **political fighting**? Heaven is for you. The government can be trusted there (Rev. 15:3). Tired of **racism**? Heaven is for you. Everyone there esteems others as better than themselves (Philip. 2:3). Tired of **people not taking responsibility**? Heaven is for you. No one makes excuses there (Prov. 28:13; Col. 3:23). Tired of **prejudice** or **bigotry** in any form? Heaven is for you. They won't exist there (Matt. 22:39; Gal. 3:28). Finally, are you just sick of all the **arguing**? Heaven is for you. All are united in truth there (1 Cor. 1:10; Philip. 2:2).

NO ACCIDENTS

God had a plan for your life before you were even born (Jer. 1:5; 29:11). It is when you discover this plan that you become your real self, the one that you were meant to be. It is then that you are at your best, and most fulfilled (John 10:10). God is continually working to bring you into that fulfilling plan. Until then, you're like a V8 engine, firing on only four cylinders. Perhaps you feel that way now. As God works to fix your V8, there are no accidents (Rom. 8:28).

MIRACLE ON "THAT" STREET

I was speaking once in South Carolina on Hebrews and our Mediator in heaven. After the presentation, an elderly woman approached me and said she wanted to find out more about this subject. I asked if she wanted to cover the deeper aspects or if she was a new believer. This dear Baptist woman chuckled and told me that she had not stepped foot in a church in 30 years, but just worshiped God in her home every week. That morning in prayer, the name of the street where this meeting was held had repeatedly been impressed on her mind, and she couldn't shake the thought. She had no idea where the street was but trusted God and just started driving until she found it, arriving just in time to hear the presentation. Again, there are no accidents. There's a reason you're reading this book. Find out what it is.

A WELCOME MAT

I'd like to roll out heaven's welcome mat for you. What you choose to do after taking a look around is up to you. The Bible reveals the way to heaven, but it also describes the glorious destination for all to see.

Perhaps you harbor some of the above barriers to looking around. As you step onto this welcome mat, I want you to lay all those barriers aside. No one has any interest in going somewhere if they don't feel they would be welcome when they arrive.

Do you fear that only people in a particular denomination will "make it" to heaven? Lay that fear aside, too; the most faithful churches don't teach any such thing.

So today, as we begin our journey through this book, let's agree to lay aside *all* barriers that would prevent us from believing that even more than a welcome mat has been rolled out for us. A "path," a "way," a "door," have all been given at infinite cost so that you - yes even you, and I, as faulty as we are - can take a look around at the things that have been prepared for us. And, if you're interested, you can go today – just as you are – and get to know the great Healer and Carpenter who prepared all of this for you.

YOU ARE WHAT YOU EAT...AND THINK

Your world might not be all you hoped it would be. But in a world full of sin, misery, and selfishness, the Scriptures call our attention away from the world and direct us to better things. The apostle Paul admonishes us:

"Finally brethren, whatsoever things are true, whatsoever things are honest, whatsoever things are just, whatsoever things are pure, whatsoever things are lovely, whatsoever things are of good report; if there be any virtue, and if there be any praise, **think on these things**" (Phil. 4:8).

Just as "you are what you eat," nutritionally speaking, so in our spiritual life we are what we behold and contemplate:

"But we all...beholding...are changed into the same image" and "as he thinketh in his heart, so is he" (2 Cor. 3:18; Prov. 23:7).

A KINGDOM OF WINNERS

The above texts are not just good suggestions. They are laws: unchangeable, inevitable. When God says something, it happens. But they are more than laws; they are promises. These give us hope that by dwelling upon spiritual things that are true, honest, just, pure, lovely, virtuous, praiseworthy and of good report, we will be transformed into the same image. Transformed into citizens of an amazing Kingdom. Everybody loves a winner. And this is a Kingdom of winners. Behold shepherd David as he handily defeats Goliath, beautiful Esther as she bravely saves her people, slave Joseph as he rises to rulership through integrity, and meek Moses as he leads an entire nation through an open sea, then watches that same sea destroy the pursuing army just in time. God wants you on the winning team. Remember that. And claim the promise:

"Whereby are given unto us exceeding great and precious promises: that by these ye might be partakers of the divine nature" (2 Pet. 1:4).

The same apostle that called us to think on holy things boldly declared his favorite theme for contemplation:

"I count all things but loss for the excellency of the knowledge of Jesus Christ my Lord" (Phil. 3:8).

This book is not just about a place - as amazing as that place is - it's also about a Person. It is written with the hope that all who read it may obtain such a living knowledge of the Redeemer that they, too, will "count all things but loss" in comparison to a relationship with Him.

It is my sincere prayer that this volume would bring you into a closer walk with your Creator, by leading you not only on a journey to your future home but ultimately to the foot of the Old, Rugged Cross. May you come to realize that the greatest thrill awaiting you is not the mansions, or the miracles, or the trips to galaxies afar, but rather the face-to-face encounters you'll have with your Maker. Heaven is "true," it is "pure," and it is "lovely." But most of all, it is your future home, to be shared with the One whose very essence is "Love" (1 John 4:8). As you get to know Him, it will become increasingly obvious why Paul directs us to "think on these things."

-CARL MARTIN

GOING HOME

"I will come again, and receive you unto myself; that where I am, there ye may be also."

-JOHN 14:3

"For the Lord himself shall descend from heaven with a shout, with the voice of the archangel, and with the trump of God: and the dead in Christ shall rise first: Then we which are alive and remain shall be caught up together with them in the clouds to meet the Lord in the air: and so shall we ever be with the Lord."

-1 THESSALONIANS 4:16-17

EVERYTHING SEEMS SURREAL. The massive, black clouds overhead churn like angry waves colliding violently in the atmosphere. The devastated earth is trembling and quaking as if it, too, is aware of the approaching power. You've studied the Bible and have known for several years that you were living in the last days, but you always put the Second Coming a bit further into the future. *Could this be it?* The small, praying company around you is wondering the same thing as you alternate between praying and gazing up into the eerie spectacle.

You know what you're watching for: "The sign of the Son of Man... coming in the clouds of heaven, with power and great glory" to take you home (Matt. 24:30). The strange, white dove that has appeared so many times now settles right beside your praying group. A beacon of peace amid the destruction. As your prayers continually ascend, your heart races in anticipation of seeing that cloud in the sky. Your petitions are suddenly interrupted by the cry of a friend. "Look, look!" he shouts. You immediately open your eyes and lift them to the eastern sky. Chills tingle your spine as you see it in the farthest edges of the firmament, beyond the angry, black clouds. It appears dark and tiny at first but gradually grows larger and brighter as it slowly moves toward earth.

Now you begin to recognize the shapes within the cloud. You are mesmerized by the scene, your eyes transfixed upward in joyous anticipation of the awesome event. You think you might actually see the tiny, blurred forms of beings atop the distant cloud, but it's hard to be sure at this point. They appear to be holding something gold, and now you see what look like wings. These are *angels* - innumerable angels - each holding a golden trumpet! You know that the greatest event in the history of the universe is now taking place, and you still cannot believe it! It is the Reaping. "And He that sat on the cloud thrust in His sickle on the earth; and the earth was reaped" (Rev. 14:16). So long talked about, so long contemplated and now it is happening! You've had dreams of this event, but the reality blows even your most vivid dreams away. Normal life is over forever.

Some of those around you are horror-stricken by the scene. They begin to wail in terror, and out of the corner of your eye, you perceive that several have started to flee. You have no idea where they are going, but you cannot take your eyes off the approaching great cloud. All you know is, this is your God, and you have waited for Him!

▲ ▲ ▲

There is a better land. By the authority of the One who created all things, there's a place that is prepared "for you." Before we continue our journey, let's find out a little more about that land and the promise to take you there. This promise was given by One who has never lied. After His resurrection, He didn't just leave and forget about this dark, sinful world. He went to prepare a place for us - for you. Coupled with this promise is the assurance that He will come again. The reason He will come again reveals something about His character: so that where He is, *there you may be also* (John 14:3). He loves you. He wants to be with you. Like a parent who desires all of the children to be present at family events, so He desires that all will be present in His eternal Kingdom. *Heaven won't be the same without you.* Let that thought sink in. Believe it. God feels that way about *you*.

So why the apparent delay? Why, if Christ is so eager to come back and take us home with Him, are we still here? The apostle Peter prophesied regarding this very question. He said, "Knowing this first, that there shall come in the last days scoffers, walking after their own lusts, And saying Where is the promise of his coming? for since the fathers fell asleep, all things continue as they were from the beginning of creation," but "The Lord is not slack concerning his promise, as some men count slackness; but is longsuffering to us-ward, not willing that any should perish, but that all should come to repentance" (2 Pet. 3:3-4,9).

That last line is the key. Jesus loves every person in this world, whether they reciprocate that love or not. He longs for each one of us to come to repentance and surrender ourselves to Him fully. He longs for us to receive Him into ourselves, to receive His perfect life into our hearts, for that is the only hope of salvation (Col. 1:27).

HIS APPEARING

The Bible gives us a clear description of the Second Coming:

> "For as the lightning cometh out of the east, and shineth even unto the west; so shall also the coming of the Son of man be" (Matt. 24:27).

> "When the Son of man shall come in his glory, and all the holy angels with him" (Matt. 25:31).

> "Behold he cometh with clouds; and every eye shall see him" (Rev. 1:7).

This event will be like nothing human eyes have ever witnessed. Shepherds did behold angels in the sky, singing to announce the first advent of Jesus (Luke 2:8-20). But this event involves *every angel in existence* and will be witnessed by every human on earth, not just a few shepherds in Bethlehem.

The King of all the universe, the One who created all things, is going to come down through the corridors of the sky accompanied by all of His angels. What a sight to behold! The glory surrounding a single angel is enough to overwhelm the senses (see Rev. 19:10; Luke 24:4-5). Just try to imagine what "ten thousand times ten thousand, and thousands of thousands" of them at once will look like (Rev. 5:11).

REUNITED

Graves will burst open on that day. "Behold, I shew you a mystery; We shall not all sleep, but we shall all be changed, In a moment, in the twinkling of an eye, at the last trump: for the trumpet shall sound, and the dead shall be raised incorruptible, and we shall be changed... then shall be brought to pass the saying that is written, Death is swallowed up in victory. O death, where is thy sting? O grave, where is thy victory?" (1 Cor. 15:51-52,54-55).

Those alive for this event will be reunited with loved ones who have died, as these precious souls come forth from their graves. All who have believed in Jesus and let Him live His life in them will be safe from the power of death forever. Funerals will, from that day forward be a forgotten concept as the redeemed dwell in the presence of the Life-giver.

As the dead in Christ are resurrected, the bodies of the living will be transformed instantly into glorious, perfect bodies.

"For our conversation is in heaven; from whence also we look for the Savior, the Lord Jesus Christ: Who shall change our vile body, that it may be fashioned like unto his glorious body" (Phil. 3:20-21).

We do not become bodiless spirits when we get to heaven. In a moment, in the "twinkling of an eye," we will be changed from the faulty, aging bodies we now have, into perfect, eternally youthful physiques, like Jesus' glorified body.

SPIRITS ON BORING CLOUDS FOREVER?

It is the misconception of what heaven will be like, and what we will be like when we get there, that causes many to marginalize it as no big deal. To some it's just a humdrum place where we float around as spirits on cotton ball clouds and strum three-stringed harps, wishing we could return to our active days back on earth. I even saw one public service billboard with a painting of a young man, laying on his chest in a cloud, chin on hands, and looking back longingly at something. Giant letters above him warned drivers to wear their seatbelts, or they would be in such a dreary, sad place as well. Such a concept makes heaven seem imaginary, unappealing and downright boring. This is why multitudes are concerned only with the current pleasures of this world, since everything here seems so much more real than any future heavenly home could be. When Jesus comes again, our bodies will be transformed into actual, tangible, glorified bodies like His own and we will forever enjoy very real activities in very real bodies.

All the faithful children of God will rejoice in victory as the glorious cloud, filled with angels and surrounding the Son of God, descends toward the earth.

"Lo, this is our God; we have waited for him, and he will save us: this is the Lord; we have waited for him, we will be glad and rejoice in his salvation" (Isa. 25:9).

Just before this spectacular event, heaven had declared that the time had come for the Son of God to return to the earth and reap – to gather up His faithful people: "Thrust in Thy sickle and reap: for the time is come for Thee to reap; for the harvest of the earth is ripe" (Rev. 14:15).

"And then shall appear the sign of the Son of man in heaven: and then shall all the tribes of the earth mourn, and they shall see the Son of man coming in the clouds of heaven with power and great glory. And he shall send his angels with a great sound of a trumpet, and they shall gather together his elect from the four winds, from one end of heaven to the other" (Matt. 24:30:31).

With that in mind, let's resume our contemplation of that wonderful day when we can finally go home forever.

▲ ▲ ▲

Now the angels, although still a great way off, are becoming more defined, and the flames that cover the base of the cloud grow brighter as it descends. The angels raise their golden trumpets and in unison shake the earth with a thunderous blast. In the center of the cloud, the glory of Jesus is finally unveiled, and His brightness outshines a thousand suns. Your best and most creative conceptions of this event have been completely eclipsed by the reality. You weren't aware that your senses could withstand such stimulus. But at the same time, you realize that your body, along with your senses, has been changed. You look down and notice a whole new physique, loaded with energy and vitality. No longer do you wear those manufactured clothes that fade and wear out. Now you are "clothed in white" as the book of Revelation said you would be. This "white robe," though, is not made from any familiar material. It shines just as Moses' face did when he had been with God on Mount Sinai. It looks as though it's made of pure light!

Now the cloud shines forth in all its dazzling splendor, the Son of God in the middle, brightest of all. The legions of angels stretch out for thousands of miles in every direction beneath the massive band of fire at the base of the cloud. Myriads of them descend toward the earth, cascading out in all directions.

You witness several touch down at a hillside graveyard in the distance as the mighty voice of Jesus calls forth His faithful children from their graves. Some of the tombstones topple as the ground bursts open beside them. Faithful men and women who died in the faith of Jesus now come forward in their glorified bodies. Their faces shine as do their robes, and many of them ecstatically hug and kiss each other, overwhelmed by the joyful reunion. The angels are right there beside them and appear to be speaking to them. Suddenly you think of several loved ones who had died. You have longed to see them again and today is the day your dream will come true! One relative was buried close by, and you can't wait to see her.

The King of the universe again attracts your attention. His majesty and beauty are naturally captivating to all true believers. No crown of thorns mars His head now. Instead, He wears the glorious crown of the King of all Creation. You cannot stop looking at His majestic countenance, as the cloud continues its descent.

But while His face shines with love to you, that same face strikes fear in the hearts of those who continually rejected the gentle promptings of His Holy Spirit. In the distance, you hear the very words of another prophecy echoed in various ways: "Hide us from the face of him that sitteth on the throne, and from the wrath of the Lamb!" (Rev. 6:16).

Now the horizon is filled white-robed multitudes rising toward the spectacular cloud. These are the resurrected saints. The sky is loaded with them, giving the appearance of countless stars. If you didn't know better, you would swear that it was snowing in reverse, there are so many. It's a magnificent sight.

The earth's surface all around you is broken up, rolling like ocean waves composed of soil and rock. Mountains have disappeared into expanding cavernous faults, and all of humankind's proud skyscrapers have been leveled. The lordly palaces and mansions, so long coveted, are now heaps of wood, stone, metal, and brick. The earth still rumbles from violent aftershocks as smoke rises from the heaps of ruin.

Suddenly you feel yourself rising off the ground by an unseen power. An angel meets you in midair and accompanies you toward the glorious, mammoth cloud. The earth below and the plans of men are in ruins, but the Lord hasn't forgotten you. He's come back to take you home, just as He promised.

The flaming base of the cloud blankets the sky just above you and extends as far as the eye can see. What will it be like to enter this holy place? Angels and people are shining all around you as they, too advance toward the magnificent destination.

Your mind races in wild anticipation as you ascend over the cloud's edge and glide over into its glorious body. This cloud is nothing like the fluffy, white things that you saw drifting in the skies all your life. This one is made of something firm that you've never seen before. And part of what gives it its shape is the shining angels themselves.

Jesus beams with joy as people are moved in close to Him at the center of the massive cloud. As much as you and all of the redeemed have waited and longed for this moment, Christ has yearned for it even more. Never again will He and His people be apart. This Creator, Architect, and Carpenter has eagerly prepared a place for them, and now He is taking them home.

As you gaze in admiration at the face of your best Friend, you suddenly feel a hand on your shoulder. You turn around and there, before you, stands your loved one who had been buried in your hometown! An angel had pointed you out to her as you appeared over the edge of the cloud. The atmosphere of love envelopes the two of you as you embrace and weep for joy. Just as you'll never have to be separated from Jesus again, so you and this person will never again have to say goodbye. The two of you now look back up to Christ as you begin to make your way toward His majestic form at the enormous cloud's center. No words are spoken, and none are needed. The energy of love in this place is so powerful it can be felt.

The flaming cloud of glory slowly begins to back away from the desolate earth. Its mission has been accomplished, and now it will voyage through the vast expanses of space toward heaven with its precious new cargo. What a trip awaits the redeemed! Much of what they have been taught about science can now be left back on earth among the rubble. Nothing in that old world could have prepared you for the things your eyes are about to behold, and your mind is about to experience.

Wonder and amazement overtake you as you and your loved one watch the stars rush by at a breathtaking speed. You don't (yet) understand the science behind the propulsion of this colossal cloud, but it doesn't really matter to you. All is in Christ's hands - whom you have learned to trust implicitly - and with Him all things are possible. An angel reveals that you are on your way to the New Jerusalem and the thought of this sends new chills down your spine. You will soon be entering the Holy City of God in heaven: the headquarters and origin of the universe! What is it going to look like? What will it feel like to walk along those famous streets of gold?

You and your relative have other loved ones and friends somewhere aboard this tremendous cloud, and you're eager to find them as well. But for now, your greatest desire is to press closer to Jesus. As you near His form, you see that He is overcome with joy. His family - the family of humans, of whom He is a part, who have willingly chosen Him over the enemy - now surround Him. Of the faithful, not a single one is missing. Not one, from any age in earth's history, is left behind. His smile is understandable. Jesus now sees before Him, the fruit of His work. The pain, suffering, and agony He endured on Calvary were for this very moment. As He beholds the beaming countenances of these millions who are now eternally secure through His blood, His face reveals that it was all well worth it to Him. This massive reunion of souls, this grand parade of the victorious, make all the pain and suffering worthwhile. The angels strike a note higher, and sing the chorus of their powerful song:

"He shall see of the travail of his soul, and shall be satisfied" (Isa. 53:11).

▲ ▲ ▲

Thought Questions:

1. What is your main takeaway from this chapter? Why is it your main takeaway?

2. Why do you suppose the myth that heaven is a boring place has been propagated over time? What are some other examples of these myths that you've heard or seen?

3. The coming cloud has opposite effects on those who witness it. What does this contrast tell you about God's character?

4. What does the grand reunion of loved ones tell you about God's promises? Who are you looking forward to reuniting with on that day?

5. What did you learn about God's will for you in this chapter? What do you feel He's impressing you to start doing differently this week to walk more closely with Him?

THE NEW JERUSALEM

"God is not ashamed to be called their God: for he hath prepared for them a city."

-HEBREWS 11:16

FORGET EVERYTHING YOU know about cities. For most of us, the thought of a city is not exactly Paradise (although I did spend part of my high school years in a California town by that very name). Trash littering the streets, vandalism defacing stores and businesses, graffiti scrawled across buildings and trains, construction and road repair jamming up traffic, migraine-inducing noise, pollution-tainted air, and of course, the crime. These cities, however, are built by humans. God has prepared a city for us with His own hands. In this city, there will be no trash, no vandalism, no graffiti. There'll be no broken-down roads in need of repair, no traffic jams, no incessant clatter of primitive machinery. Not one impure particle will taint the air or water, and of course, there will be no crime (unconverted criminals will not be there: Matt. 6:20; Rev. 21:8). The name of this city: the New Jerusalem (Rev. 21:1-2); the features of this city: incomparable.

We'll get into the details the Bible shares with us in a minute, but first, understand that it is a real city — just as real as any city you've ever visited.

I live in the beautiful city of Chattanooga, Tennessee, USA. I've also lived in Los Angeles & Paradise, California; Cayce, Mississippi and Memphis, Tennessee and each one has its own unique flavor, its own charm. Each has its own culture, events, neighborhoods, etc. The New Jerusalem is the same way. It's real. It has culture. And as massive as it is, it has plenty to see.

When asked about our own hometown, specific aspects immediately come to mind. But when we imagine the New Jerusalem, we tend to think in vague, almost fairy-tale terms. Basically, gold and silver walls and a static state of being. We've all seen the artists' renditions. Nothing could be further from the truth. One of the chief attributes of its Architect is His amazing creativity, beyond any human architect, and His love of events and activities. Consider all of the feasts days and festivals He developed. God loves social events (it's where we got our own love of them). In fact, the word "Holidays" comes from the phrase "Holy Days." Can you imagine all of the holidays we will be celebrating in heaven? And we can't even begin to conceive of all the exciting places there will be to tour in the New Jerusalem.

MORE THAN JUST THE CHATTANOOGA CHOO-CHOO

My hometown is best known for a famous train song from 1941, which became the first certified gold record in the world. That song is just about all most people know about my city. But there's a lot more to Chattanooga than a catchy Glenn Miller song. It's the same with the New Jerusalem. The Bible gives us quite a bit of information about the Holy City, but so few take time to read about it. Let's change that, right now, and take a look around.

If you came to visit me in Chattanooga, I wouldn't just show you my house, slap a postcard of the Choo-Choo into your hand, and then send you on your way, saying "you already know all this." No, I would give you the grand tour, and I'd tell you all about the place. I'd show you Coolidge Park and talk about all of its public events as we walked the longest pedestrian bridge in the world, over the Tennessee River. I'd take you to Lookout Mountain, show you Ruby Falls, and the giant Tennessee Aquarium. We'd swing by Songbirds, which *USA Today* called "the premier private collection of rare guitars in the world," and ride the Incline, the steepest passenger railway in the world.

I'm a foodie, so when you got hungry, we could stop in at Sluggo's North, a great vegan/vegetarian cafe or grab a fusion burrito at Harrison Ford's favorite local Mexican restaurant, Taco Mamacita. We could feast on the tastiest garlic rolls on earth at Provino's or dine at the best Thai restaurant in America, Rain (my favorite of all time), among the endless variety of dining choices. For Civil War buffs, we could tour the Chickamauga Battlefield or visit Point Park, and for your fine art fix, we'd stop at the Hunter Museum. *Can you tell I love my town? I'm almost done.* We could catch a Lookouts ball game and then try any one of dozens of outdoor activities. Our hiking, kayaking, rock climbing and whitewater rafting options are so numerous that Chattanooga has been voted "Best Town Ever" - twice now - by *Outside* magazine.

We'd check out Nickajack Cave, home to a colony of over 100,000 gray bats, where we'd watch my favorite animals fly out over the lake at sunset. I would tell you about how Johnny Cash crawled deep into that very cave in 1967 to commit suicide. And how, as he lay there in the blackness, he found God, gave up his drugs and started his life over again, just two months before the cave floor was permanently flooded by a dam.

During our tour, we would inevitably drive down Little Debbie Parkway, then head north until we hit Volkswagen Drive, and yes, both of those wonderful products are made right here, as well. And of course, we'd end our tour at the Choo-Choo, where you could take lots of pictures at the historic Terminal train station.

All of that is just the beginning, and that's in a town of only a few hundred thousand people, sitting on an area of about 140 square miles. Does anyone doubt that a heavenly metropolis over 700 times larger, designed by the most creative mind in the universe would have an infinitely larger variety of things to do and see? No one should doubt that, but few people ever think of it that way. So let's take a closer look at this metropolis.

THE SIZE

"The city lieth foursquare, and the length is as large as the breadth: and he measured the city with the reed, twelve thousand furlongs" (Rev. 21:16).

A furlong is one-eighth of a mile. If the city's perimeter is 12,000 furlongs, then it is 1,500 miles around. Since its length is as large as its breadth, the city has a perfectly square perimeter, 375 miles long on each side: one city, larger than the entire state of Oregon! We're also told in the same verse: "The length and the breadth and the height of it are equal." One interpretation of this is that the word "equal" here might mean "proportionate." If it does mean "equal" though, the Holy City is shaped much like a giant, golden cube, its height being equal to its length and breadth. Thus, the top of the city would sit 375 miles above the base. If this sounds like just a bunch of large numbers on paper, let's put things into perspective: consider that the clouds you see overhead (cumulus, cumulonimbus, and stratus clouds) typically start at a height of around 6,500 feet - that's far less than even two miles up. The very highest clouds (cirrus, cirrocumulus, and cirrostratus) start at around 20,000 feet, which is still less than four miles up. So even if the top of this city were just *four* miles high, it would reach a couple of miles beyond the lower clouds that we typically see floating around and even beyond the highest clouds. 40 miles high would make the city's pinnacle reach over ten times the height of the highest clouds, but this massive metropolis reaches a height of *nearly a hundred times* higher than the clouds at a staggering 375 miles. Are you beginning to see that your greatest imagination, straining to envision this city cannot begin to capture its dimensions? Even Hollywood, with its special effects and dazzling imagery of fantasy cities from worlds afar, cannot capture what it would be like to gaze upon this colossal structure.

THE WALL AND FOUNDATIONS

"And he measured the wall thereof, an hundred and forty and four cubits" (Rev. 21:16). A cubit is 18 inches. The measurement expressed here is 216 feet. Some believe this is describing the *height* of the wall, which is a possibility. However, it seems much more likely that the wall is 216 feet *thick*. For one thing, if the city itself is indeed 375 miles high, a wall rising 216 feet would seem far out of proportion - almost tiny. In fact, many of our cities today have buildings much taller than 216 feet (the tallest building in the world, the Burj Khalifa, is over ten times higher than a 216-foot wall). And yet, the prophet John, after seeing the enormous city, in all of its grandeur, described the wall as "great and high" (Rev. 21:12): an unlikely phrase for such a relatively short wall. Another clue that the wall is probably higher than 216 feet can be found in the city's foundations.

"And the wall of the city had twelve foundations" (Rev. 21:14).

Notice it said, "the *wall* of the city had twelve foundations," not "the city had twelve foundations." Another text concurs:

"And the foundations of the wall of the city were garnished with all manner of precious stones" (Rev. 21:19).

Reading on, we find that each of the twelve foundations is made of a different precious stone. Some scholars believe that these twelve foundations lie, one on top of the other, at the base of the city. Other scholars point out that the foundations are described as part of the walls, suggesting that the foundations are separate, and supported by the walls themselves, not just stacked on the ground like giant, sparkling pancakes. In other words, each foundation could be a separate *floor* in this giant city, each floor equidistant from the others (just over 30 miles apart - plenty of room for each level to have its own atmosphere and even clouds if God so desired). So then, the New Jerusalem would be one giant twelve-story structure that God Himself designed and built. In this case, the walls would, by definition, need to rise to the very top of the City.

"And the building of the wall of it was of jasper" (Rev. 21:18). Jasper is an opaque, brilliant, green stone. This tells us that even if the wall does stretch clear to the top of this metropolis, one can see inside all 12 floors by looking right through it. The word "jasper" however, falls far short of the dazzling brilliance the wall will produce. Imagine this mammoth structure towering 375 miles overhead and shining with the glory radiating from God's throne, which we are told illuminates the entire metropolis (Rev. 21:23).

"The first foundation was jasper" (Rev. 21:19). The walls are made of the same material as the first or lowest foundation. This hints once again at the possibility of each foundation being a different floor, having the first floor and walls forming the great, jasper structure upon which everything else is built.

The other foundations are made from precious stones as well with all the vibrant colors of the rainbow. Sapphire, chalcedony, emerald, sardonyx, sardius, chrysolyte, beryl, topaz, chrysoprasus, jacinth and amethyst are used for the remaining 11 floors. If some of these gems are unfamiliar to you now, that's fine; they'll be even more brilliant and glorious than you can imagine, no matter what they're called.

"And the wall of the city had twelve foundations, and in them the names of the twelve apostles of the Lamb" (Rev. 21:14).

Each foundation contains one of the names of the twelve apostles of Jesus. But why put their names in such a place? Is there any significance to this? The Bible gives us the answer: "Now therefore ye are no more strangers and foreigners, but fellowcitizens with the saints, and of the household of God; *And are built upon the **foundation** of the apostles and prophets*, Jesus Christ himself being the chief corner stone" (Eph. 2:20, emphasis supplied).

Jesus is the only Rock upon whom we are to build our faith. But the words of the apostles and the truths they handed down to us are the way we become familiar with who Jesus is. While we know that God didn't literally write out pages of the Bible Himself, He did inspire these "apostles and prophets" through the ages to do so, and He protected the integrity of the Bible. To reject the words of God's inspired prophets is to reject Christ Himself, for He speaks to us *through* the writings of the apostles and prophets. "Believe in the Lord your God, so shall ye be established; believe his prophets, so shall ye prosper," "for the testimony of Jesus is the spirit of prophecy" (2 Chron. 20:20; Rev. 19:10).

The Spirit inspiring these prophets is called the "testimony of Jesus," so heeding their words is heeding Christ's words. The eternal and unshakable nature of these twelve rock-solid foundations testifies to the validity and accuracy of the instruments through which God conveyed His Word. Do you like the beauty of jewels you see on earth today? Imagine what a thrill it will be to walk on these transparent, glistening foundations! Believe His prophets now, letting their inspired words be the foundation of your faith today, and you will walk the foundations that bear their names through eternity.

THE PEARLY GATES

"And the twelve gates were twelve pearls; every several gate was of one pearl" (Rev. 21:21).

For a sprawling city with such massive dimensions, these gates must be simply enormous. Now imagine each gate having the appearance of a lustrous pearl. The light from the throne of God will constantly flow out from the city and shimmer off each one of them.

"And had a wall great and high, and had twelve gates, and at the gates twelve angels, and names written thereon, which are the names of the twelve tribes of Israel: On the east three gates; on the north three gates; on the south three gates; and on the west three gates" (Rev. 21:12-13).

After Adam and Eve fell, by disobeying and partaking of the forbidden fruit, God sent the couple out of Eden and placed angels on the east end of the Garden to prevent them from returning to the Tree of Life and eating its fruit (Gen. 3:24). In the New Jerusalem, however, God places angels at the gates, not to keep humankind out, as before, but rather to welcome them *in,* to their eternal home. "And the gates of it shall not be shut at all by day: for there shall be no night there" (Rev. 21:25).

Upon each of these gates is written one of twelve names from the twelve tribes of Israel. Some of these names belong to men who had a record of more than their share of failures. For all eternity these gates will bear witness to the fact that although frail and erring, repentant souls who receive Jesus, experience not only forgiveness and cleansing, but also transformation and ultimately victory in the life.

The material the Lord chose for the construction of these gates is no accident either. "Again, the kingdom of heaven is like unto a merchant man, seeking goodly pearls: Who, when he had found one pearl of great price, went and sold all that he had, and bought it" (Matt. 13:45-46).

The pearl of great price is Jesus Himself. Although salvation is a free gift, it is given only to those who actually want Him, who have surrendered all to Him. He doesn't force Himself on anyone. Some forget that Jesus doesn't just *give us* salvation, He IS salvation. "He who hath the Son hath life, and he who hath not the Son hath not life" (1 John 5:12). If we "have" Jesus - not just talk about Him - we have life. And that eternal life we inherit is "IN His Son" (verse 11). Salvation isn't separate from Christ. It's not your name written somewhere. It's not mansions of gold. It's not living forever. And no, it's not even heaven. It's Jesus Himself and having Him. Those who enter through these gates will have found the great pearl in their relationship with Christ and will have given *everything they are* over to Him. Their talents, ambitions, opinions, even soul, body, and spirit, will have been consecrated fully to Him and His cause. They will have entrusted Him even with their daily happiness, believing His way is best, even if their feelings told them otherwise. "Then said Jesus unto his disciples, If any man will come after me, let him deny himself, and take up his cross and follow me," "I am crucified with Christ: nevertheless I live; yet not I, but Christ liveth in me: and the life which I now live in the flesh I live by the faith of the Son of God, who loved me, and gave himself for me." (Matt. 16:24; Gal. 2:20).

THE TREE AND RIVER OF LIFE

"In the midst of the street of it, and on either side of the river, was there the tree of life, which bare twelve manner of fruits, and yielded her fruit every month: and the leaves of the tree were for the healing of the nations" (Rev. 22:2).

The Tree of Life is described as singular, while at the same time it is "on either side of the river." This extraordinary tree, from which all the redeemed can freely eat, has trunks on opposite banks of the river, and then above this river, these trunks merge into one enormous tree.

The Bible says that this tree bears "twelve manner of fruits, and yielded her fruit every month." Are all twelve kinds of fruit growing at once, or does a totally different crop of fruit appear on each of the twelve months? When we get to the New Jerusalem, we can find out for ourselves.

When Adam and Eve fell into disobedience, they were banned from eating the fruit of this tree, for it possessed something, by God's design, that could perpetuate life. As mentioned above, the Lord placed "Cherubims" (angels), and a flaming sword to guard the way to the tree. This was done to prevent the pair from being able to "take also of the tree of life, and eat, and live for ever" (Gen. 3:22). Not only will we be given perfect, new bodies at the Second Coming, but eternal youth will be ours, with free access to this amazing tree. Perhaps you look back on your college days and wish for that same physique again. You were designed to be in top physical condition for all eternity. It is the entrance of sin into our world that has brought a breakdown of our bodies as we age, along with every sickness we encounter. Never again will anyone get sick, and there will be no more physical impairments for any of God's children.

"Then the eyes of the blind shall be opened, and the ears of the deaf shall be unstopped. Then shall the lame man leap as an hart, and the tongue of the dumb sing," "neither shall there be any more pain," "and the inhabitant shall not say, I am sick," "they shall run, and not be weary; and they shall walk, and not faint" (Isa. 35:5-6; Rev. 21:4; Isa. 33:24; 40:31).

Those who have been confined to a wheelchair will run like a deer. The formerly blind will have perfect vision, better than the best vision on earth. Those who have battled with cancer will forever have victory over their destructive foe. Physical deformities, either from birth or acquired through trauma will disappear forever. And bodies which have been deteriorated by old age (or even bad life choices) will be restored to eternal youth.

Before WWII my grandmother was a beautiful, young woman in a singing group called "The Sunshine Trio." I used to love looking at the pictures of her and the trio in their late teens to early twenties. I remember, though, my grandmother saying that as she grew older, it was like she was becoming invisible to the world. I've heard others say similar things. In our looks-crazed society, we place an inordinate amount of value on one's youth and beauty. Millions of people spend billions of dollars annually on products and procedures to hold back the clock and give them a younger appearance as time marches on. Ironically, the one source of never-ending youth and beauty is a free gift, available to all who will, by living faith, grab hold of it. Sure, it may be delayed for just a bit, but it's yours for the taking. Oh, to taste of the invigorating fruit of that tree! This is God's specific plan for you. He wants you to be there and to enjoy it forever.

But what about the river over which the tree grows? "And he shewed me a pure river of water of life, clear as crystal, proceeding out of the throne of God and of the Lamb" (Rev. 22:1). This is the River of Life, and it flows from the very throne of God Himself. God's creative power is constantly at work, supplying all the inhabitants of this city with pure, refreshing water, "clear as crystal."

Those who drink from this physical river of life will have already been tasting, in their life on old earth, the refreshing spiritual water of life that Christ had already offered: "Jesus stood and cried, saying, If any man thirst, let him come unto me, and drink" (John 7:37). And He says, "Whosoever drinketh of the water that I shall give him shall never thirst" (John 4:14).

Jesus longs to give you the spiritual, living water now so that the promise of the literal water can also be fulfilled someday soon: "For the Lamb which is in the midst of the throne shall feed them, and shall lead them unto living fountains of waters" (Rev. 7:17). To drink from that refreshing river and be filled with the eternal youth and vitality it perpetuates is an experience freely offered to all who will today give God a chance. And notice it said, "fountains of waters." Don't just imagine a single river, but glorious, flowing waterfalls and crystal, arching fountains all around. "I will give unto him that is athirst of the fountain of the water of life freely," "And whosoever will, let him take the water of life freely" (Rev. 21:6; 22:17).

THE SEA OF GLASS AND FIRE

"And before the throne there was a sea of glass like unto crystal," "And I saw as it were a sea of glass mingled with fire" (Rev. 4:6; 15:2).

The sea of glass is as clear as crystal. Most people have heard of the sea of glass, but there is something else that's even more fascinating, and most people don't catch this. Did you notice the wording of that text? This sea is either covered with fire, or it reflects the glory from the throne of God so faithfully that it appears to have fire flashing and blazing across its surface. When John saw it in vision, he could only describe it to us as "glass mingled with fire." We get a very limited picture of this sometimes near sundown on an ocean or lake; the sun reflecting off the water is almost blinding as it sparkles like millions of diamonds. This, however, is just a flicker compared to the Sea of Glass and Fire. But there's more to this fire than just a brilliant shine. Lucifer, the covering cherub (angel), is described as having been "upon the holy mountain of God" and walking "up and down in the midst of the stones of fire" while residing there (Ezek. 28:14). We often associate fire with hell, but God can use His elements any way He chooses, and it's clear from Scripture that the dazzling flames are also found in heaven.

When Christ was on this earth, He actually walked upon the water of the sea. Peter, while trusting in the power of Jesus, was able to do so as well (Matt. 14:25-31). As long as he kept his eyes fixed on Christ, he was just fine. More than just fine, he was able to do the impossible and walk on water. However, as soon as he took his eyes off Jesus and focused on the "boisterous" wind, manifested through the waves, he was afraid, and his faith temporarily slipped. The moment his faith faltered, he started to sink and cried out for Jesus to save him. True to character, Jesus reached down and grabbed hold of Peter's plummeting hand, pulling him back up beside himself. Walking on water demonstrates faith in God, not in any ability we have. It represents eyes fixed squarely upon Jesus, even in the most troubling times, and not relying on our own efforts, ideas, plans, or abilities (see Prov. 3:5-6).

The Bible describes a people who will "stand on the sea of glass, having the harps of God" (Rev. 15:2). These redeemed ones, like Peter, can actually walk on the surface of this sea. Their faith in Jesus will never slip. The very fact that they are sustained with every step will forever bear witness to their mistrust in self and their unyielding faith in their best friend.

ROBES, PALMS, AND CROWNS

The Bible tells us that the faithful children of God will be given emblems of the victory they experienced by faith, only through the blood of the Lamb. Here's how the prophet John describes them:

"After this I beheld, and, lo, a great multitude, which no man could number, of all nations, and kindreds, and people, and tongues, stood before the Lamb, clothed with white robes, and palms in their hands; And cried with a loud voice, saying, Salvation to our God which sitteth upon the throne, and unto the Lamb" (Rev. 7:9-10).

THE ROBES

These white robes will be made of something we have never seen or felt before. The essence of light itself will clothe us as the glory from the throne of God shines upon us. When Moses asked the Lord, "I beseech thee, shew me thy glory" (Ex. 33:18), God answered his request and passed before him, proclaiming His holy character. This was the incident in which God re-wrote the Ten Commandments on the tables of stone with His own finger (Deut. 10:1-4) after the first set had been physically broken. As Moses came down from the mountain after meeting and communing with God, his face shone so brightly that it actually frightened the people (see Exodus 34). This is what happens when beings dwell in the very presence of a Holy God. They reflect His light, as Jesus told us to do (Matt. 5:15-16).

Of the redeemed it is prophesied: "And they shall see his face" (Rev. 22:4). Those who have "washed their robes, and made them white in the blood of the Lamb" have allowed the "filthy rags" of their own righteousness to be replaced by the perfect righteousness of Jesus, which He worked out when He lived on this earth. They have allowed their sins to be washed as clean and "white as snow" (Rev. 7:14; Isa. 64:6; 1:18). For all eternity their very robes, your robe, will testify to the amazing mercy of Jesus in covering us with His righteousness and paying the penalty that should have fallen on us. And throughout the ceaseless ages, not one of our sins will be mentioned to us, for they will all be forgotten, as if they never were (see Ezek. 18:22; Mic. 7:19; Heb. 10:17).

PALM BRANCHES

I love palm trees. I associate them with vacations. There's something relaxing about their beautiful branches as they sway in the tropical breeze. When we lived in Southern California, they were everywhere, and I still never got tired of looking at all of them. But why are the redeemed given palm branches? The palm branch has long been a symbol of victory. When Jesus fulfilled the prophecy of Zechariah 9:9 that the King would ride into Jerusalem on a young donkey - the people "took branches of palm trees, and went forth to meet him, and cried, Hosanna: Blessed is the King of Israel that cometh in the name of the Lord" (John 12:13).

Those who inherit eternal life are described as "them that had gotten victory," "he that overcometh," "able to stand against the wiles of the devil," "able to quench all the fiery darts of the wicked," "he that endureth to the end," and "more than conquerors through him that loved us" (Rev. 15:2; 21:7; Eph. 6:11,16; Matt. 10:22;

Rom. 8:37). The heavenly palm branch they receive symbolizes not their own efforts at living the victorious life (which had failed them time and time again), but rather their complete understanding that only Jesus could give them the victory they were so utterly incapable of achieving on their own. No matter how weak, sinful and erring, the Lord tells the penitent soul, "My strength is made perfect in weakness" (2 Cor. 12:9). Some point to their weakness as evidence that they can never overcome. But Christ said that it is this very weakness that makes His own strength perfect. The weaker we are, the less we fall into the trap of depending on self, and the more His strength can work through us. Our own strength, faulty as it is, hinders His strength from doing its perfect work for, in, and through us. This message – His perfect strength of victory – will be immortalized in the palm branches.

THE CROWNS

The Bible says that the redeemed will receive crowns after the Second Coming (1 Pet. 5:4; 2 Tim. 4:8). Do you realize that you are royalty? You are a child of a King. The law of average says that many who are reading these pages are suffering right now. You are going through an extremely rough time, and you may feel like you have little or no value. You feel worthless, either through your own bad choices or through no fault of your own. Perhaps those around you have been cruel and have devastated your sense of self-worth. Jesus tells you in Rev. 3:11 to let no one take your crown. That's what these people are trying to do. They don't want you to realize your inestimable value - a value so high that the Creator of all things was willing to die a horrible, cruel death and let Himself be mocked as well, and treated as if *He* had no real value. But He reigns now and one day you will join

Him (Rev. 20:4) - *that's* how valuable you are to Him. Never forget this. He died for YOU. And He would have done so, *even if you were the only one who needed to be saved.* Did you hear that? Do you believe it? You are worth everything to Him. Now start acting like it. Today. Start believing how valuable you are in God's eyes, regardless of what hateful people say or do to you in this temporary, dark world. They don't decide your value, and even you don't decide your value. God has decided it already. He wouldn't have wasted His time creating you if you had no value, and He certainly wouldn't have sent His Son to die for something worthless.

The correlation of increased smartphone usage among teens and their rising suicide rate has borne out an alarming fact, which is that more and more young people are basing their value on what they experience on social media. The world says you must act and look a certain way to be accepted and peers are often even crueler online than in person. Even adults well past the teen years are falling further and further into depression and despondency, not realizing their value through their kinship to the King. I've often said that one of the biggest surprises in the Judgment will be when millions realize just how valuable they truly are to God and how different their lives might have been had they realized it sooner. God wants you to realize it now, while you can still let Him clean you up and place your feet on the right path, not after your life is over.

When everything seems at its lowest, both in your own life and in the depressing, chaotic world around you, that's the time Christ says to "look up, and lift up your heads, for your redemption draweth nigh" (Luke 21:28). He's coming back soon. Reader, now is the time to be "casting all your cares upon Him; for He careth for you" (1 Pet. 5:7). When you are at your lowest, remember that one day soon believers will be crowned and the redeemed "shall possess the kingdom forever" (Dan. 7:18). God wins in the end. Decide now to be on the winning team.

THOSE FAMOUS STREETS OF GOLD

"And the street of the city was pure gold, as it were transparent glass" (Rev. 21:21).

I once heard an allegory of a man who tried to "take it with him," attempting to bring into heaven bars of gold he had acquired during his life on earth. The shocked residents, looking into his bag, quizzically blurted: "You brought *pavement?*"

Most people have heard of the streets of gold, even if they've never picked up a Bible. But the above text reveals that these streets are not just run-of-the-mill gold, as great as that would be, but a unique, transparent gold. We don't know how thick the gold will be but imagine walking around on enormous, shining, golden streets that you can see right through. They'll no doubt reflect the bright images of the golden city above, as well. Speaking of that, the city itself is constructed of this same transparent, shining gold (see Rev. 21:18).

The gold upon which the redeemed will walk represents their faith, which has been tried in the fire and refined by God. Jesus admonished those in Laodicea, "I counsel thee to buy of me gold tried in the fire, that thou mayest be rich" (Rev. 3:18). And Peter, under inspiration of the Holy Spirit, advises us, "Wherein ye greatly rejoice, though now for a season, if need be, ye are in heaviness through manifold temptations: That the trial of your faith, being much more precious than of gold that perisheth, though it be tried with fire, might be found unto praise and honour and glory at the appearing of Jesus Christ" (1 Pet. 1:6-7).

"The fining pot is for silver, and the furnace for gold: but the Lord trieth the hearts" (Prov. 17:3).

"And I [God] will refine them as silver is refined, and will try them as gold is tried: they shall call on my name, and I will hear them" (Zech. 13:9).

"But he knoweth the way that I take: when he hath tried me, I shall come forth as gold" (Job 23:10).

Often the people of God find themselves, as did Job, in trials and afflictions that test their faith severely. This testing refines and strengthens them if they but hold onto their trust in the almighty God. Just as one cannot build muscle without resistance and exercise, so faith when it lies dormant, cannot flourish and grow. That chiseled guy on the cover of the muscle magazine didn't get there by eating chips and watching workout videos. Likewise, the people of God don't build their faith by just hearing about the faith of others. With each passing trial, not only does our faith increase but we more fully reflect the image of Jesus to those around us. As the gold on the heavenly streets reflects the glory and light of Jesus in the New Jerusalem, so the children of God have been called to reflect Christ on this earth (see 2 Cor. 3:18). It's been said that the way a gold refiner knows the gold is finally pure is when he can clearly see his reflection in the molten metal as he refines it. God's process - and His goal - is the same with us. He refines us to reflect His character. The Bible tells us to consider our trials as a means of building up our patience and faith during this refining process:

"My brethren, count it all joy when ye fall into divers temptations; Knowing this, that the trying of your faith worketh patience. But let patience have her perfect work, that ye may be perfect and entire, wanting nothing" (James 1:2-4).

Notice it doesn't refer to *our* work, but that we are to "let" patience have her perfect work in us so that we ultimately lack nothing. Trials are certainly not fun, but they are performing a work in us just as a baby's milk is performing a work inside that growing baby. The baby doesn't cause the molecular changes, nor is it even aware of these changes, but they are still happening. Likewise, we may not feel any character growth while patience is working on us, but it is still happening, nevertheless, and God sees it. God himself performs it, through the patience.

THE LIGHT OF LIFE

The light from the throne of God, which permeates every corner of this gigantic metropolis, will not only fascinate the senses of all who behold it but will shine as an eternal reminder of the great Plan of Salvation. His children will ever bask in these rays which brighten their new, joyful home. And just as "taking in the rays" of sunshine today releases serotonin in our brains, giving us an increased sense of well-being, so absorbing that light from God will constantly invigorate our soul as it shines forth from the Life-giver. This is the same light made available to you and me today, only then we will view it unhindered by the great expanse of space. Jesus said, "I am the light of the world: he that followeth me shall not walk in darkness, but shall have the light of life" (John 8:12).

The light which can shine upon our minds and hearts today, removing darkness, doubt, discouragement and spiritual confusion is Jesus Himself. He invites us to come to Him just as we are and let His light shine life into our souls. Just as the sunflower constantly turns its face toward the sun, soaking up the dazzling rays, so will we, as we get to know Him, find Jesus more and more appealing and keep our focus and thoughts on Him. As He is the source of all spiritual light on earth today, so He will be the source of all radiant light in the Holy City.

"And the city had no need of the sun, neither of the moon, to shine in it: for the glory of God did lighten it, and the Lamb is the light thereof. And the nations of them which are saved shall walk in the light of it," "And there shall be no more curse: but the throne of God and of the Lamb shall be in it; and his servants shall serve him: And they shall see his face; and his name shall be in their foreheads. And there shall be no night there; and they need no candle, neither light of the sun; for the Lord God giveth them light" (Rev. 21:23-24; 22:3-5).

▲ ▲ ▲

The massive cloud of fire which carries the Savior, all His angels, and now the redeemed, approaches heaven. *What will this place be like?* The suspense is overwhelming as you peer ahead toward the distant, growing light. Heaven! You have thought and dreamed about it for years on earth, and now you will actually be seeing it! It's so hard to believe that this is all real, but it is! The moment that you have been waiting for all your life is now transpiring all around you.

The cloud begins its descent upon the Sea of Glass, which stretches out for miles before the Holy City. You immediately understand why the prophet John said it was mingled with fire. The light and the radiant gold from the city bounce off the glassy surface of the crystal water so brightly, it looks as though it really is on fire - perhaps it is! What will it be like to walk in this blazing glow?

Now you and the surrounding great multitude are lowered toward its gleaming surface and the light quickly engulfs you. The golden flame-like beams blaze all around you, and it's unlike anything you've ever experienced. You realize that had you experienced anything like this on earth you would have been confused and even terrified. But since you know you are perfectly safe, you simply take in the flaming beauty of the scene. It's hard to say whether the blaze that engulfs you is fire or light, but it's a surreal sight, whatever it is, and no special effect could have ever recreated this overwhelming scene.

As your feet gently touch down, it feels soft and pleasantly cool to your toes. You smile as you slide one foot across the crystal surface. Is it a liquid or a solid? Or something in between? And if these flames are real, they surely aren't burning you. You take a step forward. The substance below you feels something like water, yet it supports you. Looking off to the horizon, you notice that not a ripple or wave appear on the visible patches of its surface that appear now and then through the flames. It is indeed as smooth as glass, and clear as crystal below the light.

Jesus, head and shoulders above all others, stands in the middle of this glassy sea, surrounded by the innumerable new residents of the New Jerusalem. The magnificent wall of the city behind, although larger in stature, is itself eclipsed by the beauty, glory, and brightness of the Savior. Human and angel alike bow before Him in love and adoration. Although He is the Son, He is fully God, deserving of worship. As you rise, you notice He is looking toward the top of the city where the Father upon His throne overlooks the scene. All eyes follow the Redeemer's upward gaze and ultimately land on the glorious light that envelops the Father Himself. You long to get a closer view and your wish will soon be granted.

But first, Jesus has something for you. He motions the vast throng of angels to bring forth the crowns, harps and palm branches of victory, which He then gives to each of the redeemed. When your turn comes, Jesus embraces you and places the crown on your head in the sight of the onlooking universe. You know you don't deserve this, and you instinctively start to reach up to cast it at His feet in humble gratitude as you've seen done in Scripture. But before you can, He gently places something into your right hand. You glance down at the golden device He's just given you. Your harp. You're getting your first close-up look at the famous stringed instrument. It looks nothing like the plain, three-stringed harps portrayed in cartoons on earth. It has many strings, and it's beautiful! You can't resist strumming it, and as the beautiful, rich sound mingles with the variant notes of the redeemed behind you - also curiously trying out their instruments - you wonder how many sounds this thing can produce and what it will sound like when all of you play together. You can't wait to find out. With palm branch in hand, you make your way back into the crowd, through the gleaming sea flames, and take your place beside your loved one, both amazed by what is taking place. And to think that all of this is just the beginning.

Now Jesus starts to lead the great multitude forward toward the entrance of the City. Although you are surrounded by people and angels on every side, there is no sense of claustrophobia that often struck you in massive crowds on earth. The passage "God is not the author of confusion, but of peace" (1 Cor. 14:33), comes back to you as you and the vast company move forward, peacefully and in order, following the Savior.

Jesus, with His mighty arm, now lays hold of one of the pearly gates and swings it back on its glittering hinges. Then the King, who prepared this amazing place for you, declares to the ransomed throng, "Come, ye blessed of my Father, inherit the kingdom prepared for you from the foundation of the world" (Matt. 25:34).

The great Shepherd then leads great multitude through the giant portal. It occurs to you that the "strait and narrow road" on earth ironically led you to the wide and accommodating gate of this place.

The massive, jasper wall is as gorgeous from the inside view as it was outside. Necks are craning all around you as everyone takes in the awesome view. This wall is thick! The other end of it - opening into the streets of the city - is over 200 feet ahead — two thirds the length of a football field. If the splendor of just the *inside* of the wall is this spectacular, what is the rest of the city going to be like? Your anticipation grows as you take in the remaining 200 feet of pure, heavenly jasper. Looking ahead, you see that some of the people have exited the tunnel, and they seem to be overwhelmed with delight and amazement as the even brighter light washes over them. Your loved one, still close by, taps your shoulder and points up to a particularly beautiful portion of the overhead stone. You had forgotten she was beside you, having been so caught up in the wonder of it all.

Now you step out into the brilliance of the Holy City. What a sight for human eyes! This metropolis is so vast, and there are so many new things to see! Grand fountains of water spray their giant arcs into the air. Lofty waterfalls, designed and constructed by the Redeemer Himself, cascade down the shimmering gold walls of some of the structures. Are these waterfalls actually branches of the River of Life originating at the throne of God? A powerful, Olympic-theme-style anthem from a million trumpets and stringed instruments fills the city as you wander from sight to sight. Such grand and instantly catchy music, yet it lacks that throb of discord so often blasted from the clunky instruments of earth. The moving composition seems to fit perfectly with this majestic and exciting yet peaceful Kingdom. So many thoughts flood your mind at once as you try to take it all in. Will you be able to get the name of this music so that you can listen to it again later? There's no need of iPods here, and you wonder without worry, how you will be able to hear such music anytime you like.

You glance down for just a second, and your attention is now transfixed on the street itself. You knew it would be transparent gold, but your preconceived image of the substance didn't even come close. You cannot, as you gaze upon it, bring to mind any material that could rival its splendor. Beneath this street, and on either side of it, you notice the foundation of jasper. Its brilliant green reflection surpasses that of the wall, for you are now nearer the throne of God, which inundates the city with spectacular light.

This thought causes you to look up toward the pinnacle of the city, and as your eyes once again behold the Father on His royal throne, you marvel at the ingenious design of this city. Although the Great White Throne is 12 floors (and nearly 400 miles) up, you can see it perfectly from this lowest level. In fact, you notice that the city has been designed, at least from your initial observations, so that the glory of God can be seen from any angle in this gigantic, intricate city. Openings appear throughout the 12 foundations, and the foundations themselves are transparent. Never, out on these streets of gold, will you be without access to a clear view of the Father and the Lamb.

Trees of all varieties fill the city. One long stretch of fountains is lined by hundreds of towering palm trees. You love palm trees. Back on earth you always associated them with vacations and good times but compared to this place, those vacation spots would now seem dark and boring. You look elsewhere and see the gorgeous willow tree, the lovely dogwood, the mighty oak. Sycamores decorate one street, while bright red and orange maples adorn another. This, of course, sparks another thought in the cascade of questions that flood your mind: do these trees change colors or do they remain brilliant in their red and orange and yellow as if it were eternally autumn? So many questions to ask the angels. You know you have eternity, but you want to know now. And each new sight creates a new barrage of questions. You know you'll get your answers, but you've always been so curious and eager to learn new things that you just can't help yourself. This land is a smorgasbord of new things, and you are now the proverbial kid in a boundless candy store of discovery.

The golden structures within this place rise to heights that dwarf the tallest earthly skyscrapers. There are more than 30 miles between each floor, and some of these buildings are several miles high. How pitiful and skinny, frail and dull, were the grandest designs humans had constructed back on earth. How temporary their existence in contrast to the perpetuity of what you now behold. Resplendent staircases of every height, shape, and design ascend throughout the city, and you wonder which to explore first at some point. The thought recurs that you need not fret over how much you can't do right away, for you have all of eternity to do these things, and to explore this city. Whatever sections remain unexplored within the first million years can be investigated in the next billion or so. Yet even then, as creative as the Lord is, you would still not have seen all that lies within the walls of this great metropolis. Truly there is no end to the handiwork of your Creator!

The multitude follows Jesus down the main street in the center of the city and moves toward something that to you, from this distance, appears to be a giant red, marble ramp of some sort, flanked by colossal pillars. Why would a miles-wide ramp be here? As you get closer, you realize that what you thought was a ramp is actually a giant red staircase lined with massive, shining pillars. It didn't occur to you that it could be a staircase from a distance because it was so incredibly wide. All your life, you knew that this city would be big, but as you gaze upon it now, you begin to grasp just how gigantic it really is. On earth, there was never a need for such a gigantic staircase, but as the large company begins to ascend its glittering steps, you realize that there is function behind the form. No city on earth would ever require a design that could accommodate a "multitude that no man can number" but things are different here. You are amazed at how such a massive crowd can so smoothly navigate the climb. No pushing and shoving, no grumbling or impatience. Most seem enraptured by the sights that surround them as they ascend the heights of the staircase. You stop for a moment and turn around to take in the city streets below with all the fabulous architecture. Is there any view in this place that is not breathtaking?

At the top of the staircase, Jesus leads this shining sea of people down another tremendous corridor. You are gradually making your way up the city floors, toward the throne Christ shares with the Father, and every step seems to be therefore more illuminated as you continuously close the distance. This giant corridor gives you a chance to look more closely at something you've seen on many of these buildings. It appears as though there are engraved signs of some sort above the doors and you want to read one of them. An unfamiliar name is carved in stone above the door frame. As you slowly try to pronounce it to yourself, a soft, deep voice from behind pronounces it correctly and says that it is the new name of one of your fellow human beings. You turn and see the smiling face of a handsome angel. He apparently had noticed your curiosity and wanted to answer your unspoken, obvious question. He then explains that soon you will be shown your own home which Jesus built especially for you. The thought of a mansion right now, however, seems to pale in comparison to the event you're about to experience. The Father and the Lamb, sitting on their throne, is an image which you have yearned to see up close and in person for so long, you can hardly believe it's about to be a reality.

After passing over various flights of stairs and exploring numerous parts of the city along the way, you see that just beyond this last enormous staircase is the Great Throne of God. Something so bright it makes the sun look like a candle shines forth from beyond the top of the stairs. Your anticipation is almost unbearable as you make your way up the final few steps. The word "light" just isn't adequate; this is something far more powerful than any light you've ever seen. Billions of angels are lifting their voices in praise as you stand at the top of the staircase in awe.

At the end of a long, golden aisle, flanked by myriads of angels, presides God the Father. He sits atop the Royal Chair in all His glory and smiles at His Son who leads the redeemed to the foot of the Throne. Jesus presents to the Father the purchase of His blood. You and the rest of the multitude bow low in the presence of the Sovereign of the universe. The Son of Man beholds with the Father the travail of His soul and is satisfied. Now all of the beings in the great city cry out at once, "Blessing, and honour, and glory, and power, be unto him that sitteth upon the throne, and unto the Lamb for ever and ever!" How long the Father has waited for this moment! How long the Son has yearned to witness this scene! The family of God, yes, the "entire family named under heaven and earth" is finally together at last. The work which Jesus did on behalf of the fallen race has yielded its precious fruit. The Father, Son, and Holy Spirit have accomplished what they set out to do. Christ's image has been restored in the fallen race and love will reign throughout eternity. There is no better place to be in all the universe than this very spot you occupy right now, and you know it. Things have never felt so absolutely *right*. Every fiber of your being is awash with joy and peace and love. You never want to leave this bright spot - *your* spot, in the one, giant family that surrounds you, completed by the awesome throne of God right before you. You try to conjure up words that can begin to describe your emotions right now but finally decide that the Word of God expressed it best in just three simple words. The three words that were true before the great rebellion ever took place and that are still true today, as the plan of salvation has come full circle: "GOD IS LOVE."

Thought Questions:

1. What is your main takeaway from this chapter? Why is it your main takeaway?

2. What does the story about the man sneaking pavement into heaven tell us about our earthly priorities? What has been pavement in your own life?

3. What do the elements of the city's construction tell you about God's character? What do the mansions or "rooms" positioned close to God tell you about Him?

4. What do the various gifts you'll receive in heaven tell you about God's promises?

5. What did you learn about God's will for you in this chapter? What do you feel He's impressing you to start doing differently this week to walk more closely with Him?

MEETING YOUR GUARDIAN

"For he shall give his angels charge over thee, to keep thee in all thy ways."

-Psalm 91:11

"Are they not all ministering spirits, sent forth to minister for them who shall be heirs of salvation?"

-Hebrews 1:14

"PROOF ANGELS EXIST: INCREDIBLE IMAGE SHOWS ETHEREAL OBJECT OVER THE SKIES OF LONDON."

THE HEADLINE IS from a 2014 news article. A 38-year-old Londoner was in her backyard garden with friends one night when she looked up and saw the moon flanked by four stars. She snapped the picture, and the result turned out looking something like an angel-shaped flash. But is this proof angels exist? Well, hardly.

And neither is the familiar cartoonish depiction of a mini angel on one shoulder, arguing with a tiny, cutesy red devil on the other. But should we rule out their existence just because of less-than-substantial examples of evidence or silly portrayals?

The Bible makes it clear that each one of us has a guardian angel. In fact, in times of danger or special need, we can be assured of the presence of multiple angels. Scripture tells us of an instance when the King of Syria, fed up with Elisha supernaturally revealing his secret military plans to Israel, decided to send "horses and chariots and a great army" to go and capture the prophet to shut him up. When the troops finally arrived, Elisha's servant saw the mighty army surrounding the entire city and frantically asked the prophet what they should do. Elisha's answer of faith is an assurance to us all: "Fear not: for they that be with us are more than they that be with them" (2 Kings 6:16). Then he calmly prayed that God would open the eyes of his fearful servant, who immediately beheld that "the mountain was full of horses and chariots of fire round about Elisha" (verse 17). I have no doubt that Elisha could not actually see that army, but his faith in God's protection allowed him to know they were there, just as surely as if he had physically witnessed them. This is the faith God will grow in us even now, as we get to know Him.

But has the almighty God, who at one time sent angelic armies, changed tactics over the years? Is He less likely today to assign angels to protect us in time of need? "I am the Lord, I change not," is the promise from God Himself (Mal. 3:6). If the faith that humans exercise toward God has diminished over the centuries, it has not altered the fact that the angels are just as available today as they were in Bible times.

Imagine how thrilling it will be to finally meet the angel who has been guarding you all your life. Have you kept that angel busy, as I have, far too many times, with foolish decisions? There's a wonderful friendship in store for you as you finally get to meet your guardian.

▲ ▲ ▲

You have been in the Holy City only a short time, and your senses are overwhelmed by all of the sights and sounds and fragrant aromas. Glorious is one of many words that come to mind as you take it all in, but words fall short when describing this place. Your attention is turned once again to the tall, handsome, friendly-looking angel that shines brightly beside you. This is the one that joined you on your ascension toward the great cloud to meet the Lord in the air at the Second Coming. It is your guardian angel, and he's eager to talk with you. He tells you his name, and you extend your hand as you start to tell him yours, but then smile as you remember that this special friend has been by your side since the day you were born. He knew your name before you did. He smiles knowingly - it's obvious to him what just dawned on you - and squeezes your hand tightly, savoring this moment as much as you are. It seems clear to both of you that a mere handshake is ridiculously formal, and you quickly replace it with a big bear hug. You immediately wonder how something so solid could remain invisible down on earth. You also wonder what he can teach you about the science of invisibility - something you thought would be so cool when you were a kid! You still think it would be cool.

As the embrace ends, you remember that since coming to this place, you've been given a "new name" (Rev. 2:17). Unlike your old name, no one else in the entire universe has this name. It was created just for you by Jesus Himself. When you first heard it, you immediately liked it and thought it somehow "fit" you. You now tell the angel your new name, and he repeats it back to you, telling you the same thing you had thought: it somehow fits you.

The two of you stroll down the streets of transparent gold amidst the celebration of the Great Homecoming. The rest of the redeemed are also getting to know their angels, and the entire city is astir with joyful reunions, angel activity, and people on the move as various genres of beautiful music flow from different parts of the city. All this activity and the cheerful sounds around you make New York city at Christmastime seem lifeless and dull by comparison.

As would be expected, you start to feel as though you've known this angel all your life. His smile radiates as he begins to tell you of the most fascinating incidents during his watch care over you. All during your life on earth you had things that seemed to go wrong, which you were determined to ask about when you got to heaven. But now the glory, peace, and joy that fill your soul make those trials seem so small and so temporary by comparison, you have trouble bringing them to mind. And how insignificant even the times of loneliness when compared to the fellowship with Jesus that you will enjoy as often as you wish. You'll also make countless friendships with the angels and the rest of the redeemed from earth, as well as exploring the endless galaxies beyond! And now to think that through it all this very *real* angel was beside you, hurting when you hurt, watching over you in danger, and living for your well-being.

Although you struggle to bring any trials or disappointments to mind, your angel does reveal some things that definitely shed some light on just such times. He mentions a few instances where you were sure that God didn't hear your prayers. Then by the gift of prophecy, the angel unfolds to you what *would have* happened, had your prayer been answered the way you desired. He reveals the ultimate loss, whether temporal or eternal, that would have resulted from always having things your way. That better-paying job you wanted, but didn't get, resulted in someone receiving the gospel from you, who wouldn't have received it had you gotten that "perfect" job and moved away. The angel asks if you had it to do over again, would you now want that prayer to have been answered at the expense of this person's soul? You clearly see his point and of course, enthusiastically answer No. You can now honestly thank God for prayers that were *not* answered the way you wanted. Your appreciation of God only grows as you realize now, more than ever, that His ways are, without exception, for your own good. All things do indeed work together for good to them that love Him (Rom. 8:28).

Next, your angel reveals a few of the times that your life was saved and you weren't even aware of it: That flat tire you had, which caused you to cross a certain intersection 23 minutes later, thus avoiding the drunk driver; that 747 whose mechanical problems were delayed while you calmly read a magazine in seat 17C, oblivious to it all; that snake whose mouth was held shut as you stepped ignorantly over it during a summer stroll through the woods. You see more and more how the hand of the Lord through His angels, was keeping you safe at every moment.

And even when injuries were permitted, (as in the case of Job and Paul and Christ), you see that it was still God's loving, miraculous power that kept you alive and sustained you through it all. Besides, even greater is your reward for all your suffering (2 Cor. 4:17; Rom. 8:18).

Your angel tells you that he and the other angels often spoke about what they would have done if they could've been human, even for just one day. The advantages there would have been with the capability of physically going and helping the sick and suffering directly and not behind the scenes as angels so often did. Of course, they at times appeared as humans to do God's work, but those times were the exception, not the rule. Humans, on the other hand, had that brief window of time where they could go out and do things to bless others face-to-face as well as directly spread the gospel to so many. How amazing that would have been, says the angel. As he speaks, you begin to see what a huge advantage, not *dis*advantage, you had as a human being born on that rebellious planet, Earth.

You approach the foot of a giant, ruby staircase that stretches up and into the colossal architecture overhead. You and your angel continue your conversation as you begin your ascent. God surely knew what He was doing when He assigned this angel to you. Your personalities seem to have so much in common that goes beyond explanation. You wonder if God put the introvert and extrovert angels with their corresponding human personalities. This is another question you can ask this new friend, who will truly be one of your closest companions through all the ages. It's a friendship that will only grow as eternity marches on.

Thought Questions:

1. What is your main takeaway from this chapter? Why is it your main takeaway?

2. What do you most look forward to asking your guardian angel? When in your life did your angel work hardest or even miraculously to protect you?

3. What does the fact that God has commissioned these beings to watch over you tell you about His character?

4. What does the comforting fact that you have a guardian angel tell you about God's promises? What does Elisha's story tell you about God's promises?

5. What did you learn about God's will for you in this chapter? What do you feel He's impressing you to start doing differently this week to walk more closely with Him?

THE RIGHTFUL REIGN

*"Yea, let God be true, but every man a liar; as it is
written, That thou mightest be justified in thy sayings,
and mightest overcome when thou art judged."*

-ROMANS 3:4

"Just and true are thy ways, thou King of saints."

-HEBREWS 11:16

"WHY WOULD A GOOD GOD LET
BAD THINGS HAPPEN TO GOOD PEOPLE?"

IN THEOLOGICAL CIRCLES, the study of this question is referred to
as **"Theodicy,"** (from Greek *theos*, "god" and *dikē*, "justice"). It's
always interesting when skeptics eagerly challenge believers with this
dilemma as if no religious person had ever thought of it before. As if
even the best of believers hadn't pondered it in the darker moments
of life (Psalm 22, for example). But mostly, as if this one question
should be enough to bankrupt the believer's entire walk with God,
whom they know and have grown to love. Volumes have been written

on the subject, but the argument usually includes questions along these lines:

Why doesn't God just stop all suffering, as I would, if I were God?

If God is perfect, and He made all things, then He also made evil, so isn't He to blame for it (or at least imperfect for not preventing it)?

How do we know God's way of governing is best, anyway?

Why are His rules so stringent? Who is He to tell us what is moral or immoral?

Often the questioning even devolves into silliness like *Can God make a boulder too heavy for Him to lift? Either way, He loses, so what kind of God is that? Tee-hee.*

Perhaps you've been challenged with some of these questions in the past or even pondered them yourself. Maybe there are a few curious atheists or agnostics still reading, and you'd like to know before you read any further, why *anyone* would choose to live under a heavenly system of such an "unjust, uncaring god." Or maybe you've adopted a set of beliefs that you feel are better suited for yourself and/or humanity than any of the antiquated stuff the Bible proposes. Fair enough. Let's take a look together...

WHAT IS BEST?

On June 23, 2016, a referendum was held in the United Kingdom, to decide whether the U.K. should leave or remain in the European Union. Many who assumed the exit plans would never succeed didn't even bother going to the polls that day, and it ended up passing by 51.9% to 48.1%. This "Brexit" vote ("Britain" + "Exit") sent shockwaves across the globe and caused Britain's Prime Minister, David Cameron, to announce his resignation that very day. Many could not believe this had happened, and not a few leaders in the E.U. were openly displeased by the move. However, Nigel Farage, the former leader of the populist U.K. Independence Party, called the vote "a victory for real people," despite the fact that 48% of the people viewed it as a defeat.

Regardless of your political views or opinion of Brexit, that controversial vote and the disparate reactions to it demonstrate how differently people can view the same event, and how rapidly our world can change. *(As a side note, the increasingly common demonizing of political foes on both sides is not helpful, and of course, people from various political parties will be in Heaven. Perhaps now would be a good time to start playing nice, since we may be neighbors in Heaven one day.)*

So, whose policies are best for running a city, or a nation, or a union of nations? Polls are ever-changing. Political, economic and social ideologies once considered taboo are becoming more and more mainstream, particularly among the youth (socialism, for example, has seen an increased "favorable" rating in the U.S., with a 2016 poll placing it at 35% overall, and a surprising 55% with voters under 30). But why? Why are we seeing increased polarization, with words like populism, liberalism, nationalism, communism, conservatism, socialism, fascism, capitalism, anarchism, etc. being thrown around as both smear labels and proposed solutions to social and political ills? Because people cannot agree on the best way to run things. No matter what direction the pendulum swings, there will always be those who oppose the trend, decrying it as unfair and/or destructive to society. Right or wrong, these impassioned, conflicting views make any prospect for a harmonious society seem increasingly slim. The more suspicious we are of government, the more suspicious we typically become of each other, of those who don't see things our way.

TRUTH AND TRUST

It all boils down to two principles, two very similar words: **Truth and Trust**. If I fully believe in something, then that, to me, is the truth. If I'm not careful, the propagation of that truth becomes so important to me that I risk falling into an "end justifies the means" mindset. I may start to believe that no matter what it takes, that policy - my truth - *must* prevail. But what if I'm wrong? What if what I thought was the truth is, in fact, not the truth? What if someone has told me something based on false or manipulated data? What if I'm pushing for a policy that is actually not good for the people, but could potentially make things worse, even though I can't see it yet from my vantage point?

The solution to this problem would be to always know all truth. To be insusceptible to lies from any party that comes at me with their proposals. Since no one has the superhuman ability to instantly discern truth from error on all issues, humans have learned to depend more on that second principle:

TRUST

Most of us are not experts in economics, tax law, health coverage, or the myriad of subjects civil servants and attorneys must research and understand inside and out. We therefore vote into office people we feel will do the footwork for us, learning what is best for We the People. We trust they won't do anything reckless that backfires on us but will constantly be working for the good of the people. Our representatives should "represent" us, as their titles suggest. But have politicians historically proven themselves to be the most trustworthy people on the planet once they get into power? When you think "honesty" is the next word that comes to your mind "politician"? (*You probably couldn't help but smile reading that far-fetched last line, particularly if you read it out loud to someone.*) While I fully believe there are honest, sincere public servants in government, we all know that politicians have historically been synonymous with self-interest and broken promises. As a politician in a movie once admitted: "When I'm not kissing babies, I'm stealing their candy."

An April, 2017 poll, conducted by the Pew Research Center found trust in government at near historic lows, with just 20% of Americans saying they trust the government to do what is right always or most of the time. And this is not a recent phenomenon. The trend has been downward overall since the polling began in 1958 when about three-quarters of those polled claimed to trust the government. As trust decreases, problems increase. And again, as we clearly see today, the less we trust the government, the more we fracture and turn on one another, with increased suspicion. These dual trust-failures in government and each other slowly tear apart the fabric of society, fulfilling Christ's principle that a house divided against itself cannot stand (Matt. 12:25).

In his excellent bestseller *The Speed of Trust*, Stephen M.R. Covey cites the actual monetary costs of broken trust in organizations, referring to them as "Low Trust Taxes." It is estimated that the price tag for lack of trust annually is $250-$300 billion for U.S. businesses and $1.1 trillion for bureaucracies. I've worked for and with companies on both ends of the trust spectrum, and I can testify that the effect on employees is evident; it becomes part of the culture. When I shared with Covey an example of extreme integrity from one of these companies, he told me he would love to use that example in an upcoming book. I told him I would have to talk to the founding family, whose story it was. After much thought, they declined, saying they didn't want to be held up as examples. When I got back with Covey, he said that their humble response made him that much more impressed with the company.

In my interaction with employees of that particular company, I can tell you that trust toward the founding family was extremely high, and it showed. Customers are impacted as well. A Watson Wyatt study shows high-trust organizations outperform low-trust organizations in total return to shareholders by 286 percent. The aforementioned company, by the way, was #1 in their field, nationwide. This is no accident. Keeping trust levels high in corporate America is hard enough. But getting the *universe* to trust you? How is that accomplished?

OF GODS AND ROBOTS

So, if 100% *truth* cannot be known or detected at all times and if 100% *trust* cannot be attained at all times, then a perfect governing system can only happen in one of three possible scenarios:

1) **Everyone is a god**. Think about it. If everyone in the system were a god, knowing the future, possessing omniscience, and interacting with perfect morality and honesty, with no possibility of making a mistake, then the system would operate with zero chance of failure. Is this an option for us? Just look at your past decisions and the actions of society around you, and you

immediately realize that no, we are not gods, possessing the list of attributes mentioned above. We must rule out option #1.

2) **Everyone is a robot**. All beings are devoid of free will and must do exactly as they are told, or programmed to do, with no possibility of deviating from the program. Even if wires, metal and computer chips weren't involved, the same flesh and blood we now possess would merely be living elements of a humanoid robot. Without free will, the city, nation or universe would operate with no chance of political polarization or war. Obedient harmony would rule the day, or rather the eternity. But at what cost? Thankfully you and I do possess a free will (Josh. 24:15; Rev. 3:20; Gal. 5:13), to exercise as we see fit, which of course places that harmony at risk. So there goes option #2.

3) **Everyone fully trusts the leader, who *is* a God**. Here we have both vital elements of Truth and Trust back in place while maintaining the free will of all individuals. If there *is* a leader who knows all things (Truth), that's a wonderful attribute to have. But can we *trust* that leader? This combination of **a)** omniscience/omnipotence creating all the rules with the citizens' best interest in mind, and **b)** complete trust in the leader to make the perfect rules - this combination is the only real possibility for utopia, outside of science fiction.

We are not all robots, and we are certainly not all gods. We are finite, fallen beings, possessing that incredibly powerful and potentially dangerous thing called a free will. That free will is capable of throwing a philosophical monkey wrench into the well-oiled machine of a perfect system (or a perfect universe) any time it chooses. Even *one* rogue individual can wreak havoc on any free system known to intelligent thought (as we'll see in chapter 9).

Whatever philosophies or ideologies of utopian government humanity has ever conjured, they will invariably run up against one of these three categories. What all governing systems boil down to is, again, these two things: TRUTH and TRUST.

God knows the end from the beginning (Isa. 46:10), and He sees the result of every incident in ways we cannot possibly know while on this earth. This is one of the reasons God doesn't always answer our prayers with a "yes." When we get to heaven and examine all of the previously-unseen pieces of life's jigsaw puzzle, we'll finally understand how all things worked together for our good (Rom. 8:28). We'll know that every time someone on the talk shows condescendingly asked, "Where was your God when this tragedy struck?" our God was right there, feeling their pain, hating the fact that it is a part of life on this earth until the Second Coming. We don't know the end from the beginning, and it is therefore quite easy and natural to blame God every time a tragedy strikes.

CRIME AND FREE WILL

We live in a sinful world, and it pains God to see our suffering. One may still ask, **but what if** God were to step in and prevent it? Let's consider if He did. This is not our home. It's a world where sin thrives and where trials and tribulations are a part of our lives (1 Pet. 4:12). He promises a perfect world one day, where every tear will be wiped away as rebellion is finally put down and every being willingly stays away from sin, that hateful thing that it is. But let's suppose that in the meantime, God simply prevented any pain and suffering because He is a benevolent God. We already discussed free will and robots. If God stopped every criminal before they committed a crime, He's still taking away their free will, even though they would be free to hate Him for it. How truly free is a will that cannot be expressed? As the saying goes "A man convinced against his will is of the same opinion still." The same would be true if he were forced against his will. This is not freedom.

BAD THINGS TO GOOD PEOPLE

But what about believers who suffer? Why not relieve all *their* suffering, every time they call out to Him for relief? Imagine if, for all of earth's history, God actually did this for all believers. How would that affect free will, the plan of salvation, and the security of the Kingdom for all eternity? What message would it send to non-believers? *Become a Christian and have no trials.* Sounds like a good deal! (Prosperity preachers have disappointed many with such false promises over the years) Soon all humanity would gravitate over to God's side for only one purpose: to avoid any suffering.

This would hinder love in two ways:

1) Now everyone in the Kingdom would basically be paid believers, bribed by a pain-free life (Satan accused Job of this: Job 1:8-11). The avoidance of pain would be the motivator, not love.

2) Satan would simply lure people into a life of sin, and then tempt them to merely claim to believe and pray for relief. God, Himself would then actually be *perpetuating* sin. He would be maintaining the same level of pain-free bliss of a future *sinless* world, right here and now, in a sin-*filled* world. No one would ever see the full consequences of sin, including all its collateral pain and suffering. The principle of Cause and Effect would be violated. God would make a cover for sin and conceal its destructive nature, the very thing He wants revealed so humans will want no part of it.

WE REAP WHAT WE SOW

Another reason for trials is consequences we bring on ourselves. We see this in the case of David (2 Sam. 24:12-13), Adam and Eve (Gen. 3:16-19), King Nebuchadnezzar (Daniel 4:27-34), and other examples all through Scripture. Some trials we bring on ourselves through bad decisions, procrastination, emotionally-charged behavior and a host of other things that follow the principle "you reap what you sow" (Gal. 6:7-9). The Pharisees took this principle too far and judged every sufferer to be a sinner, paying the price for their iniquities, even in the case of medical conditions from birth. Obviously, this approach is dubious, as Christ handily pointed out (see John 9:1-3).

REFINED IN THE FIRE

Whether collateral damage, self-induced punishment, the results of a sinful world, or as part of a bigger picture in progress - in every case we can know that God uses the situation to get our attention and refine us in the fire (Isa. 48:10; Zech. 13:9). As C.S. Lewis puts it in his classic *The Problem of Pain*: "Pain insists upon being attended to. God whispers to us in our pleasures, speaks in our conscience, but shouts in our pain: it is His megaphone to rouse a deaf world." Then, if we allow it, the refining trial will sharpen our faith and prepare us to be fitted for the mansions above. We are the jewels that make up His crown (Zech. 9:16; Isa. 62:3), and we are the elements of His temple (1 Pet. 2:5). In the earthly temple, each stone was to be chiseled in the quarry and then brought to the temple already prepared for placement (1 Kings 6:7). It was not to be modified at the temple. Likewise, God has already constructed a place for us and is now preparing, refining, chiseling and pruning us so that someday we can fit perfectly in our spot in that Kingdom (Isa. 51:1). There will be no more trials or refining once we get there.

THE PRUNING KNIFE

Every winter I prune our flower bush by the front porch down to almost nothing. And every spring it comes back with vigor, even more beautiful than before. As God purges and prunes you during trials, you will, like my rose bush in winter, seem like nothing for a moment. But as you receive the vibrant life of Christ, you will come back even better than before (John 3:30). You will begin to experience the real "you," that you were always meant to be. Jesus explained that "Every branch that beareth fruit, He [the Father] purgeth it, that it may bring forth more fruit" (John 15:2).

I once heard it put this way: although the pruning by life's trials can be painful, it is your loving Father than holds the knife.

So, *why would a good God allow bad things to happen to good people?* We've shared what the Bible has to say, so now let's visit the narrative part of this book's format and see what would happen if you could exercise the same powers that God has. Often, by looking at things from God's perspective, we begin to see why He does and doesn't do certain things. We can get further with skeptics if we ask them to put themselves in God's place for a moment, and take their argument to its logical conclusion, rather than just try to prove them wrong. Consider the following scenario carefully the next time you wonder whether or not you can trust God:

THEODICY ODYSSEY

You wake with a start in the middle of the night, soaked in sweat and screaming. The school shooting just happened a few days ago. Your little nephew was shot, along with a score of other children, and he's in critical condition at the hospital's Intensive Care Unit. Rage had filled your soul as you glared at the news footage of the shooter being dragged off in handcuffs. While politicians pointed fingers at one another, one news commentator frustratingly asked, "So where was God when all this happened?" As a believer, you were at first upset by his rhetoric, but as your nephew's condition quickly worsened, you began to replay that question in your own head. *Where* was *God when this happened? If He can't do a better job than this, then He should get off the throne and let someone else take over. How hard is it to just stop one demented criminal? If you had His power, you would have done it in an instant.* In fact, ten seconds ago you *were* doing it. Your hands were gripping the madman's neck, but the charged feeling of revenge was slowly replaced by confusion as you realized that it was not the deranged shooter in your hands, but your twisted bedsheets, crushed within your clenched fists. You've awoken from a nightmare. If only the shooting had been just a nightmare. But that part was real.

Your pounding heart begins to settle as you look around the room. On your dresser, next to a photo of you and your "little big guy" nephew, lies a crumpled sheet of paper from your journal. Normally you capture your goals, dreams and answered prayers there, but that page was torn out in frustration as you vented against God with your pen. The framed selfie of you and your nephew is now facing the wall. The sight of it staring at you during that first sleepless night was too painful. Now a strange reflection - *from the moonlight?* - shimmers off the backside of the frame. The reflection is growing, however, so this can't be from the moon. You sit up even straighter and rub your eyes for clarity. The light is not a reflection at all. The back of the frame is glowing, and it forms three unmistakable sentences:

"YOU HAVE ALL POWER. IT WILL GROW. STOP THE EVIL."

Your mind juggles a list of unrealistic reasons why the glowing words would be there as you try to make sense of the spectacle. You can't take your eyes off the sight, but suddenly you hear a child's distant scream for help. You fling the sheets off your legs and bolt out of bed to grab some clothes. As you frantically slide your jeans on, those mysterious words "You have all power" pulse brighter with an eerie glow, arresting your attention. Your utter confusion is interrupted by another scream. You dash toward your front door, reaching for the doorknob, but it swings open in front of you. *Are you losing your mind?* You hesitate for a split second, but remember that someone is in danger, and charge through the door, clearing your front porch steps.

PART 1: *TRAIN VS. CHILD - A CLASSIC DILEMMA CONFRONTS YOU*

Immediately - you're not sure how - you're at a drawbridge where a familiar scene is transpiring. A passenger train's horn blares as its blinding light shatters the darkness and illuminates something struggling near the middle of the bridge. A young child's foot is somehow caught in the tracks as the engine rushes forward, its shrieking brakes useless against the inertia behind tons of moving steel. With seconds remaining, you have no time to even get to the child, let alone free him from the tracks. This philosophical dilemma that everyone has heard since childhood is now transpiring before you. Hypothetically, you know what should be done. It's easy when discussed in a classroom setting. The many lives are worth more than just one. But this is real. *Isn't it? How did you get here?* Nevermind! You've got to do something *now*.

The drawbridge lever glows beside you. *Was it there before?* Instinct demands that you pull it, but what of the passengers? Your indecision stalls you. Every second is precious. Your hatred of this bizarre dilemma doesn't change the fact that you must do something. You just *cannot* derail a train full of people. The greater good says to let the higher number of train passengers live, even at the tragic expense of this one child.

Nausea churns your stomach. You want to turn from the awful scene and cover your ears, but you can't. You can't turn your back on a helpless child and let him die. But you can't derail a passenger train, either.

Now the child turns his face toward you. You are horrified. This is your nephew! *Here? But-...* He screams your name through tears, his terrified gaze vacillating between you and the oncoming train. The scene shifts into slow motion. Chills tingle your neck as your instinct to pull the lever rebounds. You try to rationalize. *Perhaps the train is empty!* But as you reach for the glowing lever, your new powers make you instantly aware of every passenger on board the train. You squeeze your eyes shut and shake your head frantically, trying to clear your mental vision. *How do you know all of this?* You thought you had only a couple of seconds left, but time now grinds almost to a halt, as your awareness of everyone on the train unfolds, revealing their futures. Your love for your nephew is now weighed against the number of people on this train - 23 to be exact. Strangely, you sense the love that every one of their family members has for them, and you somehow experience the collective emotions that they would feel if these precious lives were snuffed out at the bottom of the icy river, far below.

The overwhelming power of your sudden affection for the larger group of 23 quickly influences you as you snap your hand back from the lever like a hot stove. Your nephew must be sacrificed - *right?* - to avoid this greater level of death and sorrow for so many more.

A SECOND GENERATION - *PULL THAT LEVER*

As devastated as you are, it was the moral choice. Suddenly a vision of the second sentence from your room flashes into your mind. "It will GROW." Your sense that you made the right choice quickly vanishes in a flood of confusion as you see not just the future of the passengers but now the future of their children, 78, to be exact. Most of these 78 lives seem fairly normal as they simultaneously pass before you in full detail. *How does your mind comprehend all of this?* But a few of them immediately stand out.

You are horror-struck as you witness one of these yet-to-be-born individuals pack up explosives and study a building's floor plan with madness in his eyes. He finishes filling multiple bags with his deadly arsenal and drags them out his front door. Next, a headline flashes before you: "Worst Workplace Attack in U.S. History. Hundreds Perish in Bombing." Instantly the pain of the attack victims' loved ones washes over you, and the rage of weeping spouses fills your soul. That third sentence from your house now flashes before you: "Stop the Evil." Will you? You can. Only *you* can see the future. Only *you* can prevent it. You must make the decision. It's literally in your hands as they hesitantly move toward the lever.

The outrage of hundreds of loved ones intensifies and channels down your arm as you grip the lever, ready to yank. *You do hold the power to stop this madman, for if his parent on that train doesn't survive, he'll never be born, and the lives of hundreds of innocent people will be spared.*

A THIRD GENERATION - *DON'T DARE PULL THAT LEVER*

Just as you start to move the handle to stop the evil with one, decisive pull, the words "It will grow" again flash into your ever-expanding mind. Time crawls even slower as the train barely moves. The *third* generation now enters your vision. They are 317 strong, and their lives flash before you immediately. Among them is one whose technology research will save an average of 1,200 lives per year in car crashes over the subsequent 20 years until newer technology fully replaces it. *That's 24,000 lives tragically cut short if you pull that handle!* The collective pain of their families slams against you as you fall to the base of the glowing lever, hoping the vision will stop. Another descendant will prevent the child-trafficking of over 1,700 innocent lives. Still another will develop a treatment for one of the more common strains of cancer, saving over 2.5 million lives!

The aggregate pain of millions crash-lands upon you, and you feel as though you cannot breathe. Pulling the lever may save hundreds of people from the madman, but it will also permit the preventable death of millions, the blood of which - since you knew, and could easily stop it - many would place on your hands. *Surely the millions outweigh the hundreds, and the millionfold cumulative emotions certainly do, which means the lever should be left right where it is. Right?* But you haven't even begun to see the effects - good and bad - that *those* millions you save, will have on society and the future.

You hate this. You don't want this. *Let someone else do it!* The blast of the train horn resumes as time kicks back into gear. You watch in horror as your nephew shrieks and reaches out to you one last time, the blaring train closing in on him. The red front of the engine barrels ahead as every particle of metal transforms to rushing fog and engulfs the child. As the red fog drifts away, the tracks remain bare, and your nephew is gone. Only silence and the blackness of night remain.

You're exhausted. You start to pull yourself up by the lever, which snaps under your weight and you fall back to the ground. Raising the broken metal bar and examining it by moonlight, you see the sheared, rusty end where it had been joined to the base. You glance back to the tracks, which are equally rusty and notice for the first time in the darkness that tall weeds have overtaken the bridge. No train has been here for years.

PART II: *YOU NOW MAKE ALL THE RULES*

As you start to wrap your uber mind around what just occurred, you slide up to your knees and rest in this position for a moment, catching your breath in the night air, staring at your kneecaps. *This is all too weird.* Suddenly the lever slides gently from your hand and is softly placed on your shoulder. Startled, you look up and see that it is no rusty lever, but a sword, resting on your left shoulder. A pleasant man, dressed in a strange, blue robe is grinning as he waves the sword gracefully from your left shoulder to your right. He then turns and declares before an onlooking crowd that you are the rightful ruler and lawmaker. The crowd cheers as you rise from your knees, wholly bewildered by it all. *How did you get on a stage? And where are you now?*

You listen to the proceedings and quickly deduce that a war just ended, and you are now completely in charge. *What war? Where is this?* The citizens cheer your right to rule, and as you hesitantly take your place on the throne, you notice something familiar to your left.

The back of the picture from your room, on a podium for all to see. The words glow just as brightly in the daylight: "You have all power. It will grow. Stop the evil."

The man in the robe strolls over to the sign and motions toward it with his open hand. The multitude cheers even louder at these words that still baffle you, although you increasingly feel their powerful effects. *So, all these people know of your power, too? And, where are you? WHEN are you?* You can't even tell if this kingdom is future or past. Your bewilderment is suddenly interrupted by a hundred million facts about this land that wash over you. Their history, their individual problems, and yes, their future. All of their futures. You also immediately love them deeply as a people, and you would do anything for them.

This is all quite bizarre, as each citizen you meet is not a stranger at all. You know everything about them, and you care for them more than any parent could. You know their names, their history, their wants, their needs. Everything. You learn that they want you to craft the rules for this new society, seeing that you have "all power" - whatever *that* means. You are trusted implicitly. They've seen all that you've done to conquer the enemy and to make them the victors, even though to you those are all just implanted memories, clashing with your real memories of home. You feel as though you're stepping into someone else's life, midstream. But you have no idea how to get back home, and these people are counting on your newfound power. They trust you. And you inexplicably but deeply care for them.

The next day you undertake the writing of their new constitution - the document by which all will live. Your mind has expanded exponentially since arriving at this place, and it seems there is nothing you don't know - well, except one thing: *How did all of this happen to you? Why is all of this happening to you?*

Your superhuman mind immediately considers the infinite possibilities of good and evil and conceives the best rules for all, after projecting and factoring in every possible outcome of every individual, interacting with every other individual.

At last, you craft the document, and you present it before the people with much fanfare. They have eagerly gathered to witness your unveiling of the governing law. The assembled throng cheers loudly as you finish reading and explaining each policy. In one voice they enthusiastically declare, "All that you have stated, we will do!"

Your brain instantly calculates the result of their keeping that promise, and you see a society where every citizen is joyful and content. But then something strange happens. Something very strange. The scene of this crowd - millions of jubilant citizens, who could remain happy for the entire kingdom's reign - is replaced by another scene. You now foresee not what *would* happen if all followed your perfectly crafted rules, but rather what *actually will* happen when they don't. You must sit down for a moment as the darkness settles over your mind. The crowd senses something wrong. You push the vision from your thoughts and bring yourself back to the present, forcing a smile at your subjects. You'll have to contemplate all of this alone and think of a resolution at a more opportune time. Your pleasant façade seems to put the crowd back at ease. For now...

All goes well for a brief period, but eventually, there is a dispute between two individuals in one region, and you are asked to come and mediate. Although your thorough constitution spelled out what seemed quite plain to most, one individual has taken an approach that is akin to finding a loophole. But there is no loophole at all. He is skirting the plainest instructions. You love this citizen like a brother and begin explaining why the rule makes sense. He then shifts into a game that your nephew often played when you explained things that were over his head. "But why?" he asks. You explain the Why behind the logic of the rule, and he asks why about *that*. Which leads to another answer from you, which leads to another "Why" from him, one level after another. After much explanation and sharing multiple alternate futures with him, he's finally convinced. You foresee that this answer will only appease him for so long, for he is determined to be right, regardless of the evidence. You return to your palace, realizing what a chasm there is between your thoughts and theirs, and again the mysterious blackness of their future arises in your mind.

These minor skirmishes gradually multiply in your kingdom, and for a while, you personally handle them by visiting each outlier and explaining the multiple levels of "Why" to them as well as the alternate futures. Each subsequent visit, however, seems to be met with stiffer initial resistance, and each requires more and more unfolding of evidence from you. Faith is the substance of things hoped for, the evidence of things yet unseen. But an increasing number of your subjects demand to actually *see* more evidence. You know your plan is best, since you see all possible futures, and love each citizen more than their parents possibly could. But the unthinkable begins to occur: an increasing suspicion of your motives is creeping into some of them. This, despite the fact that you have only their best interest in mind and have brought them nothing but blessings.

As the testing of your constitution's integrity increases - by limited minds who do *not* know the future and do *not* know all things - you see that the level of evil is increasing as well. Soon more and more are pushing the boundaries. And not all have ill intent. Some have simply been persuaded by cunning compatriots that it is perfectly okay to disregard your policies, to just do what feels right, eventually to their own harm and the harm of others. But the effects aren't felt immediately, so they take little heed to future repercussions. This delay of consequences hardens them in their course (Eccles. 8:11).

In certain regions, they have made large portions of your constitution void by their seemingly innocent traditions. A thin foundation of rebellion is quickly and neatly being overlaid by a blanket of sincere but harmful ignorance. A growing sentiment is that they love *you*, they just don't care much for your *law*. You long for them to see that if they truly loved you and each other, they would trust you and your policies for the sake of everyone's happiness and well-being. Some even try to accuse others who express their faith in your policies of somehow lacking love, as if they must choose one or the other, law or love. They have forgotten that your policies are an *expression of* your love and that the two go hand in hand.

As you sit on your throne, contemplating your options, you now see a future shaping up as a forced binary, with two clear choices before you. The first, you have already been trying, and it is increasingly less effective (and thus, mathematically it will eventually collapse into total inefficacy). You've been explaining larger and larger swaths of infinity to increasingly suspicious, limited minds. This is but a psychological bandage. It cannot continue, and this option only delays the bitter darkness that keeps appearing on the kingdom's prophetic horizon.

The second option on the binary is one that makes you shudder. You've intentionally turned your mind from it, whenever it arose, but as Option 1 is continually failing, you've started giving it a little more thought. *But do you really have that kind of power? And do you even want that kind of power? You've never even tried it before. It seems to cross so many boundaries, but-...* Suddenly the second sentence flashes again into your mind "It Will Grow." *Hmmmmmmmm...*

Your thoughts are interrupted by a delegate from one of your farthest regions. He traveled quite a distance, and he is eager to speak with you. As he stands before you, he explains the region's list of grievances. He says that they have clear evidence that they would be better off disregarding a tiny section of your constitution and they want it removed. It is an unnecessary law. Without speaking, you mentally double-check all possible futures and see that his conclusions are wrong and yes, your way was, and still is, best. You see that what they are suggesting would lead to misery for their yet-unborn third generation, and spread its discontent to the ninth generation, spawning a bloody civil war and the loss of millions of lives.

THAT SECOND OPTION

As you open your mouth to explain yet again your logic and the future ramifications of disregarding this particular part of the constitution, it's painfully clear that this will do no good. It has become an unending round of explanations, which is counterproductive to both you and your kingdom. *The second option in the forced binary may not be so bad after all.*

Rather than even starting your explanation, you instead ask him if he is *sure* that he and the others feel that way and he impatiently repeats that yes, of course, he's sure. He starts to ramble on, but as you stare at him questioningly, concentrating deeply on his mind, a look of confusion spreads across his face as he finally goes silent. His puzzlement mysteriously abates, and he slowly speaks again. It's clear his paradigm has shifted. *Why-...why, NO...he actually doesn't feel that way. Not at ALL.* He wonders out loud why he ever even questioned anything. You smile and slowly nod your approval that he has finally come to his senses – or rather *your* senses - as you lean back into your throne. He's made the right choice, and your perfect, omniscient data backs this up. Agreeing with you has saved many future lives. He says he wonders why any of them ever questioned a leader as loving as you, and that he'll immediately go back and report to the buffoons in his region how foolish they had been. This sounds even better to you. And you're surprised you like it.

WORSE THAN REBELLION

As he gleefully leaves your presence, beaming about the good news he'll relay to his ignorant fellow citizens, the mysterious cloud of future darkness that has periodically invaded your mind disappears. It's completely gone. You see no more traumatic gloom of rebellion or war. No more pain, suffering or sorrow in any of your beloved subjects. But something even more ominous has replaced it. Although total harmony is all you now sense for your kingdom's future, the element of love has been replaced by a great void. While it's no longer a mysterious and painful darkness, it's also no longer light. Just a dull, even existence.

Suddenly you feel alone. Completely alone. Although you see a future with even more subjects as your kingdom's population grows, you also see that the loneliness remains. You see visions of grand assemblies, where they all gather in your presence for annual celebrations, but strangely you see yourself completely isolated amid the vast multitude. Isolated, because you're surrounded by an assembly of automatons, void of any free will to genuinely care about you. The loneliness overwhelms you, and you immediately regret what you did to the delegate. You realize that neither endless explanations to finite-minded, skeptical citizens nor manipulating their power of choice will work.

One thought now permeates your racing mind, and even your newfound power cannot shake it. You know the truth. You've shared the truth. But *you cannot maintain their trust in you.* You love them more than they will ever comprehend, but they are increasingly questioning everything you do. The only viable future you can conceive is one based on love, not continually tamping down their growing suspicions with more talk and rationale. That love would lead to trust, implicit trust, in what you are doing for them. But what have you just done? Where is love now in all of this? In your attempt to remove the darkness of future rebellion and misery, you sacrificed the very thing that would have held it all together: love. Love was to be the foundation of your kingdom and the cohesion of all citizens. But you have just removed the possibility of love. Love requires a free will and what you just did to that one delegate neutralized love. What of the next uprising? Which option of this binary will you resort to then? And can you even trust your own decisions anymore?

A THIRD OPTION - DEMONSTRATION

Throughout the day you contemplate this weighty dilemma, concluding that trust cannot be built merely on what you *say* is true and love cannot be gained by manipulation. Talk is cheap. And brainwashing is evil. There must be a third option. Something that actually *demonstrates* your love in a way that merely pouring out blessings cannot do. Something that reveals your love while simultaneously allowing them to practice their free will and at first even rebel against you as that love is being demonstrated. Something that will satisfy the honest, seeking, inquisitive mind, so that it willfully places its trust in you and your policies forever and truly sees that your way is best. But what could demonstrate such love? Again, you question your own ability to rule and wish someone else would take over. Someone who could come up with the perfect plan to resolve this philosophical quandary that now haunts you day and night.

In your private quarters, you fall exhausted onto your opulent, royal bed, ruminating over your great failure. You hate this power, these choices. Someone else should be in charge. Someone who can actually come up with a real plan that avoids these two pitfalls. Someone who can navigate the complexities of countless free wills experimenting with rebellion. Now *that* would take an even greater genius. And a better plan than anything you've got.

On a bedside pedestal, the framed three statements again glow brightly, mocking your dilemma and failure. "You Have All Power. It will Grow. Stop the Evil." *You've had enough!* You angrily swipe the glowing plaque off the pedestal and start to crush it with all your new power. *If you do have "all power," you'll use it to destroy this miserable thing! You hate these words. They're not for you. None of this is for you.* The letters radiate with an intensity you've not seen before as your muscles burn in your arms and neck, straining to break the mysterious sign. Never did so much power feel so utterly helpless. You're getting dizzy as you crush even harder. You close your eyes and groan as you feel the wretched thing actually start to collapse in your grasping hands. Your flickering sense of hope slowly fades to confusion as you realize that it is not the plaque in your hands at all, but your twisted bedsheets, crushed within your shaking fists. You've awoken from another nightmare.

Your face is soaked with sweat, and your heart pounds as you quickly scan the room, trying to get your bearings. It's your own room, your window, your dresser. On the dresser sits that precious picture of your sweet nephew, still facing the wall. *No glowing words!* The tan cardboard back is all that appears by the light of the rising sun through your window. You breathe deeply as you slide the rumpled, twisted sheets aside and slowly step out of bed.

Hesitantly, you approach the dresser, wondering if the glowing words will appear at any minute. *Was it really a dream?* Slowly you take the picture in your hand and turn it around. Everything's still normal... This pic is one of your favorites. It was taken on his fifth birthday. He's in your lap with his cheek against yours, beaming at the camera. You smile and cry at the same time, thinking back on that day. Your fondness makes you gaze at the picture more closely than ever, examining every pixel. For the first time, you notice in the background three tiny colorful pieces to a Bible theme puzzle you had gotten him as a present that year. You know it well; the two of you have played with it many times. He had been trying to put it together a few moments before the picture was snapped. The yellow piece is about God as Creator. "You Have All Power" it reads. The green one is about the faith of believers as they get to know and trust God: "It will Grow." The red piece is about the prophecies of Revelation and the return of Christ. "Stop the Evil." On your dresser just below, you see the note that you scrawled in anger the night before. "Where ARE you, God?"

You again ponder the bizarre nature of your dream, and suddenly your pinging ringtone breaks the silence. It's your sister, calling from the hospital. You stare at the picture as she speaks. The little guy is still in critical condition. It could go either way. The nurses said you can come by now and join the others who've gathered for prayer. Your voice cracks as you tell her you'll be right over.

You quickly get dressed and head out the door, still contemplating the dream. You reach out to a motionless door, which remains so until you turn the knob. It feels good to have to turn it. No special powers. You don't want them. God can have them. As you approach your car door, you realize that you're forgetting something. Something very important. You run back in to grab it before you leave. There it is, on your nightstand: Not glowing words, but a light unto your feet and a lamp unto your path. The love letter from your best Friend. The Bible. Black leather with a gold Cross on the front. The Cross: the demonstration of His love. His perfect plan of salvation. Quickly you tuck it in your arm and head back out the door. You do know that God can be trusted. You know this because you *know Him*. Everything is in your benevolent God's hands. And you wouldn't have it any other way.

Thought Questions:

1. What is your main takeaway from this chapter? Why is it your main takeaway?

2. What types of Theodicy questions have others challenged you with, during your walk with God? Which have you pondered yourself?

3. What do Eccles. 8:11 (*delayed punishment causes some to harden their hearts in sin*) and Rom. 3:4 (*God's ways will be justified in the end*) tell you about God's character?

4. What does Rom. 8:28 (*all things work together for good for those who love God*) tell you about God's promises?

5. What did you learn about God's will for you in this chapter? What do you feel He's impressing you to start doing differently this week to walk more closely with Him?

A HOME IN THE CITY

"In my Father's house are many mansions. If it were not so, I would have told you. I go to prepare a place for you. And if I go and prepare a place for you, I will come again, and receive you unto myself; that where I am, there ye may be also."

-JOHN 14:2-3

I'VE BEEN TO North Carolina's Biltmore Estate twice. It is the largest house in the United States, and if you haven't seen this place, I highly recommend it. Built during the height of America's Gilded Age at the end of the 1800s, it is an architectural masterpiece. The one thought that kept going through my mind as I took in its amazing design and beauty was how much greater the mansions in heaven will be. I actually ran into Ted Turner there and shook his hand, thinking, *this is probably the only man on the premises who could actually afford to build one of these.* As a billionaire, he definitely could. Fortunately for non-billionaires like me, we don't need billions. We know that right now we have something even more elaborate waiting for us to take up residency, built by the greatest Architect and Carpenter the world has ever known. We can even sing about it. "I've got a mansion, just over the hilltop, in that bright land where we'll never grow old."

Jesus has prepared a place for you. You read that right: for YOU. The One whose trade on Earth was a carpenter has built you a home that you'll enjoy far more than if you had designed it yourself. He knows what appeals to you more than you yourself know. As Creator of your particular personality, He knows exactly what design and style of home best suits your every need and want.

There is no doubt there will be mansions in heaven. When we consider who the Architect of that city is and when we read about it in Revelation 21 and 22, we know that there will be no shacks in the Kingdom of God. In fact, the grandest and most opulent homes on this old Earth will seem like dollhouses by comparison. When we look at our opening text, the actual Greek word for "mansions" is *mone*, which also means "a staying, or residence; abode." Now, the promise is that in Jesus' Father's *house* are many of these residences. This implies that the New Jerusalem - with its walls that stretch to the top of the city - is actually much like a colossal house, complete with mansions, all interconnected in one giant mass of houses and rooms.

In other words, although in size, shape, and material, these dwellings can only be described as "mansions," God has designed the city so that His entire family, all of His children, will have a place in His own enormous "house:" the New Jerusalem.

Unlike our future country homes, which will be surrounded by wide expanses of nature as far as the eye can see, these city homes will be a place where God's children can dwell among and in close fellowship with their brothers and sisters. Like any loving parent, God wants a place where all His children can be together, like the world's largest family reunion. Reader, He wants you there, as well. He's done everything He can to get you there. He invites you to be a part of the "whole family in heaven and earth," who are named after Christ Jesus (Eph. 3:14-15), and to finally abide in your own special place, right in His house.

▲ ▲ ▲

Your guardian angel has been showing you around the golden city. He has resided here for thousands of years, so what better tour guide than this? As you explore the place together, you are amazed at God's inexhaustible imagination and His boundless love for fallen humanity. Every object in sight seems to reflect the glory of God in its own way; every gift is a reminder of the ultimate Gift in the life of the Son. Of all subjects to study, the one that you are most eager to investigate is Calvary's great Sacrifice on your behalf. And yet somehow you realize that even an eternity is not long enough to comprehend all the love and self-humiliation involved in redeeming your soul and the souls of your brothers and sisters in Christ.

The great network of glorious buildings that tower all around you reveals ingenious design as well as beauty. The city is so breathtaking, only the glory of the Godhead Itself surpasses its splendor. Each floor in this grand design possesses its own unique style, its own culture if you will. Your hardest task is found in deciding which part you like the best. Regal staircases ascend into the lofty heights, gorgeous balconies decorate many of the mansions, radiant bridges span multiple buildings, and streets of gold crisscross through the labyrinth of structures. The entire place is alive with movement as angels and humans mingle along the walkways and bridges. Some of them occasionally wave from windows and balconies, as you pass below. You wave back, and the thought comes to you that as eternity rolls on, you will get to know more and more of these people and angels, until every home and every street will be filled with close friends. This thought makes exploring the place even more exciting.

Suddenly your eyes land on a house among the mansions that stops you in your tracks. This home is no larger than any of the previous places you've seen, nor does it shine any brighter. But something about the way it's laid out just seems to hold your attention. Your angel tells you that you are more than welcome to take a closer look if you'd like, and you slowly nod without a word as the two of you approach the grand building.

This edifice is several stories high, although well within its particular foundation of the great twelve. The street in front of this home is bustling with life as people and angels pass to and fro, exploring houses and buildings all along this part of the city. You'd especially liked the particular variety of trees and the unique design of the sidewalks at first glance in this part of town, even more than anywhere else you've been today. The home in front of you is truly captivating. Something about the way the various balconies are designed intrigues you. The multiple pillars in front tie into the roof in a way that curiously appeals to you. The windows are large and just the style you like. The front doors seem to say "come on in."

The angel then tells you what you already suspected: this home is yours, designed and created just for you. A sense of your great unworthiness and Christ's remarkable affection for you fills your soul. The angel then offers to give you a tour. You eagerly agree, as your curiosity grows.

You cross the busy street and begin to ascend the massive staircase with the angel. Halfway up the stairs, you get your first peek at who you assume must be your new next-door neighbor. He too is exploring his new home, and he waves from his balcony as soon as he sees you. You smile as you and your angel return the gesture. There's no need for words. You know by his expression that he is thinking the same thing you are: *I can't believe we're actually here!* You wonder not just *where* he lived back on Earth, but *when*. It could have been during your life, but perhaps he lived in the 1800s, or in medieval times, or during Jesus' day, or maybe Abraham's. You intend to find out very soon.

Above the large double doors, you see your new name inscribed in stone. You're reminded again how literal the promise was that Jesus went to prepare a place for *you*. And now you see it with your own eyes. Your greatest desire, as you look at these doors, is that He Himself should walk through them and grace this home with His presence as often as possible.

To enter the home, you don't need a key; there are no locks in this city. No need for them. All possibilities of burglary or any such crime have been forever left in the past by the free will of all the citizens here. Your angel proceeds to lead you through the spacious house. Everything is perfect, and for once that word is not just a figure of speech. Not a square inch of this place should be changed. The Designer knew exactly what He was doing; He always has.

You wonder why there are so many large, open areas as you explore the house, and the angel explains that it will be quite common for groups to get together and discuss heavenly things and various plans. This city - as headquarters of the Universe - is a very social place, and these grand rooms allow for such events and gatherings. No one will be incapable of hosting large numbers of friends and visitors due to a lack of space in the home since all homes here are designed with just such gatherings mind.

Other rooms are not so large, and some are even quaint and cozy. Every room has its purpose, and each is beautiful in its own unique way. Some have the obvious door for entrance, while others have what seem to be discreet, almost secret passages connecting them. So much to explore, not only in the massive city but even in this one house, alone.

On an upper floor, you enter your main dwelling room. Your new body has no need of sleep, so this is technically not a "*bed*room," but you still have a special room in which to go and have some quiet time if you wish. The angel unlatches the massive, pearl-colored shutters and swings them open, revealing the most breathtaking city view you have ever seen. This gorgeous vista stretches out for miles to the west, and as you step out onto the balcony, the city appears more beautiful from this angle than from anywhere else. Not only did God know what type of house matched you perfectly, but He also knew the exact view that would have the most pleasant effect on you. He's thought of everything. The math involved in arranging all the homes so that each view is perfectly suited for each individual from their particular angle - while retaining that perfection for every other individual - is incalculable.

You rest your elbows on the edge of the balcony and slowly shake your head in amazement, spellbound by the view. Suddenly you spot a close friend from Earth, walking with an angel down below and you call out her name. She looks up and smiles, then asks if that's your place. You tell her it is, and she tells you where her home is, on the other side of town, so that you can stop by in the near future. She then continues on through the city as her angel points out several magnificent structures along the way. You turn and sit down on a large, extremely comfortable chair beside the angel. Taking a deep breath of the pure, fresh city air (usually a contradiction in terms on Earth), you lean back in your seat. You and your angel remain silent for a moment as you take it all in. The soft melody of the music drifting up from somewhere on the streets below seems perfectly fitting for this amazing moment. The distant glistening of the city's western horizon once again brings your thoughts to God. How well He knows you. How much He loves you. At last, you have found a home, a place to forever call your own. After your long pilgrimage on Earth - which now seems like but a moment - your journey is ended. You are truly "home." And now a new journey has begun: your real journey. If you could have kept this thought uppermost in your mind when on earth it would have reminded you how temporary that terrestrial home really was. Now you reside in your *real* home, and it suits you perfectly. In your Father's house there really are many mansions for His children. And the Master Carpenter made this one just for you.

Thought Questions:

1. What is your main takeaway from this chapter? Why is it your main takeaway?

2. How does the principle of Matt. 6:21 (*where your treasure is, your heart is*) relate to the mansions in heaven?

3. Our opening verse, John 14:2-3, says Christ is building your specific home in heaven so that you can be there with Him. What does this tell you about His character?

4. What does the fact that God knows you better than you know yourself tell you about God's promises?

5. What did you learn about God's will for you in this chapter? What do you feel He's impressing you to start doing differently this week to walk more closely with Him?

REVERSAL OF FORTUNE

"Blessed are they that mourn: for they shall be comforted."

-MATTHEW 5:4

WE ALL LOVE rags to riches stories. We love ugly duckling stories. Whether poverty or health or looks or acceptance, we like to see the downtrodden and bullied finally overcome their circumstances and experience success. One of the most basic rules I learned in screenwriting class was to make the audience care about the main character. Why? Because if the audience feels bad for them when things go wrong, they'll cheer for them when things finally turn around. A common criticism by movie reviewers is that they didn't give a care about the main character or whether or not they fell off a cliff, much less reached their goal.

Fortunately, we don't have to work to make God care about us when life has dealt us a bad hand. He shares our pain, no matter how deep. And today there is plenty of pain to go around. The news is almost unbearable to watch these days. Scanning just the headlines as they flash onto your phone eliminates the visual impact the full video footage, but the pain so often detailed in digital font still drives the point home: this is not a world of happiness. Children are being abused. Women are being harassed and assaulted. Men, women, and children are being murdered. Attempted suicide is climbing at an alarming rate, particularly among teens, who have tragically been convinced that they have no real value. Some mothers are even convicted of killing their own babies. Wars and natural disasters are snuffing out the lives of thousands, and health problems shorten or ruin the lives of millions.

As bad as all this is, we are seeing only the tip of the iceberg. Imagine how the Lord must feel; He sees it all. Not one person's feelings are crushed without Him taking notice. Not one child is mistreated without Him seeing. Not one woman is beaten beyond His eyesight. If He notices and cares about a sparrow that falls from a tree, how much more does He notice and care about your pain (Matt. 10:29-31)? All of the suffering in this world, experienced by every human from the greatest to the weakest, He sees and records. But more than that, He feels. It hurts Jesus actually more than it hurts the one in pain. After all, who would you rather have suffer: a loved one or yourself? It's the same with God. He hates to witness all the pain and heartache that occur daily in this world. We would do well to remember that there is a limit to how far He will allow the suffering to continue. Soon He will return in the clouds of glory to "give every man according as his work shall be" (Rev. 22:12).

On that day all suffering will end. Those who languish in pain and misery now, who are abused and mistreated at the hands of others, who suffer from physical and mental disabilities, will very soon have a reversal of fortune.

Reader, are you one such person? Maybe your trials don't involve physical abuse or faltering health, but rather verbal or mental abuse or chronic hatefulness. Or perhaps your suffering has nothing to do with people intentionally mistreating you, but you are just going through an extremely rough time right now: your job situation, your money problems, your addictions, your wayward or estranged loved ones. Perhaps you are serving a long prison sentence, separated from family and friends. Whether physical or mental, trial or temptation, our Lord pronounces a special blessing upon you if you are somehow suffering. He says that though you may mourn now, if you give yourself over to Him you will indeed be comforted in the land of beginning again. And He assures you that "your sorrow shall be turned into joy" (John 16:20). The comfort He promises, you can claim right now, in this old world. Always remember that the same Jesus who desires to walk with you beside the river of life in heaven is walking beside you today, though you may not always sense it. He promised to never leave you or forsake you, no matter what (Heb. 13:5). Christ declared that He came to this world so that you might have a more abundant life (see John 10:10). The Christian is strengthened through the trials, for they possess something that non-believers utterly lack: a Rock upon whom to place their burdens, a Shepherd who tenderly watches His sheep, an Intercessor to forgive their sins.

In fact, one of the names given to the Holy Spirit by Christ Himself is "the Comforter" (John 16:7). If we can grasp this thought, then when trials come - no matter how severe or apparently permanent - we can be comforted by the fact that God is still in charge and will soon put an end to all injustice in this life, which no one said would be fair.

"Beloved, think it not strange concerning the fiery trial which is to try you, as though some strange thing happened unto you: But rejoice, inasmuch as ye are partakers of Christ's sufferings: that, when his glory shall be revealed, ye may be glad also with exceeding joy" (1 Pet. 4:12-13).

▲ ▲ ▲

You have been in the New Jerusalem for only a short time. Your guardian angel is taking you on another personal tour of the glorious metropolis, and now he says he has a few people he would like to show you. You follow him, eager to see what he has in mind.

The city is so immense that even inside its walls there are rolling fields of green grass and countless acres of giant trees. A group of people dressed in shining white gather beneath the boughs of one such tree. Close by, several little ones help each other scale the back of a grand lion, who sits patiently among them as they play.

Your angel points out one of the children: a little boy you estimate to be about 8 years old. He explains that this child was abused for most of his short life. The drunken father had made a habit of slapping the child around for every little thing. Even if something was broken by accident, and even if not this child's fault, "daddy" would inflict wounds on the boy that would take days, sometimes weeks, to heal.

Now the child's face just radiates with joy. In the old earth, several of his little teeth had been knocked out. But here his playful smile reveals a complete set of pearly-whites. He laughs with glee as he finally mounts the majestic creature and strokes its gorgeous mane. The painful past is gone. The joyous future is now a reality.

You step again onto main street, its transparent gold surface sparkling under your feet. A little farther down the busy road, the angel points out a beautiful woman robed in white, smiling as she talks with her former guardian. He explains that this lovely woman was nearly devoid of any self-worth in the old world. Often, she had been teased for her disfigured face, which had been badly wounded in a car accident when she was only a toddler. She had no real friends all through grade school, and high school was a living nightmare with almost non-stop bullying. The college years had proven only slightly better. Often, she had contemplated suicide and felt that no one would notice her departure. In fact, based on the occasional news report of similar situations, she expected a few might even make jokes about it after she was gone if she were to actually go through with it. But just after college someone had befriended her and treated her like a real person of value, equal in every way. That same someone ultimately led her to Christ, who finally gave her peace and a knowledge of her true worth. She discovered that when the King of the universe comes all the way down to earth and dies for your sake, you must not be such a worthless person after all. She understood for the first time that she was indeed a princess, a daughter of the King. And now this royal child stands among true friends, looking every bit the part of the beautiful princess she always was.

As the angel finishes the girl's story, two boys and a girl run by at an incredible speed, laughing as they go. Your angel tells you that these three had been paralyzed on earth and that they now excel in speed. For all eternity their strong legs will be a testimony to the power and benevolence of God. Their exceptional speed reminds you of God's character and how He more than makes up for the trials all face on earth. The lame excel in speed here. The blind have the most amazing eyesight. The deaf have the best hearing in the universe. The mute now sing the most beautiful songs. Just as everything Job lost was *more than* restored by God in the Bible story (Job 42:10,12), the people of earth have now been more than compensated for the particular trials they experienced on earth. This joyful thought makes perfect sense to you as these three dash across the field.

Your eyes follow them as they run past a great, marble table loaded with food and they quickly disappear over the next hilltop. At the marble table sits a large group of people, talking and laughing with glee. Your angel reveals that these are just a fraction of those Christians who had died of starvation in the third world countries of the old earth. The bodies of these people are now filled with strength and energy, and it's obvious from the buffet spread out before them that a lack of food will never again be a problem.

Up ahead and to the right of the street you see what looks like a giant park. Thousands upon thousands of people and angels are gathered here, and soon you understand why. At the northern end of the park, a gentle hill covered with orange poppies rises from the plain. Jesus sits upon this hill and in his lap are several little children. The crowd listens eagerly as He reveals some of the things He has planned for them. He must have just recently come to this park, for as the people become aware of His location, they quickly descend on the place. The crowd is growing by the minute.

Your angel points out a little girl sitting on the knee of the Savior. What better place in all the universe to be? What safer place is there in all creation? The angel informs you that this girl's family had been taken captive during one of the old earth wars and she had witnessed the torture and death of her father. The barbaric and inhumane treatment that she and her mother were subjected to for months on end was worse than death itself, which also ultimately came to her by a cruel hand at a tender age. Incomparably evil were the deeds that men could do when the passion of war and lust burned through their veins. Demons enjoyed inhabiting such men and urging them on in their cruel endeavors.

But now this little innocent child sits on the lap of the Lord, her mother and father reclining beside Him among the flowers. Smiles rest on every face in this new land, and all have forgotten the trials of days gone by. The cursed lot that so many had to bear, and the fortune of countless suffering souls, has, for all eternity, been reversed.

"And God shall wipe away all tears from their eyes; and there shall be no more death, neither sorrow, nor crying, neither shall there be any more pain: for the former things are passed away" (Rev. 21:4).

"And the former shall not be remembered, nor come into mind" (Isa. 65:17).

Thought Questions:

1. What is your main takeaway from this chapter? Why is it your main takeaway?

2. As you look at the world around you, what specific fortunes would you like to see reversed in the suffering of others? In your own life?

3. What does God's notice of a sparrow falling tell you about His character toward suffering humans today?

4. What does Rev. 21:4 (*no more tears in heaven*) tell you about the promises of God?

5. What did you learn about God's will for you in this chapter? What do you feel He's impressing you to start doing differently this week to walk more closely with Him?

THE JOY OF THY LORD

*"His lord said unto him, Well done, good and faithful
servant; thou hast been faithful over a few things, I
will make thee ruler over many things: enter thou into
the joy of thy lord."*

-MATTHEW 25:23

I ONCE READ AN account of a passenger ship that came into a city
port from a distant land. There were two very different people pro-
filed in the article. The first, a man who was wealthy and famous,
stepped onto the gangplank to disembark and was met with great
cheers of adoration from the onlooking crowd. This man was, after
all, famous. Many other passengers filed off the ship, most greeted by
loved ones and small groups, but none equaled that first VIP's recep-
tion. Finally, after everyone else had disembarked and all were leaving
the dock, a weary, worn missionary stepped onto the same ramp, and
not a soul was there to welcome him. No one there cared about this
man, nor gave him any accolades. But what had he been doing for the
past few years overseas? Telling others about the gospel and bringing

them into the Kingdom. And for each one of those, we're told the angels in heaven rejoice, although the earth might give little notice (Luke 15:7,10). This meek man understood "the joy of our Lord."

What exactly is the joy of our Lord? What is it we will "enter into" when we get to heaven? The Bible gives us some clues.

"Looking unto Jesus, the author and finisher of our faith; who for the joy that was set before him endured the cross" (Heb. 12:2).

According to the Bible, the joy of our Lord is found in saving lost souls. Jesus endured the Cross by contemplating the future joy brought about in the final redemption of the human race. For Him, true joy is found in beholding all of those who will gain eternal life through His work on their behalf.

Another thing that brings Him joy is seeing His children accept the Sacrifice provided for their sins, repenting of those sins, and turning away from them.

"Likewise I say unto you, there is joy in the presence of the angels of God over one sinner that repenteth" (Luke 15:10).

God and angels rejoice over one sinner that repents here on earth today - *one* sinner. They are not indifferent to the lives and actions of individuals, neither are they dependent upon a great reformation on Earth to ignite their interest in us. No, we are told that even one person who comes to God in sincere confession and repentance of sin can evoke joy in heaven.

"Now unto him that is able to keep you from falling, and to present you faultless before the presence of his glory with exceeding joy" (Jude 24).

Not only does the sinner's acceptance of His death on the Cross bring joy to our Lord, not only does the sinner's repentance bring Him joy, but we're told that His ability to give us victory over sin brings Him "exceeding joy." He loves us too much to merely forgive us and then leave us chained to the sins that so easily beset us. He wants to break those chains, to set the captives free, to abide in us so that we no longer do those soul-destroying things. It is in this victory which He works out through us, that He finds exceeding joy.

Thus, if we are to enter into His joy when He comes back to receive His servants, we should be entering into His joy here, while souls are perishing all around us. Not only *should* we be, we *will* be. What brings Christ joy will also bring us joy when we have "the mind of Christ," (1 Cor. 2:16) which we can have now.

"Let him know that he which converteth the sinner from the error of his way shall save a soul from death, and shall hide a multitude of sins" (James 5:20). The Lord calls upon us to seek out His lost sheep. We are all God's children, and the only true way to enter into His joy is to partake in His reaching out to the lost: those who don't yet know Him. This act, done in the love of God, with patience and no criticism or judging, will surely bear its fruit and bring us a joy that we will eternally share with the Savior. Jesus even prayed that "they might have *my joy* fulfilled in themselves" (John 17:13).

While Christ is to forever be the focus of all praise, honor, and glory, the redeemed will enjoy seeing the fruits of their labors and will also be appreciated by others for their own labors. Many souls will in that day approach the humble instrument that God used and thank him or her for their influence and guidance which led to the foot of the Cross. Many children will gladly proclaim of their mother and/ or father, "It is because of your efforts, your loving guidance, your Christ-centered priorities and principles in my upbringing, that I am here today."

In other cases, it is the parents who embrace the child in gratitude for the perseverance which they demonstrated by the grace of God. Friends, co-workers, relatives, and acquaintances will not be forgetful of the person or people so influential in their lives. Some people will, for the first time, be made aware of the prayers which had been ascending to heaven on their behalf from a concerned loved one.

In heaven, it won't even matter what job we had in this life, or how many cars we owned; what degrees we attained from colleges and universities or how many awards we garnered; how handsome or beautiful we were, or whether we achieved any scholarly recognition or worldly fame. The only question that will matter, as far as our course of action is concerned, is whether or not, through the grace of Christ, we advanced the cause of God and glorified Him. Did we reach out to uplift our fellow human beings? Were we fully submitted to the will of our Father in heaven? Did we, by our words and lives, reveal the crucified Savior to a dying world around us? Only on that day will we truly get a clear view of the bigger picture. Only then will we realize just how much the Holy Spirit influenced others by the way we lived our lives. And only then will we truly share in the fullness of our Lord's joy.

"And they that be wise shall shine as the brightness of the firmament; and they that turn many to righteousness as the stars for ever and ever" (Dan. 12:3).

▲ ▲ ▲

You are on your way to the great Marriage Supper with several dear friends and loved ones when suddenly you spot the person who brought you to Christ. She is also walking toward the grand table and then she looks your way. Your eyes meet, and her face lights up as she recognizes you. Immediately she runs over and embraces you. This is not out of character for her, as lovingkindness was a normal part of her personality, even in the old earth. Love and appreciation flow freely from your lips as you express how much she means to you. No shred of pride emanates from your friend about how she brought you to the Lord - just humble praise to God for bringing *you* into *her* life. This is, and was, a person deeply aware of the fact that without Jesus we can do nothing. You know this to be true, for had she been trying to influence you with merely her own abilities, there would have been no appeal to her testimony.

You both keep repeating that you can't believe you're finally here, and you quickly plan a time when you can get together and just sit back and talk. Suddenly there's a tap on your shoulder, and you turn to see a beautiful young woman, her face radiant with joy. You don't immediately recognize her, so she proceeds to explain that the last time you saw her she was in her nineties, and you had kindly volunteered to come over and work around the house for her. While there, you had given her a small book which showed her how to have a relationship with Jesus. That little act planted the seed which led to her acceptance of Christ. You had no idea what the results would be, but you had given it to her and prayed about it, trusting in God to do His part. That was the last time you ever saw this elderly woman, until right now. What a change has taken place! Such a beautiful young lady stands before you in her luminous white robe; it's hard to believe this is the same person. But now that she has revealed herself, you can see, particularly in her eyes, a resemblance to that elderly woman from so many years ago. She wraps her arms around you in a warm embrace and acts as though she doesn't want to let go. It is starting to become very clear to you what eternal consequences even small decisions could have back on earth, and you're so glad you didn't decide it was too much hassle to go and help out an elderly woman in need.

The two of you loosen your embrace, and she joins your group on your trek toward the giant Marriage Supper table. As you make your way down the wide, golden street lined with palm trees, you spot another friend from the old earth. You recognize him immediately, for you had been quite close. He and another man you don't recognize hurry over to you, and he also gives you a hefty bear hug. You quickly introduce him to your new friend, and he begins to explain to her how you brought him to Christ as well. He tells her that at first he was taken back when you started talking about Jesus. He thought you were becoming too strait-laced, a newborn Jesus freak. But eventually your cheerful disposition and helpful spirit were far too contagious for him, and he had to find out more about who Jesus *really* was for himself, beyond all the clichés. Your secret prayers also had a steady and powerful influence on his heart, although he didn't find out about those prayers until years later.

He now introduces you to his friend, who begins to explain how your pal had led *him* to Christ. His story underscores the fact that each person who is brought into the Kingdom cannot help but bring others in as well. It's the same principle as physical seeds that take root, grow and ultimately bear fruit, creating more seeds that naturally spread and keep the cycle going. By the grace of God, this process had been continuously repeated throughout earth's history. The value of even one soul is more apparent than ever as you realize the multiplication factor involved. Not only did you directly influence all of those you introduced to Jesus, but you indirectly influenced all of the ones they influenced, and all of the people *they* influenced, and so on, and so on. In fact, you quickly learn that one of the people that this man brought to Christ eventually became an effective evangelist, who brought thousands to the Lord (who then brought even more). You now witness these same thousands on the other side of a hilltop, thanking the evangelist for his powerful messages. And you thought you had done so very little with your limited time on earth. Throughout the ages, these countless, precious souls will stand as eternal reminders of just how impactful every act on earth really was.

As you stroll along, talking with your friends, you see in the distance, among a band of angels, a woman whose harsh attitude toward you had been met with kindness in return. Her presence here is the fruit of that kindness, which led her to Christ. Over there by one of the grand fountains walks that formerly homeless man whom you fed and to whom you spoke of Jesus' love. He went on to study the Bible with you and ultimately got his life back on track.

By the Tree of Life in the center of the City stands a woman who had been enslaved by a horrible addiction and who found no freedom in the messages of her counselors. She had been lulled to sleep by the belief that this addiction was just a part of who she was, and that she should never expect to gain the victory. The Holy Spirit had prompted you to go and speak from the Scriptures the words of encouragement that yes, indeed, Jesus is able to "proclaim liberty to the captives" and to "keep you from falling." By faith, her life had been transformed.

And over by the banks of the River of Life stands that former religious hypocrite. He had been notoriously judgmental in his criticism of others, which caused many to avoid his presence. But you and another friend sought him out and invited him to your weekly small study group. He saw in your group something that he knew had been missing in his scholarly religious life, and you showed him that the "something" was Jesus.

During the latter part of your life on the earth, you found it impossible to just keep the love of God inside. You were so liberated by it and joyful in it that you just could not keep quiet. This love didn't originate in you but was a supernatural gift from God that flowed *through* you. What a privilege it had been to promote the cause of God! And how thankful you will always be that while there was still time to make a difference, that privilege had been given to you. Only now do you fully comprehend the true joy of the Kingdom of God. It's not merely experiencing all of the wonderful things God has prepared for you; it is found in both fellowship with your Creator, and seeing with your own eyes, the happiness experienced by those for whom you prayed, worked, and cared. This was the will of God for His children. Of such is the Kingdom of heaven.

Thought Questions:

1. What is your main takeaway from this chapter? Why is it your main takeaway?

2. Who shared the gospel with you and how did they do it? What is your favorite way of sharing it with others?

3. What does Hebrews 12:2 (*Christ endured the Cross by contemplating your salvation*) tell you about His character? What about all of heaven rejoicing at your repentance?

4. What does Jude 24 (*Christ gives you victory*) tell you about the promises of God?

5. What did you learn about God's will for you in this chapter? What do you feel He's impressing you to start doing differently this week to walk more closely with Him?

THE MARRIAGE SUPPER

"Blessed are they which are called unto the marriage supper of the Lamb."

-Revelation 19:9

"The kingdom of heaven is like unto a certain king, which made a marriage for his son, and sent forth his servants to call them that were bidden to come to the wedding: and they would not come. Again he sent forth other servants, saying, Tell them which are bidden, Behold, I have prepared my dinner: my oxen and my fatlings are killed, and all things are made ready: come into the marriage. But they made light of it, and went their ways, one to his farm, another to his merchandise."

-Matthew 22:2-5

My favorite dish in the world is my brother-in-law Doug's Tamale Pie. I'm a foodie, so I don't say such a thing lightly.

I like it so much that *I've even included his recipe in the back of this book as a bonus.* I maintain a list of "Eight Great" favorite foods in the world, some homemade and some from restaurants (most made by my wife, who is an excellent cook). I'm such a foodie that I once set up a web page to bring my favorite fast food restaurant to Chattanooga (It's Del Taco if you must know, and I get the green burrito, minus cheese with extra sauce). Supposedly there are several on the way, but we'll see. I'm such a foodie that when I'm on a business trip, I immediately scope out the local non-chain restaurants to try something new. But the top of this list is Doug's Tamale Pie.

Now suppose I made a great big crock pot of that culinary wonder and brought you a plate of it. I tell you, "Friend, taste and see how good this is." You breathe in the aroma and start to salivate. It smells great, and you're practically starving. But lifting your fork seems like too much work, so you ask me to just taste it *for you*, and then tell you what it tastes like. That's just as good, right?

TASTE AND SEE

As silly as that may seem, it is exactly what many of us do with a generous offer from God. He says specifically "Taste and see that the Lord is good" (Ps. 34:8). But instead of doing so, we rely on the testimonies and experiences of others, who assure us that God really is good. We don't actually see for ourselves, *taste* for ourselves, and we miss the blessing. As we consider the feast that Christ wants to spread out before us, let's keep Psalm 34:8 uppermost in our minds.

Christ not only returned to heaven to prepare a place for you, but He's also planned a great feast for you when you get there. And never has there been a feast like this.

"He shall feed his flock like a shepherd," "And I say unto you, that many shall come from the east and west, and shall sit down with Abraham, and Isaac, and Jacob, in the kingdom of heaven," "That ye may eat and drink at my table in my kingdom" (Isa. 40:11; Matt. 8:11; Luke 22:30).

So, is this a real feast with real food? According to the Bible, the answer is most definitely, yes. Jesus declared, "But I say unto you, I will not drink henceforth of this fruit of the vine, until that day when I drink it new with you in my Father's kingdom" ("until the kingdom of God shall come") (Matt. 26:29; Luke 22:18). Jesus will drink the "fruit of the vine" with His followers in heaven, just as He drank it with them at the Last Supper. And after His resurrection, Jesus, in His glorified body, was given real food by the disciples. "And he took it, and did eat before them" (Luke 24:43). Our bodies will be like Christ's (see Phil. 3:21), and since His glorified body consumed food, ours will as well. "And they shall plant vineyards, and eat the fruit of them" (Isa. 65:21).

The food at this supper will be like what they enjoyed in the Garden of Eden. Before death entered our world through disobedience, the food, like the rest of the planet, was perfect, having just come from the Creator's hand. God invented our taste buds, and He invented food of all varieties to match those taste buds. He could have easily designed us to take in nutrients through soaking our hands in the mud three times a day, or swallowing three seeds per day, or countless other mundane ways, bypassing the need for taste buds altogether. But He didn't do this. He invented pleasure, and He forever linked the act of eating with a high amount of pleasure. Does anyone think that the level of pleasure when we eat in heaven will be less than what we experienced here on earth? The fruits and vegetables we eat today from the grocery store after miles of shipping and days of storage aren't nearly as tasty as fresh, vine- or tree-ripened food. And yet even the latter is nothing compared to the delicacies that await us in heaven. For thousands of years, the foods we eat have been getting further and further away from their original taste that Adam and Eve enjoyed. In fact, in just the last 100 years, the soil of the world's best farmlands has been so depleted of nutrients that many of the older generations claim they can even taste a difference.

What is your favorite fruit? Cherries? Peaches? Blueberries? Watermelon? Bananas? Whatever it is, forget everything you know about it. The flavor there will make the sweetest, most succulent fruit here taste like sawdust. For many people, the idea of eating natural foods in heaven seems boring, because they have survived on a diet of junk food for so long, their taste buds have been per- verted. What they don't realize is that even their favorite high cho- lesterol, artery-packing, health-destroying food is, by comparison, bland and tasteless. Blueberry pie à la mode? Eating it in heaven would be sheer punishment due to lack of flavor. Deep-dish pizza with everything on it? The taste buds would hardly notice it. Hot cinnamon rolls with frosting oozing down the sides? Yes, even this scrumptious favorite pales in comparison to what is in store for you. We must continually grasp the thought that "Eye hath not seen, nor ear heard, [nor mouth tasted,] neither have entered into the heart of man, the things which God hath prepared **for them that love him**" (1 Cor. 2:9).

GOOD REASONS TO MISS OUT?

The above text brings us to our next and more important question: Do you love Him? The parable of the Marriage Supper describes those who were initially invited. It says of them, "they would not come," "they made light of it, and went their ways, one to his farm, and another to his merchandise" (Matt. 22:3,5).

Sharing the Marriage Supper with Christ is more than just sitting down to eat and drink the delicacies of Paradise. It is receiving Him into our hearts today, and counting everything else in this world as nothing, by comparison (see Philip. 3:8). Notice that those who did not want to come to the feast went to their "farm" and "merchandise." The "farm" represents our work, our achievements, the things that occupy our time and minds. Are we putting these things above God? If so, we are as surely making idols for ourselves as the heathens did centuries ago. "Thou shalt have no other gods before me" is the first of the Ten Commandments (Ex. 20:3). No one comes to the Wedding Feast who does not put the King of the feast first in his or her life. The Lord forces Himself upon no one; it must be a willing decision.

The "merchandise" represents all of the material things we so often cherish above salvation itself. These too can become another god before Him who alone should occupy the throne of our hearts. In the same parable recorded in Luke, we get even more excuses for missing out on the Great Supper. One had just bought some land that he put ahead of the feast (investments). Another had just purchased five yoke of oxen that he felt he should put to good use right away (our livelihood). Still another had just married and had placed his spouse above his opportunity to attend the feast (loved ones over God) (See Luke 14:16-20 & Matt. 10:37).

Long is the list of reasons to be absent from the Marriage Supper which Jesus has so graciously planned for us. Many are the excuses for our delay in putting Christ first. Remember this: There will always be a good reason to do the wrong thing. But these "good" reasons should never override the *right* thing. To accept Jesus as our personal Savior and to abide in Him daily is the only chance we have to sit down with Him at the Great Feast. And here is where faith enters into the picture. God knows that we need material things. He knows that we have our careers. He knows that we cherish our loved ones, as well we should. But when we give ourselves fully to Him, placing Him above all of those things, He will make sure that all of our needs are met (see Philip. 4:19). There is no safer place to put our careers, our material possessions, our health and yes, our loved ones than in the powerful hands of our God, who cares more about them than we do and who knows exactly what is best.

WITHOUT A WEDDING GARMENT

In the Marriage Supper parable, not only do we find people making excuses, but we actually discover one man who thought he could attend the feast without the wedding garment. The king who prepared the feast notices this man, and says to him, "Friend, how camest thou in hither not having a wedding garment?" (Matt. 22:12). The guest was "speechless," and was cast out of the feast into "outer darkness." We'll learn more about this outer darkness in chapter 24, "Strange Fire."

Without the wedding garment - the robe of Christ's righteousness - we will never sit down at that fabulous supper. Anything less than Christ's righteousness covering us represents our own attempts at righteousness which the Bible describes as "filthy rags" (Isa. 64:6). At the same time, this robe that Christ offers will never cover chosen, ongoing sin, but rather is a reflection of the Holy Spirit dwelling in us. And the Holy Spirit in us causes us to walk in God's statutes and keep His judgments so that we no longer walk after our favorite sins (See Ezek. 36:26; Gal. 5:16; Acts 5:32).

"He that covereth his sins shall not prosper: but whoso confesseth and forsaketh them shall have mercy" (Prov. 28:13).

"Blessed is he that watcheth, and keepeth his garments" (Rev.16:15).

"To Him that overcometh will I give to eat of the hidden manna" (Rev. 2:17).

Jesus longs to sup with you at the Wedding Feast that is soon to take place. He's standing at the door of your heart. He's asking you to invite Him in and give yourself completely to the One who will never let you down.

"Behold, I stand at the door, and knock: if any man hear my voice, and open the door, I will come in to him, and will sup with him, and he with me" (Rev. 3:20).

▲ ▲ ▲

You walk amidst the vast multitude that is following Jesus to the great Wedding Feast table. As Christ approaches the banquet, He calls out for all the redeemed to come join in the supper that He has prepared. Everyone shouts, "Alleluia! Glory!" as the procession continues to move forward and surround the giant table.

This table flashes with the most brilliant, pure silver, and it appears to be many miles in length. As you approach the grand setting, you notice that a place has been prepared just for you. Your new name is written in the most beautiful style of handwriting, and you wonder if the Savior Himself wrote it. You will ask Him about this later.

There is something exciting about being surrounded by such a giant, energetic sea of people. You haven't been here long, and you still haven't gotten used to seeing such a great multitude gathered together in one place. The table shines increasingly brighter as all the redeemed press close to its reflective surface to find their place. The light from their robes seems to set the silver table ablaze in shimmering white.

As you sit at your place, you again contemplate the Savior making all of this possible. Even at this grand feast, not one thought of self-righteousness creeps into your mind. This is the case with all of the saved. All praise and glory and honor go to the Lamb who was slain for your sins. The blessings He pours out on His children just keep on coming.

You lean forward and peer to your left, down the massive table. What a sight! A glorious, silver surface many miles in length, attended by all of these people! You look to your right: the view is equally impressive. It is astounding to think that every person in the history of the world who was ultimately cleansed by the blood of the Lamb is now sitting at this same table. Moses sits among this assembly. David can be found here. Joseph, Rahab, Noah, Rachel, Paul - even Adam, the father of the entire human race - all have their place at this very table in this surreal moment.

Spread out before you is the most delightful food your eyes have ever beheld. There are the grapes, so giant and plump. The large, ripe figs look delicious, as do the golden-brown almonds, walnuts, and cashews. The peaches, pomegranates, cherries, dates, strawberries, and all the other fruits appear ready to burst their skins with their sweet fillings. And in a tall goblet, you see the fruit of the vine - the delicious grape juice - that Christ was so fond of on the earth. Today He will drink it with all His faithful children, just as He promised. You can hardly wait for the feast to start.

Innumerable shouts of joy and praise rise from the table in gratitude to God. Here there is no need to "say grace" or "say the blessing" before eating since you can just thank Him in person. And this food has no need to be blessed; it's already perfect. The shouts continue to rise as Jesus makes His way along the massive table. He's fulfilling His promise to give the overcomers a share of the heavenly manna. He has no need to carry a giant basket, for just as He miraculously multiplied the bread on the earth for the "5,000", He can multiply it here for this multitude. Your heart skips a beat as you see that He is now working His way near your part of the table!

Finally, the Son of God reaches down onto your plate and places the most lovely, delicate, piece of fluffy, white food you have ever seen. You are about to get your first taste of heavenly manna, and it looks delicious. But what really catches your eye is the nail print in the Savior's hand which holds the manna. What an image to behold. The One whose hands were pierced for you, now stands beside you, serving you with that very same hand. You are not overcome by a shameful weight of guilt, for Jesus has taken care of all that. Rather, a sense of love and gratitude for this Man washes over you. He gave His life so that you could be here with Him in this moment and for eternity. You wish for nothing more than to spend time with your wonderful Friend, and it stirs your heart to know that it is exactly what He wants as well.

The Marriage Supper of the King is now a reality. The Wedding Feast is underway. All who accepted the gracious invitation are present for this grand event. Every guest is clothed with the wedding garment. As you taste the succulent food spread out across the table and consider the hands that prepared it, you thank the Lord that you have not missed the wonderful banquet. The great Shepherd feeds His flock and gives them a taste of the heavenly manna as promised. "Blessed are they which are called unto the marriage supper of the Lamb." Blessed shall they always be.

Thought Questions:

1. What is your main takeaway from this chapter? Why is it your main takeaway?

2. Which type of excuses for not attending the Wedding Feast do you find most easily hinder you from putting God first? Career? Worldly plans? Material possessions? Investments? Your livelihood? Your loved ones?
3. What does the fact that God throws a celebratory feast for your arrival into heaven tell you about His character?
4. Christ provides the garment of His own righteousness for the Wedding Feast. What does this tell you about His promises?
5. What did you learn about God's will for you in this chapter? What do you feel He's impressing you to start doing differently this week to walk more closely with Him?

BEFORE THE BEGINNING

"And He said unto them, I beheld Satan as lightning fall from heaven."

-LUKE 10:18

"How are thou fallen from heaven, O Lucifer, son of the morning! How art thou cut down to the ground, which didst weaken the nations!"

-ISAIAH 14:12

T HE BIBLE'S FIRST words are: "In the beginning, God created the heavens and the earth." It tells us that you didn't descend from a primordial pool of sludge that lacked 1) a plan, 2) the intelligence to carry out a plan, and 3) most of the molecular elements contained in the end product. You are a child of your parents, who are children of their parents, and such it has been, all the way back to a genetic pair created by God at "the beginning" of this earth's history. But what about before that? What was going on before the beginning of this world's history? And while we are studying Heaven and all that the Bible tells us about our future home, wouldn't it help to know a little bit about the history of Heaven itself? If God is eager to bring everything full circle and get us back into His physical Kingdom, wouldn't it enhance our understanding to discover why that Kingdom was at risk in the first place? Why are we cosmically separated from Paradise right now and only reading about that wonderful place while confined to this dark, cruel world of sin and suffering?

WHY THE WAR IN HEAVEN?

It's fascinating to think about the fact that the very first war actually occurred, not on earth, but eons ago in Heaven:

"And there was war in heaven: Michael and his angels fought against the dragon; and the dragon fought and his angels, And prevailed not; neither was their place found any more in heaven. And the great dragon was cast out, that old serpent, called the Devil, and Satan, which deceiveth the whole world: he was cast out into the earth, and his angels were cast out with him" (Rev. 12:7-9).

But why was there a war in such a holy place, where everyone got along so well, and everything was perfect? We said in chapter 4, "The Rightful Reign," that we would come back to the question of why a perfect God would allow evil to even begin in His otherwise-perfect universe. We'll also address the allegation that if God is Creator of all and knows all, then isn't He to blame for all of the evil in the world today?

Let's start our quest by going back as far as our finite minds can take us, based on the information revealed in the Scriptures. Keep in mind as we do so, that "The secret things belong unto the Lord our God: but those things which are revealed belong unto us and to our children forever, that we may do all the words of this law," and "how unsearchable are His judgments, and His ways past finding out" (Deut. 29:29; Rom. 11:33).

God hasn't revealed every detail about eternity past to us because there are some things we are just not ready or capable of receiving at this point. He only gives us what we can handle at any given stage (see John 16:12; 1 Cor. 3:2 & 10:13). But He has given us the information we need to understand the gospel and His plan of salvation. The things that have been revealed "belong to us," but there are things which have not yet been revealed, so understand that our knowledge of eternity past will be imperfect at best. Let's proceed, then, focusing on what we do know.

LOVE: THE FOUNDATION AND GLUE

God IS Love (1 John 4:8). This is the very core of His being. It is the foundation of His government and the glue of His Kingdom. Love, residing in the hearts of all intelligent creatures, keeps the well-oiled machine of the universe running harmoniously, without issue. Love is outward-focused and willingly seeks to give, and bless others rather than take, and focus on self (see 1 Cor. 13). The absence of love in hearts is the one and only thing that can disrupt that harmony and, in fact, did disrupt that harmony.

Love is not solitary, and since God is love, He desired to exercise and share that love with intelligent beings, capable of willingly reciprocating that love. Love is not static; it grows over time and over larger numbers of beings to love. God wanted a universe full of intelligent beings who could share His love, so He set about creating life. But one such being - the highest-ranking angel - was called "Lucifer" which means "Shining one, light bearer" (see Strong's Concordance). You doubtless know what eventually happened to Lucifer, who became Satan and was ultimately cast out of Heaven. So, did God create a devil? Why did He allow this red, pitchfork-wielding, bat-winged, horned creature to exist if He knew that he would ruin the bliss of Heaven?

First of all, notice that his name indicated brightness and light. The Bible says of him: "Thou wast perfect in thy ways from the day that thou wast created, till iniquity was found in thee" (Ezek. 28:15). No, God didn't create a red devil with bat's wings and horns (and the Bible never portrays him like that, even after his fall). He created a perfect, beautiful angel to be the covering cherub (Ezek. 28:14) standing next to the throne of God. The covering cherub is the highest position of an angel, which is what Lucifer was created to be. But it said he was perfect "till iniquity was found" in him. Iniquity is sin, and sin is the transgression of God's law (1 John 3:4). Lucifer started off perfect from the hand of God, but then this mystery called sin (2 Thess. 2:7) was found in him. He began to dwell on his own brightness and beauty (Ezek. 28:17) and eventually decided that he should be in the place of God. He thought that he would like to take God's place on His throne and in fact "be" like God with all of His powerful attributes. Essentially, he wanted to be God and was unsatisfied with his position as "merely" the highest of all created beings. Read it in his own words:

COVETING GOD'S POSITION

"I will ascend into heaven, I will exalt my throne above the stars of God: I will sit also upon the mount of the congregation, in the sides of the north: I will ascend above the heights of the clouds; I will be like the most High" (Isa. 14:13-14).

I had a schoolteacher, Mr. Swafford, who said that Satan had "I" problems. We thought he meant the devil needed "eye"glasses until he explained by writing the word "Lucifer" on the board and then expanding the center letter of the covering cherub's name. My father also pointed out that in a universe focused on service to others, the above quote seems out of place with five "I"s crammed in there. It's clear where his priorities were.

So why is Lucifer (his name being changed to "Satan" after his fall, which means "adversary" or "accuser") still around, allowed to tempt and wreak havoc in our world? Why didn't God simply wipe him out, the minute Lucifer started expressing doubts about God's rulership? Think about it for a moment. When Lucifer was having baseless doubts about God and started spreading those doubts in the minds of other angels to recruit them for the great war, God had three options.

OPTION 1. ZAP THE TRANSGRESSOR

The first option - so often cited by critics - is that God should have just zapped Lucifer out of existence. Evil appears, and evil is destroyed. Simple enough. It's what any noble being would do, right? For the sake of universal stability. Well, not exactly. Put yourself in the place of any of the other angels as you witness the scene. The God you always thought of as loving and honest, suddenly killing the first being who doubts Him? Remember, the accusation had been that Lucifer should be in God's position and that God's way - His law - was not best. Just as his narrative is beginning to gain steam and his seeds of doubt are being considered, he is destroyed. Imagine yourself and the other angels looking around at each other in shock as the accusations of Lucifer - that God is unfair - are still ringing in your ears. Would this really solve the problem of evil? Would this solidify love in the hearts of all other beings of the universe? Or would it merely cause them to repress their real feelings that Lucifer just might have been onto something and that maybe God had something to hide? The very act of silencing Lucifer would have, in fact, given the angels their first shred of evidence that perhaps the accusations were true. If you were smart, you would not have wiped out Lucifer at this stage, and neither did God.

OPTION 2. ZAP THE BRAIN CELLS

What about option two? God could have just immediately taken over Lucifer's thoughts and instantly brainwashed him to stop thinking that way and go back to thinking God's way. Basically, suspend his free will. I'm not a fan of the movies anymore, but my friend Viggo designed the Neuralyzer for the film *Men in Black*. This fictitious handheld device can zap the recent memory of its target, putting them in a temporary hypnotic state, where they are susceptible to suggestion and the implantation of false memories. For humans, this option is mere Hollywood fiction, but for the Creator, this was a very real possibility. Should He have done it? Should He have told Himself "the end justifies the means," since He knew Lucifer's doubts were, in fact, unfounded? What does this do to love? The moment the memory is zapped, and the brain is tweaked to go against what that free agent wanted to think, the dreadful path has been laid for robot land. Ask yourself: Would you do this to your loved ones? Would you take over their minds if you could and make them loyal to you and love you, even if it were against their will? Of course you wouldn't. Unless you have an unhealthy lust for dictatorial power (in which case you would never have gotten this far in this book), you would have no desire to control their thoughts like that. You wouldn't do it, and neither did God.

OPTION 3. LOVE

That leaves us with option three, the only option that love could have chosen. Since love is the foundation of God's government and the glue that holds His Kingdom together, love is something that could never be sacrificed in the long term for the sake of short-term gains. Yes, wiping Satan out would have put down evil for the time being. And zapping his memory and free will would have "cured" his lust for power. But both of these options destroy something even greater, which is love and the future possibility of love. If the truth were to be known to all inhabitants of the universe once and for all, then Satan had to be allowed to explain his erroneous, self-destructive theories to anyone who would listen. Truth is, unfortunately, not a prerequisite for influence. Satan's lies could be spread far and wide, just as easily as the truth had been. We've all heard the saying that a lie can travel around the world before the truth can put its boots on. Such has always been the case, and the "father of lies" (John 8:44) discovered this very quickly.

God knows the future. He knew that "the lie" (2 Thess. 2:11), the main lie behind every sin - that God's way is not best - would be traveling through the streets of heaven and eventually across planet earth many times before the truth could ultimately be borne out by experience. Anything short of this would be either a militant power-play or divine brainwashing on God's part, neither of which is an option for Love. God saw the future of woe and misery that sin, the transgression of His law, would bring. But He also saw beyond the misery to a time where all intelligent beings on earth and in the angelic, cosmic realm, would see for themselves the utter foolishness of sin and the self-destructive nature of rejecting God's perfect will. God is the Life-giver. He, in fact, IS our life (Col. 3:4). So, our choice to push Him away is actually our choice to push life away. The wages of sin is death (Rom. 6:23) because sin separates us from God (Isa. 59:2), who is Life.

If you had perfect love for all living beings, perfect wisdom and knowledge, and a clear vision of the future, revealing the outcome of all three options, you too would choose option three. It's the only smart thing to do, and the only loving option. Although philosophers and skeptics have invented countless religious theories to muddy the water and confuse the mind, it all boils down to the simple question of: *Can God be trusted that His way is best?* God's response to the rebellion of Satan is one more piece of evidence that the answer to that question is Yes. God did as you would have done, knowing all things. He took the course that would keep the free will free, and simultaneously ensure that this mystery of iniquity would not rise up again a second time (Nah. 1:9).

Ironically, as Satan was allowed to continue his existence, one of his favorite tactics became convincing humans that he actually doesn't exist. While Peter warns us explicitly to "Be sober, be vigilant; because your adversary the devil, as a roaring lion, walketh about, seeking whom he may devour" (1 Peter 5:8), the enemy knows that it's hard to be watchful and vigilant about something that isn't real. A 2013 YouGov poll revealed that nearly 20% of Christians don't even believe Satan exists. And a recent online article penned by a Christian pastor was entitled "The Modern Church Doesn't Need a Make-Believe Devil." This, in spite of the fact that demons are men-tioned 63 times in the New Testament alone and Satan is referenced over 30 times. He is real, and he's seeking prey.

Some wonder why God didn't just refrain from creating any beings in the first place, knowing what He knew. But love cannot exist alone. The redeemed, that "great multitude that no man can number," will ultimately stand before His throne, along with the "ten thousand times ten thousand and thousands of thousands" of angels who chose love over self. These should not have their existence denied because of others who would not choose love. God's fairness demanded this. His love assured this.

One day "the books will be open," (Daniel 7:10; Rev. 20:12) and all of the redeemed will have a chance to look over the same history that the angels have seen unfold before them. It is the history of the great controversy between Christ and Satan, between good and evil, God's way and the self-destructive way. When those books are open, you will see, in a format far superior to any earth video, exactly what happened before the beginning of earth's creation. You will see what happens when the highest "covering" angel covets the throne of God and decides that he knows better than Omniscience. You will witness just where this "full circle" began as you behold the history of your heavenly home. And when you see the mystery of iniquity do its deadly work, you will agree, with all the unfallen beings in the universe, that sin should not rise up again the second time. Based on the Scriptures, that scene will look something like this:

▲ ▲ ▲

A handsome, young prince stands before the Throne of the Universe. He has everything his heart desires. You are dazzled by the beautiful jewels that adorn his shining figure. His privileges are unrivaled by any created being. He loves the Creator with all his heart. As the highest angel, He loves and serves the creatures he oversees. If ever a created being were a reflection of God, it is this prince. His name is Lucifer, meaning "the bright and shining one." Completely content, as he has been for a span of eons, he delights in singing songs and leading the sea of shining faces in the angelic choir. A master of music is he, with his "tabrets and pipes" that were "prepared in thee in the day thou wast created," and with "the noise of thy viols (stringed instruments)" (Ezek. 28:13; Isa. 14:11). And that mighty, creative intellect has often focused on composing songs of such an elevating nature that they affect the very soul of both singer and audience alike. The countless worlds scattered across the expanses of the universe have been blessed by the orchestral sounds of this creative, musical genius.

All is harmony in the vast reaches of the galaxies. Each being is content with their own position. One pulse of harmony beats throughout the universe. The system of the Kingdom operates like a well-oiled machine.

The two great wheels of love (Matt. 22:36-40) move and motivate the entire cosmos in harmony:

1) **Love to God**
2) **Love to one another**

These two principles resulted in willing submission to God's will and in joyfully blessing all others. As long as these two principles of love reigned in the hearts of all, through the Holy Spirit, there would be no chance of discord or disruption in the stream of joy that flowed out to every inhabitant. None had ever tried to operate outside of the realm of these two foundational pillars. And why would they? Everything God ordered resulted in a blessing for the obedient one. By faith - the blending of belief and trust - they knew that God had their best interest in mind and they loved Him all the more for it.

THE FIRST MYSTERY

But a change is soon to take place. This prince, given more privileges and gifts than any other, would one day take note of his beauty and it would affect his mind in a way it never had before.

It started off as a small thing. Leading the angelic choir as he stood before the Throne, he noticed that, as usual, all the singing angels were beholding and praising the Creator, seated right behind him. Their eyes barely missed him as they focused on the Life-giver, and Lucifer contemplated his own beauty, shining out before them as they sang. *What if their eyes - and just a tiny bit of the praise - were to be directed at him someday during these beautiful songs? Just for a moment?* Strange thought at first, and certainly not what Lucifer sought after. *But what if?* He quickly casts such a random thought out and continues leading the choir in praise to God.

You see that time has passed and Lucifer is now walking amid the stones of fire, contemplating a new song he is eager to compose. Little does he realize how this same brilliant musical talent will be wielded by him one day on a distant, fallen world to lure many subjects of a new species away from the very Creator he so adores. As he contemplates the new tune, he can't help but recall the fleeting thought of all those angels potentially focusing on him someday as they sing those moving songs of praise, rather than on God. The dazzling brightness of His own beauty again flashes into his mind, only this time he lets this thought just rest there for a moment. Not only does his physical splendor surpass the other angels, but, as he thinks about it, so does his intellect. He has been blessed with these gifts and starts to wonder if the other angels really appreciate him as they should. He doesn't like where these thoughts are leading, and quickly shakes them off again, at least for the time being.

Again the scene changes, and Lucifer, with the other angels, is hearing for the first time that God is planning yet another race of beings. The covering cherub's interest is heightened by the words, and he concentrates intently on the face of God as the Creator lovingly shares His plan. The angels are excited by the thought. This is wonderful! A new, intelligent life form, unlike the angels. They love it when He reveals His plans for new creations, and this time, it turns out, the new race will be made in the image of God! They will be able to reproduce others after themselves, something even angels cannot do. The new plan sounds amazing to all, and they're eager to witness the creation of these new beings. As countless angelic voices around him enthusiastically discuss the new plan, you notice Lucifer seems a bit more solemn than the others, but quickly forces a smile before turning away to concentrate for a moment. He must gather his thoughts.

As soon as the announcement concludes, he leaves the crowd of angels to be alone for a bit. He's not so sure what to think about all of this. *A new race? Made in God's own image? Isn't that what he, Lucifer, the "bright and shining one" was? And what's this about their supposed ability to reproduce themselves? And multiply? Even he can't do that. It sounds dangerously close to creation itself, and only God can create. Will they be - banish the thought - higher than himself?* This prospect drives him still further from the distant assembly as he seeks to escape even the sound of their cheers. He doesn't like his thoughts. He doesn't like the new plan, but he doesn't like his own reaction to it, either. This is all unfamiliar territory. *Why does he not cheer like the other angels,* he wonders. *Is it because they aren't intelligent enough to know what is going on here: that God might,* might, *eventually position these new beings to be higher than angels themselves? And what if He did? Why should they care? Doesn't God know best? After all, the other angels have always been pleased with Lucifer being in a higher position. Shouldn't all be satisfied with whatever position God, in His wisdom, assigns?*

You look on as the battle in Lucifer's mind plays out before you. A thousand conflicting thoughts, clashing in that brilliant mind. *He should just go talk to God. Yes, yes, that's what he should do. God would understand. God would help him and explain everything so that it's all okay. But then again, God didn't even consult him with this plan of these new beings, did He? And why not? Isn't he the covering cherub? Don't his ideas matter to God? Wouldn't his input be valuable? God should be honoring him more than He has.*

The scene again changes, and you see that God did not leave Lucifer in distress. God's principles are unchanging, and just like in your case, God offered to "instruct and teach" Lucifer in "the way that he should go" (Ps. 32:8) and He was "not willing that any should perish" (2 Pet. 3:9), including this questioning cherub. You see that God bore long with the vacillating angel, just as He did with you during your rebellious time on earth. Even longer. Consistent with His character, He gives Lucifer every bit of evidence that His way is best, and that selfless love is the only way to live. You see that it seems to work for a time and even though you know how all this turns out, you almost wonder how it could ever be when you see him embrace Christ and thank Him for explaining things so clearly and patiently.

But again the scene changes and Lucifer is once more alone. He's spending less time at the Throne lately, and his free will is frantically exploring its options. The mental gate - still blocking the path of doubt, which he has pondered so many times - he now opens and peers deep into the distant, mysterious blackness, to which the path leads. *What is down there? A life, existing at odds with its own Source. A rejection of the path of light and life laid down by the Creator of all life.* Lucifer is confused. He knows that the only evidence he's ever had is that of a loving God who has always instructed him benevolently and never held back any "good thing" he needs (Ps. 84:11). But then again, he is being held back from a position equal to God. *Why not go down this path? Why not just find out for himself and no longer take God's word for it?*

Little does Lucifer realize that the battle taking place in his mind at this moment would be repeated billions of times in the minds of all fallen beings on a planet called Earth. Every sin ever knowingly committed required a decision on this very question: Is God's way best? It is the question at the center of every Bible story in Scripture. And it would one day be the final test for humans on planet earth at the very end of time when all would be compelled to either accept the " mark of the beast" or be prohibited from buying or selling (Rev. 13:17). And ultimately, loyalty to God and His law - "God's way" - would cause those who hadn't received the "mark" to be targeted for death (Rev. 13:15). You remember those events well, having gone through the "time of trouble such as never was, since there was a nation" (Dan. 12:1), just before seeing Christ return in the cloud. And you know by experience that the solution to that question is to get to know Jesus. It is about a relationship with Him. It is to walk with God as Enoch did. And unlike the fallen humans on earth in your day, Lucifer *had* known God. He *did* have a relationship with Him. He *had* walked with Him, even closer and longer than Enoch had. The rebel angel is without excuse. Sin itself, that mystery that no one can explain, is without excuse, or it would cease to be sin (John 9:41; James 4:17).

As Lucifer gazes longingly at that mysterious darkness of rebellion in his self-deluded mind, he ultimately decides to walk through the gate and trod that path. You witness him place his free will in opposition to God. His decision is made. It's time to take action. He leaves his solitary place, determined to spread his new, venomous ideas to the other angels. He will exalt his own throne. His position had been high, but he is determined to be like the *Most* High.

Scene after scene passes before you as Lucifer advances to drop seeds of doubt into the minds of individual angels. He has always been fully trusted by all the angels, and this previous trust works to his advantage as you witness varying reactions to his new theories. Each seems confused at first, but some are more easily swayed than others to trust the wily cherub. As word gets back to the Throne, God, of course, already knew, and even now He bears long with Lucifer, explaining to the angels where this new philosophy will lead. He is, however, allowing the accuser the freedom of speech heaven has always maintained.

The scenes continue to reveal a growing dissatisfaction, and ultimately, fully one-third of the angels are in agreement with Lucifer (Rev. 12:14) and are ready to side with him no matter what. The two-thirds who are loyal to the Creator are seen pleading with their best friends to reconsider their baseless positions. As has always been the case, even throughout your old planet's history, reality meets fable head on, but every conceivable tactic and clever angle are utilized to make the falsehood seem believable and even logical. The motives of those aligned with truth are questioned. Emotions are given a high priority. Contrary to God's design, where emotions are a *result* of principles carried out or violated, these emotions are now *guiding* them, *replacing* principles, as facts give way to feelings. The very discontent that Lucifer implanted into their minds, with no evidence whatsoever, is now pointed to as the only evidence needed to demand change in God's way of doing things. Circular reasoning, so often wielded on earth by the unscrupulous, is artfully crafted and honed by the arch deceiver.

Time advances and the scene now explodes in a burst of light as you step back, witnessing the infamous War in Heaven. The cancer of sin has done its damage, and God, in His mercy has drawn a line.

He offers those who choose love to remain in their positions. Those who wish to reject love and replace it with this mysterious dark agency, "iniquity," are free to start their own kingdom elsewhere.

They have opted out of God's way of love, and for the sake of love, must no longer hinder love's progress in this Kingdom. But Lucifer, now "Satan" has other plans, and has been emboldened by God's mercy and forbearance, mistaking it for weakness and a refusal to mete out any consequences. No one had ever rejected love before. He did. No one had ever lied before. He did. And no one had ever ended a life before, so what should stop him and his army now? The battle rages before you as God, in His foresight and wisdom, again refrains from stepping in and immediately annihilating the insurgents.

The rebel angels seem both surprised that God does not do what He could easily do with His unlimited power - squash their uprising immediately - and at the same time, they've counted on His unending love and patience. The confused rebels are outnumbered 2-to-1, but the loyal angels are not eager to drive them out, although they know they must do so if the rebels seek war. Each wields a powerful, flaming sword that you had read about in Scripture. The silly lightsabers of Hollywood never knew what power was. Just one of these flaming swords was so powerful it wiped out 185,000 soldiers (Isa. 37:36). And you now witness billions of them clashing in a sea of flashing fire. The gold of the Holy City is obscured by the smoke of war as the battleground erupts like a thousand vertical mushroom clouds in every corner of the metropolis.

The insurgent army of billions is not slain, but instead cast out amid the tears of the victors and given the opportunity to demonstrate the proposed superiority of this new path outside of the Kingdom. You see Satan looking over the sea of bitter faces which are glaring back at him, waiting for his words of instruction and hope. He has cost them their positions, and they are now much lower than before, not lofty and exalted as he had promised. Satan, of course, knows this is bad, and it shows. He knows that this isn't turning out as he had hoped, even though he knew overthrowing God seemed like a fool's errand. He begins to speak but notices the fallen angels are looking over his shoulder, and suddenly he hears something that he's never heard before. It's a distant metal clanking sound, and it's coming from the Holy City. He turns to see what it is, and those giant gates of pearl, always open and welcoming to all who would enter are now closed for the first time. The visual image only reinforces the tragic truth of their situation, and he slowly turns back to face what is now an army of demons, angrily waiting for his response to their terrible defeat and ever-worsening condition.

Meanwhile, far above, at the top of the City walls, Christ is comforting a host of grieving angels as they sadly gaze out into the distance at the losing army. The victorious angels are not celebrating their victory at all, but rather weeping for their vanquished friends below. They despair at the vacancies that now riddle the city mansions, and the Son of God shares their sorrow. One angel stands next to Christ and sadly mentions the empty rooms, to which the Lord replies that the vacancies will not remain forever, for there will be others. The city will once again be full one day. The angel seems confused by Christ's answer and asks Him who will they be, and from where will they come?

As you watch the scene, you realize that this same question has been asked down through the ages from the fall of humans right up until the last decision for Christ on planet earth: Who will they be, and from where will they come? As these same holy angels were eventually assigned humans to guard over the millennia, they pondered this question. Will it be this person, in this house? Will it be that person, in that era? Oh, how they had hoped so. The rich, the poor, the old, the young, every race, creed and color, "every nation, kindred, tongue and people" (Rev. 14:6), they were all welcomed to receive the perfect life of Christ in place of their own sinful experience. All were invited to opt back into the family and Kingdom from which their Eden ancestors fell. None could obey their way back into the

Kingdom or even be forgiven back into the Kingdom. They must be born into it. And Christ had made that new birth possible, through His own death and resurrection (Rom. 6:4; Col 2:12). As you now witness the results of the rebellion in Heaven, you again wonder how you could have ever doubted His love or thought sin was a good idea - even in the smallest things.

Your attention is drawn back down to the black cloud of demons drifting further from the shining city. Satan actually does have a plan, it turns out, and of course, you know that it involves a beautiful garden with him inhabiting a serpent. He reminds these spirits of darkness that the coming, new species would be able to "be fruitful and multiply." The descendants of these would be the result of a law that applied to every creature in the new world: "every seed after its kind" (Gen. 1:11,28). In other words, if (and at this point it seemed like a big " IF") they could get the parents of the race to rebel, the descendants would, by definition, have the same fallen nature as the parents! And if that were the case, then these new fallen ones could multiply and perhaps get their numbers high enough to equal the loyal angels who had just cast them out of the Kingdom. Little does he realize at this moment that one day, in the distant future, he indeed would return to these very same gates with this same demonic army, joined by legions of descendants of the new race he is referring to right now. And their numbers would be "as the sand of the sea" (Rev. 20:7-9). What he also doesn't yet realize is that his expanded army would then suffer a second defeat. This next defeat, however, would end in permanent destruction from the presence of God and the Lamb, and "the blackness of darkness forever" (2 Thess. 1:9; Jude 1:13 - more in chapter 24 "Strange Fire").

Satan seems impressed with his own brilliance, as the plan emerges from his lips. He emphasizes that he will capitalize on the emotions and physical senses of the first couple, downplaying God's words and casting doubt on His motives. Across the sea of faces, expressions of rage gradually succumb to visages of flickering hope. Could it be? Could this plan actually work? Why not? He had convinced all in this army to doubt God's love and reject His will. Perhaps he could do the same with this coming new life form...

As you contrast the holy sadness within the city walls with the evil scheming on the massive, black cloud, you realize you've just witnessed the grim closing of the first chapter in the cosmic conflict between Christ and Satan. Everything is much clearer now than ever before. You know that all of your questions will be answered now that the books are opened, and history is unfolding before your eyes. The next chapter is the part where your own species enters the picture. It is where Satan slithers up a tree in a garden and unleashes this mystery called iniquity onto the free will of the human race, injecting it into their DNA. It's where he temporarily lays claim to the fallen planet as "the prince of this world" (John 14:30) and "the prince of the power of the air" (Eph. 2:2), while simultaneously convincing millions that he doesn't even exist. Yes, the second chapter is one with which you are much more familiar. In fact, nearly all earthlings were familiar with it. For it opens with one of the most famous statements in all of human history: "In the beginning, God created the heavens and the earth..."

Thought Questions:

1. What is your main takeaway from this chapter? Why is it your main takeaway?

2. What attacks on God's character do we see today, similar to the ones Satan used on Him before the War in Heaven? What similar methods of argument against the truth? Have you ever used the wrong method to promote the truth? And why do you think Satan works so hard to make people believe he doesn't exist?

3. What does God's forbearance with Lucifer's free will and rebellion tell us about His wisdom and character?

4. What does the ultimate triumph of truth in the universe, with sin not rising up the second time, tell you about the promises of God?

5. What did you learn about God's will for you in this chapter? What do you feel He's impressing you to start doing differently this week to walk more closely with Him?

BEHOLD ALL THINGS NEW

"And he that sat upon the throne said, Behold, I make all things new."

-REVELATION 21:5

HOLLYWOOD HAS SOME pretty amazing special effects, without a doubt. But their best in the business could never conjure up anything even close to the spectacle of earth's creation. No human being has ever witnessed the creation of a planet. In the first five days of earth's history, God spoke many things into existence. He started with "Let there be light," and proceeded to bring forth the atmosphere, the land, the plant life, the sun, moon and stars, the marine life of the deep and the birds that fill the skies. It wasn't until the sixth day - His last day of creating, and after the animals that had been made earlier that day - that human beings were formed. Thus, by the time Adam and Eve took their first breath, the entire planet was up and running.

Their home, as it were, had been built before their arrival. The only thing they saw God "make" was the Sabbath day, the day after their creation (Mark 2:27; Gen. 2:2-3). They weren't privileged to see any of the other amazing things come from the Creator's hand during the previous five days, or even earlier that day.

But this will not be the case when the earth is made new the second time. Although Jesus returned to heaven to prepare a place for you in the New Jerusalem, which ultimately descends to the earth (Rev. 21:2), we are promised that one day this entire planet will be made new, and right before our eyes.

"And I saw a new heaven and a new earth: for the first heaven and the first earth were passed away" (Rev. 21:1).

The prophet John faithfully records what he saw in vision, and this is in harmony with the words of two other Bible prophets, Peter and Isaiah: "Nevertheless we, according to his promise, look for new heavens and a new earth, wherein dwelleth righteousness" (2 Pet. 2:3:13); "For behold, I create new heavens and a new earth... the new heavens and the new earth, which I will make..." (Isa. 65:17; 66:22).

After the Holy City comes down to earth from heaven and the final judgment is executed (see chapter 24, "Strange Fire"), then all of the redeemed will be able to watch the creative power of God in action. "Behold," says the Lord, or, "Watch what is going to happen now." And then He says, "I make all things new." Nothing in this old world is worth missing out on that event. Jesus has the power to re-create this planet, but never forget this: it cannot be truly complete without you there. You are among those that Christ wants to place on the surface of that new earth, as citizens of His glorious, peaceful Kingdom. You are God's child, and when families get together, the parents desire nothing more than to have all the children present, with none missing. Determine today that by the grace of God you will be there when the Father, Son, and Holy Spirit once again make all things new.

▲ ▲ ▲

You are standing atop the lofty western wall of the New Jerusalem, peering down at the surface of the earth, far, far below. The brilliant jasper shimmers under your feet. Suddenly you hear a voice, as beautiful as many waters, as mighty as thunder. "Behold!" It rumbles across the golden sky, like peals of thunder, "I make all things new!"

You eagerly inch closer to the edge of the wall beside three of your closest companions and all four guardian angels as the words continue to roll across the face of the earth. The God you serve has the power to create with just a word, and He proceeds to tell the earth exactly what to do.

"Let there be light!" He commands. Now the light that shines from the Throne bursts out from the city and bathes the entire earth with its brilliant rays. There will never again be the need for a sun on this planet, for "the Lord God giveth them light" (Rev. 22:5).

You listen as God commands the lakes and rivers to appear. Every atom and cell obey Him as molecules transform into the material of His choosing. Glistening water, seeming to appear from nothing, begins to coalesce and grow before you, from sparkling, white rivulets to bubbly rushing streams into gorgeous flowing rivers, which converge in various places, forming crystal blue ponds and lakes. This time the earth will not have the majority of its surface cloaked by the oceans, however (Rev. 21:1). These bodies of water are still enormous, but they don't rob humans of the bulk of land surface as they did after the great Flood (Gen. 7:11). You gaze upon the scene as watery blue regions dot various parts of the new earth.

Next, the Lord commands that new trees and fresh plant life should appear. A lush carpet of green, garnished with trees of every variety, rolls out from the base of the city. It is an awesome sight. The creative energy involved shakes the very atmosphere, and the sound is overpowering, yet not painful to the ears. To see a tree formed from nothingness is quite a thing to "behold." These trees are perfect, and you look forward to tasting their fruit and climbing some of the larger ones very soon. No doubt you will recline under many varieties of them in the future during some of your private talks with Jesus.

Flowers begin to sprout up, splashing the various landscapes with their vivid colors. Some of the rolling hills are speckled with red, while others wear shades of blue. The level plains that stretch out for miles are also covered with a panoply of floral beauty. One field is loaded with bright white daisies, and the bank of a tiny creek is lined with yellow daffodils. The tulips and roses, the lilies and carnations, all have their place in this spectacular new world.

Again, the mighty voice calls forth life, only this time they are lives on the move. Graceful birds of every size, color, and variety now burst into the skies with their amazing air show, and some in their spectacular flight formations seem to pay homage to their Creator. Others land in the freshly-made trees and begin to sing and chirp in delight. Still others fly toward you and up over the walls of the city on a quest to explore that vast domain. One lands on your shoulder and playfully rubs its head against your neck. It appears to be a small reddish-brown falcon of some sort, and you reach over to gently lift him onto your wrist. No fear resides within this bird. Unlike the wild fowls of old earth, these birds love the companionship of people. As you move him in front of your face, you start to ponder what you should name your new friend. You get distracted, however, as another, much larger bird soars directly over your head and into the city. Its wingspan must be 20 feet or more, and you try and recognize this species from the old earth. But before it lands, your attention is diverted again by that powerful, deep voice you love to hear.

The Creator commands that the land animals appear, and now the green of the earth below begins to stir with activity. Vast herds of buffalo come forth, the breath of life just bursting from their lungs. The landscape erupts with life as the thundering, brown sea of buffalo curves toward the south in spectacular formation. The sound of millions of hooves mingles with thousands of other herds that are charging across the plains and hills and down into the valleys.

Horses, antelope, elephants, zebras, sheep, deer, every beautiful and perfect creature that moves in numbers, comes forth to beautify the planet and fill it with motion. All of God's creatures are appearing. The bears, lions, kangaroos, wolves, rabbits, and squirrels, along with innumerable other creatures, materialize before your eyes and right away begin to enjoy their tailor-made habitat in perfect harmony.

Far below, streaming out of the three Western Gates, you notice that some of the redeemed have started to exit the city and explore the wonders of God's creation. The angels grab the hands of you and your three friends and step over the edge of the wall for an exhilarating ride, plunging down to the surface. You remember those "wingsuits" that humans wore on old earth, but this flight puts that extreme sport to shame. Your falcon friend quickly takes flight and follows your lead, joining your group as you gently touch down on the newly-created grassy surface.

You notice a group of brown bears playing beside a churning, white river in the distance and you eagerly head off toward them. As you do so, a giant herd of horses overtakes you, and you find yourself surrounded by thousands of pounding hooves, thundering on all sides, stirring up a wind that tussles your hair and you laugh, smoothing your hair back as they storm past you. You have no fear of any bodily harm, and you stop to experience this thrill. Several of your friends are only a few feet away, and you look at each other in mutual amazement as the stampede rumbles by on all sides. Finally, the last few horses gallop past, and as you watch them head toward the horizon, it occurs to you that later on, you can ride any of them that you wish. There are no fees to pay, no lessons required, and no chance of any injuries.

Suddenly an enormous lion leaps in front of you, and he's followed by dozens more. They're chasing one another like giant, playful kittens, and you decide to join them. You dash up the side of a hill and then down the other side, surrounded by the tribe of massive felines. Several of them roar as they head toward the giant valley below. You are amazed that you can actually keep up with them and you increase your speed as the incline steepens. At the bottom, a few of them playfully lunge at each other. One turns and charges back up the hill, and you quickly try to catch him. At the top of the hill, you stop to scan this view of the new world as the lion quickly circles you and then calmly plops down by your side, taking in the view with you.

Eventually, the bears by the distant river once again attract your attention, and you start back down the hill to give them a visit. As you approach them, one lumbers over to greet you. She is smaller than the other bears, and she rises up on two legs to lick your face playfully. Then the two of you race toward the river, where the other bears are gathered. Not one of them scampers away as you charge toward them. You are eternally and harmoniously sharing this wondrous, new habitat, and nothing will ever ruin that.

The light from the throne of God and the Lamb gives everything a beautiful golden hue much like the last hour before sundown on old earth, only brighter and more glorious. You sit beside the river's edge, leaning against a giant redwood. As the falcon settles once again onto your shoulder, a few new thoughts come to mind. The massive rocks that make up the riverbed will never, ever bear the selfish marks of graffiti. The tree you lean against will never be burned for pastureland. A thorn-free rose which you pick will never die. The massive herds that roam the prairies will never be hunted, poached, or diminish in number. This water rushing in front of you will always be safe to drink. The air that you breathe will never contain a trace of pollution. All is in God's hands. The planet is safe forever; danger is eternally a thing of the past. What a wonderful place is this home planet of yours. Behold, all things are new.

Thought Questions:

1. What is your main takeaway from this chapter? Why is it your main takeaway?

2. When the New Jerusalem comes down to the earth, heaven comes to earth, for where God is, heaven is. How does this fact shed light on Luke 17:21 (*"The kingdom of God is within you"*)?

3. What does the fact that God replaces this dark, sinful earth with a new, perfect earth tell you about His character? Why do you think He moves His headquarters to our planet?

4. God can actually speak things into existence. What does this tell you about the power of His Word and His promises?

5. What did you learn about God's will for you in this chapter? What do you feel He's impressing you to start doing differently this week to walk more closely with Him?

INHERITANCE OF THE MEEK

"Blessed are the meek: for they shall inherit the earth."

-MATTHEW 5:5

"But the meek shall inherit the earth; and shall delight themselves in the abundance of peace."

-PSALM 37:11

WHAT IS YOUR favorite type of landscape? If you could have a thousand acres of undeveloped property anywhere in the world, where would it be? Think about all the places that you've been or seen on travel shows. Would you choose rolling green hills? The lofty mountains? The forests? The plains? The jungle?

LANDSCAPES

On a recent trip to the big island of Hawaii, our family was amazed to discover such a wide variety of these extremely diverse landscapes all compacted onto that one island. Starting at the airport, our drive consisted of black lava rocks as far as the eye could see. Eventually, the view morphed into your basic desert with cactus dotting the dry landscape and the occasional wild goat trotting by. After that, we saw rolling green hills and trees, which my son accurately described as almost indistinguishable from our land near Chattanooga, Tennessee. And gradually the rolling green hills turned to a thick, tropical terrain covered with jungle foliage and palm trees. And although we never saw any, there also are parts of this same island that are even covered in snow!

When I was a kid, I remember traveling across the country from Tennessee to California more than once and even back then, what always stood out for me was the amazing diversity of landscapes and climates from one coast to the other. And I loved them all. Each region had its own unique charm. I remember as we drove across the deserts of the southwest I marveled at the giant red rocks rising up toward the western sky, many of them balanced in ways that seemed to defy gravity. As I took in the rugged, rocky terrain, I couldn't help but think about the cowboy and Native American images from the 1800s. This was a completely different world for me. I even used some of my mom's empty spice bottles to collect dirt from each state along the way (and yes, I did keep them out of the cabinets when we returned, avoiding culinary disaster). But the California coast, in particular, seemed wonderful to me. I won't deny that part of it could have been the mansions of Beverly Hills and Hollywood that dazzled my impressionable young mind, but the land itself, and the sandy white beaches always appealed to me. Later, when I lived there as an adult, I relished our quick jaunts up the Pacific Coast Highway to beautiful Santa Barbara, which remains to this day one of my favorite towns. Eventually, when

I returned with my wife and kids to my home state of Tennessee, it seemed to strike me for the first time just how beautiful that southern state was. Absence makes the heart grow fonder, they say, and the rolling, green hills and winding rivers, along with the gorgeous fall colors now seemed exceptionally beautiful to me.

I do love to visit large cities with their bustling mix of modern architecture and global culture, but there is something liberating about finding yourself surrounded by vast expanses of open land, untouched by modern development. Real estate agents are quick to point out one obvious selling point about land, which is "they aren't making any more of it." As we saw in the previous chapter, though, God promises He *will* be making more of it, and part of that new land will be just for you.

Land has always been one of the most sought-after, precious resources to the human race. More wars have been fought over land than anything else in history, and it was, in fact, a promised "land" that the Israelites sought during their 40 years in the wilderness.

FAITHFUL STEWARDS?

At the very dawn of humanity, God put Adam and Eve in a garden so that they could "dress it and keep it" (Gen. 2:15). Humans were created to enjoy the land and have done so ever since. We were also to be faithful stewards of the land and the animals (Gen. 1:26-28). He told the first couple not only to be fruitful and multiply and replenish the earth but also to "subdue it." To rule over it faithfully and take care of it. He didn't design a beautiful world just for the human race to turn around and destroy it. And yet, the Bible predicted that at the time of Christ's return, human beings would have been so unfaithful in their stewardship that they would be described as those that "destroy the earth" (Rev. 11:18).

A few hundred years ago, and for most of earth's history, that prediction would have seemed a bit far-fetched. The earth was far too massive for mere humans to do much large-scale damage to it. But as our numbers have increased exponentially, our technological advances have multiplied, and our manufacturing capabilities have exploded. We are now seeing that prediction come to its fruition. And this is not about climate change. Regardless of one's views on that controversial subject, all can agree that pollution has been a serious problem for this planet. One need only visit the cities, where large numbers of people reside, to see the effects of mismanaged trash and neglected decay. In some areas, we have made improvements, but we still have a long way to go, and in general, humans have not proven to be very faithful stewards. We are truly destroying the inheritance of the meek.

In the New Earth, the inhabitants will appreciate the beauty of nature, regardless of the particular landscape and they can be trusted by God to have dominion over that new land forever and ever. They will cherish their inheritance because they cherish their Creator.

Just as in the case of your City home, the Lord knows more about your favorite type of land than you do. When the earth is made new, He will lead you to the land that you have inherited by His merits. He will have designed this landscape with you in mind, and as we saw in chapter 10, "Behold All Things New," you will actually be there to witness the recreation of the New Earth.

When we think we really want something, like a certain piece of property or a house or car, we find that after we have it, the excitement slowly fades. In some cases, we begin to wonder why that particular thing was so important to us and soon we're infatuated with something else. Not so with the land you will inherit. Never in a trillion years will you begin to grow tired of it. Never will you find another plot that suits your fancy better. The Lord will be giving you the land that fits your desires and personality better than any other land in the New Earth (or the entire universe for that matter). Were you to pick your land, you would choose incorrectly. You might come close to a perfect match, but you would still be off, not knowing every other stretch of land on the planet, nor your own shifting interests. But your Father knows you better than you know yourself. After all, He created your tastes and desires, and He knows exactly what will make you the happiest. The greatest thing of all about the land you will inherit and the house that you will build on that land is the opportunity to invite Jesus over for a visit. If He is a welcome guest of yours now, He will be a regular guest of yours then.

You are walking with Christ along a hillside covered with brilliant orange poppies. They wave in the gentle breeze as you stroll by. Jesus puts His hand on your shoulder as you talk to each other. His words are so kind, and you've never been more at ease in your life. This man - this real man who walks beside you - actually came down to the old earth and allowed Himself to take your punishment. All of those sins that you committed He took upon Himself. By His stripes from the whip, you were saved and ultimately healed. You almost understand how He could take the sins of others. But *your* sins? Your life on earth had so many regrets, so many grievous sins, particularly considering the light of truth that you had, it always seemed too good to be true in your particular case. You wonder now how you ever could have thought that He didn't care. Or how you could have thought of Him at times as an impersonal Savior. Now it is just you and Him, one on one, and there's not another soul in sight. He is as real and personable as even your closest friends on old earth, and He loves you more than they possibly could, because His love is, and always has been, unconditional. It was through Him that you ultimately realized your true value.

The hand on your shoulder still bears the mark of that fateful day - the day your sins drove that nail through the flesh. Yet you feel no lingering guilt, no nagging "if only"s. Jesus is not One to remind you and condemn you for what your sin did, but rather He promised to forgive you and to completely cleanse you from all unrighteousness (see 1 John 1:9). He even went a step further and promised that He would remember your sins "no more" (Heb. 10:17). They are gone - cast "into the depths of the sea" (Mic. 7:19). Having put on His righteousness, you are accounted and treated as if you had never sinned. Is this justice? Not at all. God's mercy withheld the justice you deserved and instead gave you pardon. But was justice done away with, simply forgotten? Did God just say, "Oh well, everyone makes mistakes"? Not in the slightest. He cannot govern a lasting Kingdom this way. No kingdom or government could survive in such a way. The sentence still had to be paid in its fullness; God's unchanging justice called for this. But the full price fell upon the One who now walks beside you in this meadow - the One who is bringing you to your land which you possess because of His sacrifice.

He waves that nail-scarred hand forward and points out that your land is just over this next hill. The fact that He created it with you in mind is so typical of your Savior - always thinking about the welfare of His children. Ownership of the land is trivial in comparison with the reward of getting to spend an eternity with Him. You cannot take your eyes off Him as you make your way toward the top of the hill. His face just radiates with love, and He makes every other friend seem like a stranger by comparison.

At the top of the ridge, your eyes fall upon the land that has been purchased and designed for you. As perfect and beautiful as all the rest of this new earth has been, the magnificent vista that now spreads out before you tops everything! Your mind, created by this

Man beside you, is magnetically drawn and attracted to the landscape in front of you which He also created. A perfect match!

The bright, hilly prairie that rolls out before you is covered with wildflowers of every kind and thousands of colorful butterflies flit from petal to petal. Jesus explains that the land stretches out farther than your eyes can see, and He plans to show you around the entire terrain. The idea of a continued private walk thrills your heart much more than the prospect of all this land that you have inherited.

As you stroll across the prairie, you reach down now and then and pick a few of your new wildflowers, which will never die. Theirs is the most wonderful scent you have ever experienced, and it seems to energize you more with each breath. Some of these sunny hills possess a surreal familiarity as if you've been here before or seen this place somehow. Perhaps you had dreamed about such a place once as a small child, and of course, Christ knew that, too.

You reach the crest of yet another ridge which reveals a sprawling valley, flanking a gorgeous, winding river. The light from God's distant throne reflects back down from the sky and sparkles off the flowing river like a million tumbling diamonds as a small bear scampers out and shakes the water off. Beyond this scene is a lofty mountain range adorned with several waterfalls of various size and height. This must have been visible in the distance all along, but your attention has been captivated by all the other sights until now. Jesus explains that yes, even these mountains are given to you, and the forest that lines their base, as well.

Sensations of gratitude and love again wash over you as you look once more at the Savior. His own eyes have been on you; He always loves seeing your reaction to His gifts. You are His precious jewel, His child, one created in His own image. This bond that you have will only grow stronger with every walk you share on this beautiful new land.

You fall at His feet in adoration, but He lifts you up and embraces you. You're home now, forever to live in peace and safety. Again, you wonder how you could have ever doubted His love on old earth. He leads you down the hill to drink of the water from your sparkling river. He still has much to show you, and He's eager to see your reaction. As you reach the base of the hill and continue toward the river, He starts to sing one of your favorite New Earth hymns. The song is all about love - a love that will grow through all eternity.

Thought Questions:

1. What is your main takeaway from this chapter? Why is it your main takeaway?

2. What type of terrain is your favorite, if you could have a thousand acres anywhere on earth? Mountains? Beachfront? Rolling Hills? Desert? Islands? Lakefront? Forrest? Jungle? Prairie? Why would you choose as you do?
3. God selects the meek to inherit and be stewards of the earth. What does this tell you about His character?
4. Whenever you walk with Christ in the land you inherit, you know He will remember your sins no more. What does this tell you about His promises?
5. What did you learn about God's will for you in this chapter? What do you feel He's impressing you to start doing differently this week to walk more closely with Him?

COUNTRY HOME

"And they shall build houses, and inhabit them; they shall plant vineyards and eat the fruit of them."

-Isaiah 65:21

My father and I did an amazing thing on our countryside land in Apison, Tennessee when I was growing up. We built an entire three-story red barn out of hundreds, if not thousands of wooden pallets. To be accurate, they weren't the only thing we used, but they were a significant component. Each pallet had to be dismantled with a crowbar, and my twelve-year-old hands got so good at that, I could do it in my sleep. At the time, I didn't like the work, especially on those cold, winter mornings. But looking back, that long project definitely gave us more father-son time for talks than anything else we could have done. Dads, I highly recommend doing something similar with your own sons while you can, especially in the busy, digital-dominated world we live in today. Do special things with your daughters as well. Moms and dads who give their daughters and sons their time are providing them with the thing they need more than anything money can buy. It is through your time with them that you place their feet on the path to the Kingdom. The pastor, the teacher, and the youth leader can never come close to the influence you have.

Building that barn was a wonderful experience, but building one's own home is even more rewarding. To design and build your own house (or at least pay for someone to carry out your chosen floor plans) is a dream for millions of people. The good news is, the Bible makes it clear you'll not only have a home in the New Jerusalem built by Christ (John 14:2-3; Heb. 11:16; Rev. 21:2), but also the opportunity to build your own home out in the country, where you can plant vineyards, fruit trees, gardens, and anything else you desire.

BUILDING THE DREAM

As I said, owning a home is a dream that millions of people will never realize in this old world. Hard working though they may be, the money just never seems to be quite sufficient for the actual purchase of a house. And even among those who are fortunate enough to buy a home, only a small percentage enjoy the experience of actually designing it themselves and building it to meet those specifications.

Often, we read in the news about people who have inherited some grand estate upon the death of a loved one, and we tend to think less about their loss and more about their great gain. Sadly, this is frequently the case with our visions of heaven as well. We love to imagine all of the things we will receive without considering the ultimate cost to the Savior. This is not to say that Christ wants us to be gloomy and despondent. Quite the opposite. When we contemplate just how undeserving we are and couple that with how gracious He is, our joy and gratitude will be apparent to all our acquaintances. Whoever is forgiven of much, the same loves Jesus much (Luke 7:47). But when we consider the sin that cost Jesus His life, and just how dangerous and deadly it really is, we won't be quite so willing to play with it and regard it as a small matter. If Jesus is truly our Friend (and only His friends will be there: John 17:3; 15:14-15), then we will never take for granted the great Sacrifice, only to dwell upon the inheritance.

WHEN BILLIONAIRES MOVE IN

Imagine if you were a billionaire and your wayward adult child contacted you after years of completely ignoring you. For what seemed like an eternity, he had shown no interest in you, but suddenly your phone rings and it's him telling you how much he misses and loves you. At first your heart thrills over this unexpected reunion, but soon you discover the real reason for the call. He says they're about to foreclose on his home, and he desperately needs some money, like, yesterday! You ask him how much and he tells you over two million dollars. You gasp that he allowed himself to get that far into debt and that now he is about to lose it, but you decide this might be a chance to permanently reconnect and you offer him the money. He thanks you profusely, reminding you how much he loves you. You then tell him that you're so glad he loves you and that you would like to come stay with him over the summer to get caught up on things. You figure he would agree to this, since, after all, you are basically purchasing his house and he loves you so much. His silence is deafening, but he finally speaks, discouraging your extended visit. You deduce from his stammering excuses that your money was good enough for him, but you are not. If you stay with him, it would really cramp his style.

Many of us do this with Jesus. We love the idea of the mansions and land we will inherit and the fact that we pay no price for our sins, thanks to His sacrifice. We may even talk about Him frequently or put His name all over our ministry. But to receive Him into our hearts so that He can begin to live His life in us, well, that would just cramp our style. The only reason we feel this way is that we do not know Him. We do not yet realize the total fulfillment that comes from letting Him live His life in us. And in reality, we do not realize the love involved in His ultimate sacrifice to save us for eternity.

It would be well for us to spend some quiet time every day in contemplation of what Jesus did in our behalf, especially the final scenes of His life. Then the best part of thinking about our heavenly mansion becomes the anticipation of frequently seeing Jesus when He visits us in that very place. Friendship is a wonderful thing, and love is even greater. For all eternity we will testify to the fact that "Greater love hath no man than this, that a man lay down his life for his friends" (John 15:13). And "there is a friend that sticketh closer than a brother" (Prov. 18:24). That Friend will always be Jesus.

▲ ▲ ▲

You have surveyed your land several times and are choosing the best place to build. The Holy Spirit seems to be impressing you of a certain spot, and as your eyes stop there, you can just imagine the layout in your mind's eye. Yes, yes, indeed, this is the place. This gentle hill is slightly higher than the others, and its level top is wide and accommodating. This spot will offer a 360-degree view of your land, which spreads out beyond the horizon on all sides.

Your blueprints have all been designed and laid out, but not only on primitive paper. Although you've sketched them out with some friends at one of your favorite hangouts downtown in the City, they are also recorded in your mind. Your memory is always accurate and doesn't dim over time. You know the exact dimensions of the floor plans and you decide that this is, without a doubt, the spot to break ground and start building. Unlike old earth, you need no building permit, so you can begin construction right away.

But these projects are always joint ventures, much like the old "barn raising" events in the old earth. You have spent much of your time during similar jaunts from the Holy City helping some of your friends construct their own houses on their new land. The joy comes from an entire group getting together, discussing the steps of the event, singing, working and watching the palatial structure go up as a team effort. Last week, in fact, you put the finishing touches on one friend's place, and the whole gang agreed to come to your land today and start all over. Working together to help various friends' house plans come to fruition has not only provided wonderful social opportunities but has also given you a ton of fresh ideas for your own home.

After much anticipation, that time has finally come, and several of your closest friends arrive. You explain your design to them, sharing your original sketches and dimensions and they are all eager to see this marvelous house completed. You remind them that they are, of course, welcome to help themselves to all your orchards and gardens and anything else they find on your land. More and more friends arrive, and the project finally begins. Some have even brought a variety of instruments to provide music at various times. Every event is yet another excuse for music, and you notice that some of your favorite musicians have even shown up.

As the days go by, your house is transforming from design to reality, and at each stage, you are increasingly eager to see the finished product. During this period, you still have friends' homes in the works, and you gladly take turns on each place. Each of your friends has some of the same people helping, but also others that they know. Thus with each undertaking, you make new friends, some of whom then join your project. Each group is continually growing as the friends multiply.

Finally, the day has come for your much-anticipated housewarming event. As always, there is music in the air to celebrate this event. The finishing touches are complete, and the gang that started off as several dozen has now grown to several hundred. Each one of these workers has become a close friend, and soon you will be helping some of the newer friends start their own homes.

Jesus Himself is present for this event. He stands by the front door, and the two of you look out over the vast crowd that has come for the housewarming (and to see Jesus). You invited Him here, and you want to give Him the first tour.

Together, you enter your new house, and you immediately show Him the special chair that you have designed just for Him. Only He is to sit in that particular seat, and you hope to have it occupied as often as possible.

Again, you are oblivious to the things around you as you walk in His presence. The house means nothing to you if not for a place to invite Him to come and visit.

A train of guests follows you on your tour, and they notice that each room contains some item in honor of Christ. The entire house is actually one giant architectural tribute to the grace that He has provided and an expression of gratitude for His love. Just as the city that He designed is replete with symbolism of His love for you, so this house incorporates symbolism of your love for Him.

Having explored all four floors, you and Christ exit the home and mingle with the celebrating crowd all around. Not only are people there, but your guardian angel and a host of his angel friends have come to join the festival. They, too love these events.

Before departing, several friends remind you that when you decide to build any additions to this mansion, just let them know and they'll be happy to help. Giving is the spirit that pervades the population of this New Earth. That which constantly fills the minds of all is love for God and for each other. Service to others and laying aside self are common attributes here, quite the antithesis of the way things were on Old Earth.

As the crowd gradually disperses, not one shred of trash appears anywhere. Nothing looks junked-up or misused in any way. In fact, each person brought something for either the house or the land, and the grand estate is actually more attractive now than it was before anyone showed up. This is just how things are done here.

The last friend says goodbye, and you and the Savior walk back into your new home. You want Him to stay as long as possible because you love talking with your best Friend. You treasure just being in His presence. Besides, there's a brand new chair in your living room that's just waiting to be occupied.

Thought Questions:

1. What is your main takeaway from this chapter? Why is it your main takeaway?

2. What style of architecture is your favorite? What features would you incorporate if money and time were no object?
3. What does Christ standing at the door and knocking, desiring to live His life in you tell you about His character?
4. What does our opening text, Isaiah 65:21, tell us about God's promises?
5. What did you learn about God's will for you in this chapter? What do you feel He's impressing you to start doing differently this week to walk more closely with Him?

THE SPEED OF Λ THOUGHT

"And it shall come to pass, that before they call, I will answer; and while they are yet speaking, I will hear."

-ISAIAH 65:24

"And when they were come up out of the water, the Spirit of the Lord caught away Philip, that the eunuch saw him no more: and he went on his way rejoicing. But Philip was found at Azotus [40 miles away]."

-ACTS 8:39-40

TELEPORTING. WHO WOULDN'T want to try it, if it were safe? For now, it's just the stuff of science fiction. One screenplay I was working on in Hollywood was about a group of boys who had a machine that worked much like the transporter on *Star Trek*. This machine could "beam" anyone who had a small, portable device somewhere on themselves to anywhere else on earth through the miracle of advanced technology (and science fiction). Many sci-fi buffs and physicists have debated the future plausibility of such a device. One that could actually separate every molecule in a human being, send those molecules through the air or outer space, and then reassemble them exactly as they were, somewhere else without terminating the life of the traveler. Good luck with that. But God doesn't need luck, and He's already performed this at least once, as recorded in Scripture. More on that in a moment.

God longs to give us more good gifts than we could ever imagine (Matt. 7:11). This is hard for us to believe sometimes, but it's true, and the Bible is clear on this point. Most parents long to see their kids happy and fulfilled, and our heavenly Father is no exception. The reason He created all of the beings of the universe (including you) was so that He could experience a love relationship with them and shower them with blessings. There is nothing He enjoys more than seeing His children happy. But so often the things that we think will make us happy in this world would really not be in our best interest. When we get to heaven, our minds will be sanctified, and our requests won't be tainted with selfishness. We will always ask according to God's will, and we have the promise that *anything* asked in harmony with His will is granted (see 1 John 5:14-15). In that day God will be able to safely say Yes to all of our requests, knowing that none of them could possibly lead to anything that would cause us or anyone else to stumble.

Isaiah 65:24 tells us that one day God will actually answer our prayers before we even ask them. He sometimes does so even now, but that's another topic. The Lord knows our thoughts and can see the future. He knows what we are about to desire before we even desire it. For a heavenly example, imagine if you were on a planet in a distant part of His endless universe and you suddenly wanted to be in the presence of God's throne. You could instantly be there at the speed of a thought. God could answer that request before you even got the words out. Impossible you say? With God, all things are possible (Mark 10:27). Science fiction you say? God has already performed this miracle in the case of the disciple Philip. Read about how God instantly transported Philip from a pool of water between Jerusalem and Gaza to a city 40 miles away called Azotus in Acts 8:26-40. See also Luke 24:31; John 20:26; 6:16-21 for similar miracles.

How long till our technology on earth can do this? We'll let the scientists and sci-fi buffs spend hours in online forums theorizing and battling it out. I'll just trust that what God did for Philip two thousand years ago, He can easily do for me in Heaven. Our heavenly Father - who created every molecule in us and all the laws of physics - is truly able to do more than we could ever ask or think (Eph. 3:20).

▲ ▲ ▲

You are exploring the mammoth base of a beautiful, winding canyon whose walls are streaked with various shades of red, brown and black. God's creative designs are ever before you, and you are continually learning more about His power and genius through observing these designs. Various rock formations line the edges of the canyon, and you are sitting atop one whose massive, colorful arches caught your eye. You recently started a unique rock collection, and now you are finding all sorts of specimens to add to your growing display at home. Gold and silver are commonplace, but now you are finding stones that you've never seen before, never even knew existed. Many of these actually didn't exist in old earth. In school, you had learned that all matter on earth was made up of 103 known elements. But here you regularly discover new and unusual elements, and your heavenly

Father is continuously making more, simply by speaking the Word: the transparent gold of the city streets being one example.

In your dusty hand is one particularly beautiful, radiant stone that your diligent search has just uncovered. It is composed of what look like millions of tiny mirrors which make this rock appear to take on different shapes and sizes, depending upon the angle from which it is viewed. This is definitely one of the most amazing rocks you have found to date. You can't wait to get it back to your home and place it beside the others. But first, you want to talk to your heavenly Father about how He created such a thing and find out more about the science involved here. You decide that you would now like to be in His presence at the top of the New Jerusalem, and you have faith that you will be.

Instantly you are before the dazzling throne of light, and you reverently bow in love before approaching the Creator. A widening grin covers your face as you hold up the fascinating rock. Your Father returns the smile, knowingly. He is fully aware that you enjoy and collect these things, and He explains that He had placed that one at that particular spot just for you. Lovingly and patiently He explains the science behind this rock, and as your mind begins to grasp the concept, your admiration for Him increases. You love everything about Him. He never tires of explaining new discoveries, and your love for Him will continue to grow throughout the ceaseless ages. How blessed you are, to be able to call Him "Father."

You remain by His throne for a period of time that escapes your concept. Time becomes irrelevant in His presence. There is nothing you enjoy more than just being with Him. It's a healthy addiction. Like David, you can honestly say, "One thing have I desired of the Lord, that I will seek after; that I may dwell in the house of the Lord all the days of my life, to behold the beauty of the Lord, and to enquire in His temple" (Ps. 27:4). This is your favorite place in all the universe.

He tells you He has a surprise for you at your home, and you eagerly think of going there to see what it is. You love all of His surprises, many of them tailor-made just for you. Instantly you are at your country home, in your rock collection room. Each of the thousands of rocks has its own story to tell. Each was the result of one of your exciting expeditions. Each helps to reveal more clearly the infinite mind and creativity of your Father. You see a perfect spot for your new stone, and you place it there as its image morphs into an oval shape. The oval transforms to a variety of shapes as you observe it from various points in the room. The light from the window engulfs the stone, igniting its millions of tiny mirrors and bounces forth onto the walls, outshining the reflections the other stones. You take a step back in awe and gaze at the kaleidoscope of colors sparkling on the white wall as if they were alive and dancing. You take a seat and admire the scene, settling into the comfortable chair as you contemplate the recent words of your Father explaining the physics of how this dynamic effect in a stable rock is possible.

As you take in the scene, your eyes eventually fall on an unfamiliar object. That's right, the surprise! The surprise that God had mentioned! No longer sidetracked by the dazzling light from your new rock, you spring out of the chair to check this thing out. At the base of your collection sits a gorgeous, ruby-red stone. Curiosity overtakes you as you slowly kneel beside it to get a better look. Upon closer investigation, you realize that this is, in fact, *half* of a cut stone. The stone is ultra-light. No, it is *weightless*. And its components must contain, among other things, something like helium, since it remains in the air wherever your hand releases it, mimicking a rock in space with no gravity. Plucking it out of the air, you flip the mysterious stone over and discover that it is shaped like a treasure map which gives clues to where the other half is. Your heart races as you wonder what the Lord has conceived to take place when the two halves are connected.

This map displays an area you have yet to explore. What will this place be like? What kind of creative masterpieces will be in this land? What will its culture be like? Your smile widens in anticipation, for you know that wherever it is, the answer is just a thought away.

Thought Questions:

1. What is your main takeaway from this chapter? Why is it your main takeaway?

2. God has already performed this physics-defying transporting miracle with Philip. Since "with God all things are possible," what other imaginative things might we be able to experience in heaven?

3. David could have had practically anything he desired on earth. Yet he wanted nothing more than to seek the Lord and be in His presence, beholding and inquiring of Him. What does this tell us about God and His character?

4. What does the fact that God can answer us before we even call out to Him (Isa. 65:24) tell us about His promises?

5. What did you learn about God's will for you in this chapter? What do you feel He's impressing you to start doing differently this week to walk more closely with Him?

WORKING THE LAND

*"They shall plant vineyards and eat the fruit of them...
mine elect shall long enjoy the work of their hands."*

-ISAIAH 65:21-22

M Y MOTHER HAS always loved working the land. I remember, even when we lived in Memphis and had only a small, suburban front yard, she planted a willow tree and watered it every day, letting the hose just drip on it for hours at a time. That thing grew like crazy, and she often received compliments from neighbors about its beauty. Later, when we moved to the other end of Tennessee (Apison) and had plenty of land to work with, she had a ball. She planted even more willow trees there and a variety of other bushes and trees, including a small row of pines that are now five-stories high. My sister Linda lives there now, and she has carried on the tradition by planting even more (fruit) trees with her husband Doug, of Tamale Pie fame (see chapter 8, "The Marriage Supper"). If you currently love working the land, you're in for eons of opportunities to carry out your greatest plans.

GOODBYE WEEDS

As we've explored in previous chapters, God knows exactly what would please you, even more than you do. He knows what type of land would best suit you and bring you peak enjoyment. But He doesn't expect you to just sit idle on the land and eventually fall into boredom. His promise is: "Long will you enjoy the work of your hands." And God always keeps His promises. But don't worry; as you "work" the land, it will be nothing like burdensome toil and sweat we experience today. It will be a refreshing and creative venture, increasingly fulfilling. It was only *after* Adam and Eve disobeyed that the ground was cursed so that our enjoyment would be hindered by thorns and weeds. God said, "Cursed is the ground for thy sake; in sorrow shalt thou eat of it all the days of thy life; thorns and thistles shall it bring forth to thee... In the sweat of thy face shalt thou eat bread" (Gen. 3:17-19).

Not just by the sweat of our brow, but our *face*. This is hard work, as anyone who has labored on a farm can attest. These thorns, thistles, and weeds of every kind have been a burden to everyone who has worked the land since that fateful day. And the battle with tenacious weeds still continues. These pesky plants thrive even in the most unfavorable conditions and seem to assault any attempt at a landscaped lawn, flowerbed or food garden. Throughout the Bible, we see that thorns are a constant reminder and symbol of sin itself (see Matt. 13:7,22; 27:29; Heb. 6:8; Prov. 22:5). Working the land today, although rewarding, definitely has its share of frustrations.

As it was before the fall, so it will be again after the new Creation. To work the land will then bring us utter joy and satisfaction. And the ground itself will no longer produce those obnoxious weeds, thorns, and thistles. No, in the new earth, the soil will cooperate with our efforts to the fullest, and we will continually find real joy in working the land.

THE WORLD'S HAPPIEST PEOPLE

I once read an article on happiness which cited a study, ranking personal activities that generated the highest levels of sustained happiness and contentment. It looked at everything from sports to traveling, to collecting and every major hobby or leisure activity in between. Can you guess which one took the number one spot on that list? Gardening. Despite all the things mankind has concocted to entertain and occupy the time, the garden remains the top choice for evoking joy, satisfaction, and happiness, believe it or not.

Many celebrities who have attained such levels of wealth and fame that one might think their interests would never include something as simple as gardening have even touted their passion for working the soil. Julia Roberts, Jake Gyllenhaal, Martha Stewart, Ringo Starr, Nicole Kidman, Sienna Miller, Prince Charles, Oprah Winfrey, Lauren Conrad, Jessica Alba, Oscar de la Renta, Suzanne Somers, Zooey Deschanel, Mindy Kaling, Shakira, Savannah Miller, Ellen DeGeneres, Tori Spelling and many others have been quite vocal in their praise of this activity. George Harrison, with all the trappings of fame and riches surrounding him as one of the Beatles, even said that working in the garden was his favorite time of all. Although some of these people may have never acknowledged God, they discovered through experience that God knew what He was doing when He put our first parents in a garden.

A recent poll in the U.K. from *Gardeners World* magazine found that 80 percent of gardeners felt satisfied with their lives, compared with 67 percent of non-gardeners. 90 percent of gardeners felt that the activity improved their mood and the study also showed that gardeners were less likely to display signs associated with depression or unhappiness. The editor of the magazine said, "We have long suspected it, but our research means we can definitely say gardening makes you happy." Other university studies have validated that engagement with "green places" is good for the health. One professor even recommended that individuals "self-medicate" more with what she referred to as "green exercise."

Psychologically, surrounding ourselves with nature clearly has a positive impact, there's no doubt. But other research has found that there also may be benefits in the actual soil itself. Recent studies have shown that microbes found in the soil have an effect on the brain similar to the antidepressant drug Prozac, but of course without any of the side effects. The microbes under study are called Mycobacterium vaccae, and they may have a link to increased serotonin production. Serotonin is the natural brain chemical associated with a feeling of well-being and contentment. It should be noted that sun exposure also releases serotonin (15 minutes increases this natural drug *eight*fold - why do you think your mood is so elevated when you lay out at the beach?), so the time in the garden can make you feel better in multiple ways! As a Chinese proverb puts it: "If you wish to be happy forever, become a gardener."

Besides the vineyards promised in Scripture, there will no doubt be opportunities to work with whatever plant life your heart desires. Cultivate a garden filled with all your favorite foods. Plant as many trees as you want, whatever variety you like. There will be no risk of any species not thriving in your part of the world, for there will be no death in the new earth, and that includes the trees. And sprinkler systems will forever be a thing of the past. No plant there will suffer from dehydration, for the living water flowing from the throne of God will continually refresh the entire planet. Every plant in sight will be vibrant and healthy.

Finally, the land itself can be altered by you. Do you wish to divert a new creek off of that broad river? Go ahead. Would you like to dig a tunnel through part of your mountains? Feel free. Or how about a bright, sandy, palm-covered island in the middle of one of your giant lakes? Build a Caribbean-style treehouse on it. Hang a comfy hammock there. And imagine the variety of beautiful, tropical birds such an island will attract. You can do whatever you please. The land has been given to you, and unlike the land of the old earth, it can never be taken away. Long will you enjoy the work of your hands.

▲ ▲ ▲

You are admiring the beautiful, glorious horizon as you finish planting the small honeysuckle bush along the grove of almond trees by a tiny pond. It reminds you of those rare sunsets on the old earth when the sky just radiated with streaks of gold and orange. Some called it the "golden hour." Your God is certainly a God of infinite creativity, and He is constantly revealing new and beautiful scenes across the earth. You think about that friend who came by to visit a while back, and you remember how you had agreed that this particular hue was one of your favorites. You wonder if she too is admiring the sky right now and experiencing this same blessing.

The land itself rivals the beauty of the sky, and you pause to take in the scene. Trees, shrubs, and wildflowers of endless variety adorn the landscape with vivid color. While the fresh blossoms of spring are ever before you, the brilliance of autumn splashes over every red and golden leaf as they rustle in the gentle breeze.

Leaning back down to the honeysuckle, you take in a deep breath and savor the aroma. The fragrance is mild and sweet yet invigorating. It occurs to you that although you never grow tired in the new earth, there are certain things, like this honeysuckle fragrance, that seem to energize you even more.

The tiny pond beside the honeysuckle is the home to several water turtles which you have named, as well as multitudes of bright, colorful fish, and a family of black and brown ducks. Somewhere in here is a playful freshwater stingray, which you always enjoy feeding when he appears. This is one of your favorite spots to bring visitors. It is quiet and calm, and the ducks just love the attention. No matter what you and your guests talk about here, the subject frequently turns to Jesus. Your admiration for Him has been growing with each new discovery, and His love seems to be revealed more clearly with the passing of time. The Cross of Calvary is your science and your song; His sacrifice, a mystery continually unfolding to your mind.

A stone's throw from the pond lies the food garden, loaded with your favorite delicacies. Your eyes scan the progress as you approach this natural grocery store. On either side of the garden are the fruit trees. Large, plump cherries, apples, peaches, dates, figs, and the rest of your favorite fruits weigh down the branches and await your picking. Their scent drifts through the garden on a gentle breeze. Along the far edge of the orchard are the bushes and vines. Giant blackberries, blueberries, raspberries, and other such treats almost obscure the bushes with their ample clusters. Their luscious taste reminds you of that homemade cobbler you used to eat, only much more flavorful. And these treats require no added sugar and will never clog your arteries. Then, of course, there are the famous grapevines. You enjoy a wide variety of grapes from these diverse vines, but you also make as much refreshing grape juice as you or your friends could ever want. Even Christ Himself has shared this "fruit of the vine" with you on numerous occasions, just as He promised when He was on the old earth.

You also have a few vanilla plants for some of your favorite recipes. And several maple trees produce their syrup for a luscious maple bread that is a favorite in these parts. The honeybees have also provided their golden treat in several hives among the trees. You often enjoy watching these diligent creatures fly from flower to flower as they carry on their work. And now you have no fear of that infamous sting since they have no reason or drive to harm you.

At your feet in the garden, you notice an immense, green-striped watermelon, growing under the shade of a lemon tree. You gently slide your hand over it, feeling its surface, then thump it to make sure it's ripe. You did this on old earth, not sure what to even listen for, but it seemed like the thing to do. When anyone was watching, you'd sometimes say, "Yep, that sounds ripe!" hoping your prediction was accurate. But here your ears are keen to the telling sound, and you know what you're doing. Satisfied that it's ready for consumption, you crack it open on a nearby stone, revealing the brilliant red interior and then break off a tiny piece for a test. This refreshing, cool, sweet flavor cannot be compared to any melon you tasted on the old earth. You don't even need to salt it like you did back then. The taste is perfect like it is. In fact, it's even better than your last melon here! Is the food here getting better with time, or is your appreciation capacity simply expanding? Perhaps your taste buds are constantly improving. Whatever the reason, every meal you have seems better than the last.

You lift half of the melon and start heading toward home, leaving the other half for your cousin who had said he wanted to see your garden and is coming by a little later. He normally prefers the bright yellow melons over the red ones, but you told him that this latest batch will give his yellows a run for their money, and he said he'd come by today to see for himself. There is no concern of the crisp, luscious fruit drying out in the open air, or being devoured by bugs. When you come back to this spot, the melon will still be as fresh as when you first cracked it open. And the insects here obediently stick to their work in their own areas, just as God has designed.

Nearing your home, you cross the small iron-and-emerald bridge that you built over your circle-creek. A while back you decided that you would like to have a creek flowing in a continuous giant circle all the way around your estate. You designed and created a large channel that ultimately formed this circle about a quarter-mile out from the perimeter of your home. Then you diverted the water from one of your rivers into the new creek. Knowing that with God all things are possible, you studied the science of gravitational and magnetic pull, and trusted in God to make it happen. Once the water flowed into the new channel, something amazing happened. By the previously-untapped laws of physics and the power of God, it didn't merely settle into a donut-shaped lake but rather flowed on continuously in this formation. Many of your guests have enjoyed swimming or just relaxing in the giant circle-creek, and you love to watch their expressions when they finally notice its full, unique design.

God's power can also make the rivers flow uphill, and you have already designed an area on one of your highest mountains that allows for just that. You see it on the horizon as you walk up the marble stairs to your front entry: three giant, distinct rivers that actually flow *up* to the top of the lofty mount, and then diverge in three different directions. One river turns left at the peak and snakes along the top of the mountain range, eventually ending up at your second-largest lake at the southern base of the mountain range. Giant trees of various sorts line either side of this river, giving it extra beauty for those who might want to explore the mountaintop via the peaceful tributary. You chose and planted the specific type of trees you thought should go there. The second river becomes much shallower as it crosses the peak and spans far out, cascading down the other side of the mountain at a 45-degree angle, creating acres of white water and a cool, refreshing mist. Many of your guests have ridden this shallow river all the way to the bottom; it's one of the more popular rides on your land. The third river accelerates near the top as it curves hard to the right and then actually arcs up into the air over 100 feet beyond the summit before eventually splashing down into the head of another deep river far below. Extreme sports on old earth never offered a ride like this! All three rivers regularly transport guests to the top after the eager riders decide which thrill they'd like to try. Most experience all three again and again.

Each design and project you undertake is done so with three things in mind: glorifying the love and power of God, bringing joy to your fellow human beings, and enjoying the work of your own hands.

Before entering your house, you stop and relax in a comfy blue chair, positioned near the left front pillar, overlooking the mountains. A palm branch fan turns slowly overhead, powered by all-natural resources. From here you can see almost all of your land, and the pink-orange streaks in the sky are giving way to a shimmering gold. Another cool bite of watermelon fills your mouth as you lean back and contemplate the Creator of all things. From the wonderfully sweet food you enjoy to the marble on which your feet rest; from the mountain range that graces the horizon, to the very sky that shimmers in dazzling color; all have come from the hand of your best Friend and Redeemer. You truly serve a creative God. And long will you enjoy the work of your hands.

Thought Questions:

1. What is your main takeaway from this chapter? Why is it your main takeaway?

2. Have you ever had and/or worked in a garden of any kind? How was your experience? Good? Bad? Why do you think so many rich and famous people still prefer the quiet of a garden?
3. God placed Adam and Eve not in a state of sedentary idleness, but in a garden with active responsibilities to work the land. What does this tell you about His character? What does His curse on the land after their disobedience tell you about Him?

4. What does our opening text, Isaiah 65:22 (*you will "long enjoy" the work of your hands*) tell you about God's promises?

5. What did you learn about God's will for you in this chapter? What do you feel He's impressing you to start doing differently this week to walk more closely with Him?

INNER SPACE

"Dost thou know...the wondrous works of him which is perfect in knowledge?"

-JOB 37:16

"[He] doeth great things past finding out; yea, and wonders without number."

-JOB 9:10

W HEN I WAS in school, I must admit there were few things I found less appealing than biology. The idea of cutting open a dead frog and having to learn the names of all those reeking parts was not my idea of a good time. One thing I did discover, however, was that there was, without exception, a design involved in every aspect of animals, minerals, and plant life. It seemed that no matter how small the object - even under a microscope - an organized, elaborate plan was evident.

VIEWING GOD'S CREATION

When we consider the incredible variety of life forms that cover the earth, we begin to realize just how many intricate, unique systems must be involved in the inner workings of these entities. In the beginning, Adam and Eve were continually viewing God's perfection and creativity apparent in all of His handiwork. Every created thing attested to the infinite wisdom of its Designer. The opportunity to study the treasury of nature up close and uncover the countless secrets it contains was one of the greatest blessings bestowed on the first couple. Their studies weren't hindered by all of the limitations we have today. With perfect minds and superior faculties, they were able to learn from nature in ways we can't even begin to imagine. In ways we will be experiencing, however, in the world to come.

My sister, Marylee is an amazing photographer. Her pictures have won awards, and she has a keen eye for capturing images at just the right time and angle. Her husband, Gary is incredible, too. His photos were published in a giant coffee table book about Knoxville. Together they produce a gorgeous photo calendar every year, and I can't even begin to list all of the other places that have published and awarded these two.

There's something about fascinating images, angles, colors, and perspectives that attract the human mind. And what we now can see is quite limiting, compared to our visual abilities in heaven. Even now, humans with a rare fourth cone cell in their eyes (tetrachromats) can see far more colors than most people, who have only three cone cells (trichromats). Also, certain Aborigines have been shown to have superior vision, with one particular Aborigine man on record capable of reading at a distance four times further away than those with "normal" eyesight. And according to the record keepers at Guinness, one

Veronica Seider is capable of vision 20 times better than a normal person, with eyes that work almost like a telescope or microscope. Seider is able to identify people at a distance of more than a mile away.

I'm partially-colorblind, and I've seen several YouTube videos of guys with my same type of colorblindness trying on special glasses that are supposed to correct this problem. Invariably, when they first don them, they're overwhelmed by their first sight of such rich colors and begin to weep for joy. I've been tempted to get a pair, but they're not cheap ($600 at last check), and I'd have to be sure and try them on with no cameras around!

If that is the reaction of just *color* enhancement, imagine how emotional it will be when our faculties are all enhanced, and we can see the intricate details of God's designs with eyes that can do even more amazing things.

My friend Jack Faatz was reading the first edition of this book and sent me an online *National Geographic* article from Feb. 23, 2018, entitled "Pictures Capture the Invisible Glow of Flowers." You can Google it and see the magnificent photos yourself. The photographer used a process called *ultraviolet-induced visible fluorescence photography*, which causes the plants to fluoresce, so the light you see glowing is actually radiating from the flower itself. Amazing what Marylee and Gary and National Geographic can do with cameras today to see nature in unique and innovative ways. Imagine what we can do when we get to heaven and can explore nature on so many levels in ways that we can't even dream of today.

ABSENCE OF INTELLIGENCE?

The staunch evolutionist would ultimately suffer endless rounds of frustration in heaven, for they would constantly be trying to explain away all of the Creator's designs as accidents. They would forfeit the blessing of seeing God's hand in all His imaginative works.

If you were shipwrecked on an island and discovered a collection of rocks laid out to form letters that spell "HELP," you would immediately know that these rocks didn't just accidentally fall into place like that after a tropical storm. The fact that the end result clearly had a function, purpose and design tells you that the rocks were placed there by an intelligent being who had this *result* in mind. In 2011, scientists uncovered in the deserts of northwestern Kenya what they deemed to be the oldest handmade stone tools, which, according to their calculations, actually predated their timeframe for human existence. The irony is that this very evidence they used to determine that these were, in fact, handmade tools, is the type of evidence they rule out when discussing human origins - intelligent design. The idea that these stone artifacts weren't random stones that just happened to take the shape of functional tools (using evolutionary laws of probability) was never even considered. No serious scientist would look at these artifacts and even try to postulate such a hypothesis. Their credibility would vanish. And yet nature's designs, infinitely more complex than crude stone tools, are deemed products of a completely random result, with no initial design in mind.

"INFINITE DIVISIBILITY"?

Consider this fact for a moment: if you were to choose just one item - animal, mineral, or plant - and decided to study it, examining the smaller and smaller components within that object, you could keep yourself busy for years and still never learn all of its secrets. How can this be? It's called the concept of "Infinite Divisibility." Both Plato and Aristotle discussed this concept in theory and many philosophers and physicists have debated it over the years. Quantum physics pioneer Max Planck (1858-1947) suggested that there is, indeed a minimum size to which something can be divided and reduced, now referred to as "Planck Length," but the debate continues as science uncovers more and more secrets. If Infinite Divisibility is correct, then regardless of how small any portion of matter gets, it can always be divided in half. No matter how many times you split the element, you would never reach an ultimate "foundation" to it all - no starting point. Try to wrap your mind around that one.

Another thing to consider is the mysterious nature of the elements themselves, and how they interact with one another. Pure sodium, for example, will burn and explode if it gets wet (YouTube it, just for fun). Chlorine, on the other hand, is usually a gas and is quite caustic. Neither of these is something you should ever consume for obvious reasons (being even more harmful than some of the online consumption "challenges" that abandon common sense). But combine the two and their physical properties completely change, to create something you will likely consume in some form today: sodium-chloride, which is table salt. Now imagine all the new elements we'll discover that aren't even available on earth today, and how they might react when combined or altered.

In heaven, when we can study nature firsthand, at levels far surpassing what our current technology allows, and discuss our findings with the Creator, we can settle old earthly debates and questions once and for all. And then there will be still more science challenges to ponder in our insatiable quest for knowledge. But whatever we discover, there is no doubt that it will reveal more and more about the intelligent design implemented by our heavenly Father.

You are taking a walk through the flower garden behind your country estate, and you come across a vibrant, yellow rosebush, the seeds of which you had long ago planted. Charmed by its bright blossoms, you pluck one of the flowers. The fact that the genetic code and properties for all of this beauty were stored within those tiny seeds intrigues you. You decide to examine the contents of one of the remaining seeds. You have no need for a microscope because, with your new body, all your senses are far keener than the most advanced lab equipment of old earth. You simply adjust your eyes and begin to observe the wonders of this complex thing called a seed. Your eyes now increase their magnification as you begin to study the very cells that make up the inner components of the seed. You marvel at the detail and intricacy of such a tiny, tiny thing.

You have just begun another journey into inner space. Just as the Creator's universe has no outer edge, no matter how far out you journey (if it did, what is that "edge" made of, and how thick is *it*?), this inner universe has no end (or rather, beginning) no matter how far *in* you go. Since there are no time schedules to adhere to, you decide to continue your journey down into the universe of this rose seed.

You can stop at any stage inward and look around in detail or zoom in at high speed and watch the stages pass before you in rapid succession. You've done this before with other plants and animals, so some of this looks familiar to you. It's an education all in itself to learn and compare the inner workings of a variety of life forms, each revealing the perfect plan laid out by God in all He touches.

Now you allow your eyes to zoom in faster and further than you ever have before, and you find yourself in a strange, new world. These bits of matter, now a million times smaller than an atom, are completely new to you, and the intricate design is beautiful. You pause for a moment to take in the scene. No need to take any notes. Your memory stores data perfectly and eons from now you'll be able to recall every one of these scenes in perfect detail. As you observe the complex system, you can testify to the statement that God's ways are definitely "past finding out" (Job 9:10), for you understand that there is no end to this matter-splitting study. The Creator is so infinite in time, dimension and wisdom that He was there before you, designing even these infinitesimal life-support stages, although they themselves have no starting point. He created the systems that support these, and the systems that support those, and so on for infinity. Now *that* is an awesome God!

With the distant ringing of your door chimes on the other side of your home, you realize that you have a visitor. No problem: you simply set your focus so that it will automatically return to this stage of micro-vision when you resume your study. You turn from the flower garden to go greet your guest. As you contemplate the endless creativity of God, you know that you will have lots of new things to share with your visitor. Perhaps this person will join you on your next incredible journey through the living kaleidoscope of God's creation: a journey into the boundless universe of inner space.

Thought Questions:

1. What is your main takeaway from this chapter? Why is it your main takeaway?

2. With God all things are possible. We got a glimpse of what might happen if God were to enhance our visual abilities. What other senses or faculties might He enhance and

what might it be like to experience those abilities? Consider Samson's strength (Judges 13-16) and Elijah's sprint-to-marathon (1 Kings 18:46) for starters.

3. What do God's amazing designs, from the infinitesimal elements that compose the atom to the cosmic systems comprised of galaxies, tell you about His intelligence, creativity, and character?

4. What does the fact that some of God's ways are "past finding out" tell you about His promises?

5. What did you learn about God's will for you in this chapter? What do you feel He's impressing you to start doing differently this week to walk more closely with Him?

BIBLE HEROES

"And I say unto you, that many shall come from the east and west, and shall sit down with Abraham, and Isaac, and Jacob, in the kingdom of heaven."

-MATTHEW 8:11

Wᴴᴇɴ I ᴡᴀꜱ a kid, I thought Samson was the coolest character in the Bible. Beating up all those Philistines and pulling a giant city gate straight out of the ground was right up my alley. It didn't take me long, however, to reach an age where I realized Samson was actually one of the weakest characters in all of Scripture. Jesus, the meek and lowly Savior (Matt. 11:29), ended up being the strongest one, by far.

I have a lot of questions for Samson and for so many of the Bible characters. Have you ever wanted to ask one of the characters in the Bible a question? Perhaps ask them why they did or didn't do a certain thing? What was it like for Noah and his family to be completely alone on the earth after the flood? When Adam and Eve were cast out of Eden, how often did they go back to the entrance of the Garden and peer past the flaming sword at their former home? What was it like for Mary and Joseph to raise Jesus?

Well, when you get to heaven, you can ask them. You can even discuss things that you and certain ones have in common. Perhaps trials that the two of you both endured. Have you been falsely accused and suffered dearly for it? Talk to Joseph, he's been there. Was your reputation marred by ignorant gossipers, who got it all wrong? Talk to Mary about her blessed pregnancy. Were you shamed by gossipers because of your own bad decisions, and longed for forgiveness, ultimately finding it in Christ? Talk to the woman caught in adultery, whom He saved from the stoning. Were you framed by cunning business associates? Talk to Daniel, he can relate. No matter the trials you've been through, a Bible character has been there, at least on some level (1 Cor. 10:13). It might even bring you comfort to read about them now, before you get to see them face-to-face and start a real friendship. The friendships you'll share with the Bible heroes might even be closer than any relationship you, or they, had on earth. How can this be? Because you'll have all eternity for your friendship with Joseph to grow. Your love for your dear friend Esther will continually increase as the eons pass. And as the ages roll on, you will become more and more familiar with the personality of your close friend David.

Yes, the Lord promises us that we will have plenty of opportunities to speak to and build relationships with Bible characters. Your voice will unite with theirs as you frequently sing the praises of the One who made it possible.

▲ ▲ ▲

You are walking with Daniel along a massive, golden bridge which spans one of the new earth's larger rivers. The two of you are on your way to the Great Throne Room of the Father and the Lamb in the New Jerusalem. You have many friends in this place, but somehow you and Daniel seem to have an extra special friendship. Many times, you have discussed his visions recorded in the book of the Bible which bears his name. How thankful you are that he was true to his post and accurately recorded what he was shown. The role that he was assigned during his allotted time on the earth was carried out faithfully by the grace of God. One of the things that has become quite clear to you since arriving here is the fact that everyone who was ever born on planet earth had a specific plan for their life. The tragic part is that so few ever sought to know from God what that plan was. But for those who did seek, it was always made plain. The Savior had made this perfectly clear in Matthew 7:7: a promise you still cherish even today.

Although your sinful record was completely erased by God, as if it never was, you do know that much of your life had been wasted before you allowed Jesus to really take control. You had made many professions of faith, but they were all shallow until you fully grasped the need for complete and utter surrender to Him. The Lord in His wonderful mercy had then fulfilled His promise to show you His will for your life, and eventually, your path was made known. He had strengthened you to redeem the time (Eph. 5:16) and carry out His specific plan for you.

Now you and Daniel are once again discussing this very topic. How amazing is God, you declare, to have worked through such unworthy vessels. You are relieved that it's not constantly lorded over you that Daniel's life was spotted with far less sin than your own. No condescension takes place in this land, for all are aware of their own unworthiness. Christ accepted you when you came to Him in repentance as though you had no spotted past and as if you had literally been born at that moment. Thus, there is no asterisk placed by your name in the books of heaven, reading *Barely Made It*, or *Forgiven,*

But Reluctantly So. No, the Lord had taken you where you were and started afresh. He delighted in His mercy toward you and kept His eyes on you and your future life with Him. You and Daniel cannot stop talking about your love for Jesus and His love for the two of you. You still can't fully grasp how Christ was able to literally take your sins upon Himself and clean up the record as if you lived His perfect life, but you intend to study the Plan of Salvation, even more, today when you reach the New Jerusalem.

Floating peacefully downstream beneath you in a heavenly vessel is a friend you met in the Holy City when you first entered its gates. She is a woman who lived during the days of the prophet Samuel, and your personalities just seemed to hit it off. She smiles and waves as she recognizes you. You never dreamed that you would have so many friends here from other time periods on earth. You have discovered that people are people, and the special bond all of the redeemed have with the Savior only binds each friendship even closer.

Now you and Daniel proceed down the golden steps of the bridge onto the lush, green grass which stretches out for miles at the base of the New Jerusalem. Several angel friends greet you in passing. The soft grass feels warm under your feet as you head toward the hill on which the city sits. As many times as you have returned to this city, you never tire of beholding its splendor. The place is so immense that despite all your years here, you have yet to see the entire thing. Rooms and roads, alleys and balconies, buildings, bridges, and staircases fill the glorious place and they just never seem to end.

As you approach the Simeon gate on the southern wall, you see the apostle John speaking to an angel. His writings also brought you closer to the Lord, and you have thanked him as well for being faithful to the part he was to play in the great Plan. One of the things you remember about John is that he was extremely interested in speaking to you. He had seen visions - which he faithfully recorded in the book of Revelation - about the people who would be alive at the very end of the world, and here he had been able to speak to you in person. He had asked you all sorts of questions about what it was like to be among the group that went through the great Time of Trouble and were alive at the Second Coming. This is the group to which the people of God had wanted to belong since the ascension of Christ. What a privilege, he had exclaimed, to be among those who gave the final warning to the earth before the return of the Lord! You had always been envious of the Bible characters for the times in which they lived, but you have consistently been told by them that you lived in the most amazing time of all - the last days of the earth's history.

The beloved apostle grins as he recognizes you. He and Daniel briefly talk once again about the similarities in their visions. The Lord had used these two men to give the clearest picture to the last generation on earth of what the end would be like. They have a special bond as well.

Passing through the majestic pearl gate, you enter into the busy, golden street. Happy people are milling about the place, some exploring its infinite secrets, some conversing with one another, and some on their way to or from the Great Throne Room. Faces shine from being in the very presence of the Life-giver; from head to toe, they gleam with pure energy. An impromptu choir has started to sing over beside one of the great fountains that line the sidewalks. They are singing one of your favorite songs and you and Daniel join in as you pass by.

Just stepping down from one of the many giant staircases are Peter and Noah. Peter is asking Noah some questions about the days in which he lived. At first, you were surprised at how many Bible characters were eager to interview other Bible characters when they got there. But after all, people are people.

Finally, the two of you reach the Great Throne Room, and as you enter, you see Adam, the father of the race, on his way out. This is your great-great-multiple-times-grandpa standing here, and you will always have a special place in your heart for him. Everywhere he goes he sees his descendants, and he seems determined to develop intimate relationships with all. Suddenly an idea comes to you: you will start with your parents and try to trace your line all the way back to Adam to see if you can locate all of them here in at least one unbroken line. With each previous generation above you, the possibilities double, so this will make for quite a complex and fun project. You have already met many of your ancestors, which makes this new idea seem even better and maybe you'll complete it even faster than you thought. But then again, what does time matter?

You embrace the tall, handsome figure and Daniel does the same. His fall and all of the woe he brought into the world by his single act of disobedience was long ago cleaned from his record. For 930 years on old earth, he witnessed the horrible consequences of disobedience to God. It seemed a great load to bear, but now he sees only joy and happiness - all of it, thanks to the Savior.

You and Daniel approach the throne and bow reverently in the presence of infinite Holiness. You then rise, eager to begin your latest inquiries about the Plan of Salvation. The theme is inexhaustible and grows more and more fascinating as you study it. Love, you have experienced, is not a static thing, but grows and in fact multiplies as it is exercised.

You and the prophet take turns asking questions, which the Father and Son patiently and eloquently answer. What a privilege it is to speak to the Deity face-to-face! And what a blessing it is to be asking your questions with a man you once only read about in the Old Testament: a man whom you now call "friend."

Thought Questions:

1. What is your main takeaway from this chapter? Why is it your main takeaway?

2. Which Bible characters would you particularly like to talk to someday and why? What would you ask or tell them?

3. God used flawed individuals who made many mistakes, rather than just angels to accomplish His plans. What does this strategy tell you about His character?

4. Many Bible characters who will be in the Kingdom, actually did horrifically sinful things. What does this tell you about God's promises?

5. What did you learn about God's will for you in this chapter? What do you feel He's impressing you to start doing differently this week to walk more closely with Him?

MARINE LIFE

*"They that go down to the sea in ships, that do business
in great waters; These see the works of the Lord, and
his wonders in the deep."*

-Psalm 107:23-24

I LOVE SHARKS. LET me rephrase that. I *fear* and love sharks. I never
saw the thriller *Jaws* in the theater (it was before my time), but I
remember as a kid seeing Jaws-themed trailers and promotions on
TV, and the one thing that stood out was the famous score by John
Williams. Two ominous, deep notes. You know them; they started off
verrrrrry slow... and then sped up as the Great White moved in for
the kill. There are few kids who haven't hummed that "buuuuum-
BUM...buuuuum-BUM..." around their friends when swimming at
the beach. And everyone knows exactly what it means. Suddenly the
water seems a little deeper, a little cooler, a little darker.

When I was learning to surf in Southern California, this was constantly on my mind. Local news reports of beach attacks only rein-
forced my fears. And yet, I'm fascinated by these powerful creatures.

Of course, their mindless-killer reputation has been exaggerated (Peter Benchley, author of *Jaws*, has said he regrets vilifying them). There are even a few brave souls who've been recorded swimming "cage-free" with Great Whites. I would love to face my fear one day and see one of these amazing creatures up close (I'll take the cage approach, thank you). But what I really look forward to is the day when I can swim with as many of them as I want in the cool, clear waters of the new earth. Then I can rest assured that the wild animals - including sharks - won't hurt me (Isa. 11:8-9).

The prophet John saw the new earth in vision and declared that "there was no more sea" (Rev. 21:1). This was most likely the case before the flood, as well. When God destroyed the world with a flood, it involved more than a simple 40-day rainstorm. The Bible testifies that "the same day were all the fountains of the great deep broken up, and the windows of heaven were opened." This reveals that not only did the water plunge down from the sky, but the bodies of water on earth cracked open in the "great deep" and began to overflow at a tremendous rate. In addition, the water that came from the sky itself had its source in more than mere rain clouds.

In the creation account, we get a glimpse of the Creator at work: "And God said, Let there be a firmament in the midst of the waters, and let it divide the waters from the waters. And God made the firmament, and divided the waters which were under the firmament from the waters which were above the firmament: and it was so" (Gen. 1:6-7).

Many scholars believe this refers to more than just the water content in clouds, especially since there was no rain back then. It is very likely that there was a far greater amount of water - in fact, a *layer* of water - at the outer edge of our atmosphere. Again, before the flood there had been no rain, because "the Lord God had not caused it to rain upon the ground...but there went up a mist from the earth, and watered the whole face of the ground" (Gen. 2:5-6). This is another reason so few of the antediluvians believed Noah's predictions of water falling from the sky; it had never happened before. A mist or dew had simply formed on the ground every morning and kept everything watered.

Before the flood, there wasn't nearly as much uninhabitable land under water as there is today. Between two-thirds and three-fourths of the planet's surface is now covered by the seas. In the new earth, it will not be so. But does this mean there won't be any large lakes or sea creatures as we know them today? No more dolphins or stingrays or sea lions? It seems unlikely that God would do away with such marvelous animals simply because there won't be vast oceans covering the land. These creatures obviously descended from other creatures that were in the water at Creation, before there were vast oceans covering the land.

I have no doubt that there will be dolphins - and sharks - in the new earth. But according to the Word of God, their habitat will not rule the planet as it does today. The world will then be as it was in the beginning: a place created primarily for human habitation. We have no need to wonder if God will prevent us from enjoying the thrill of swimming with the wonderful creatures that now roam our oceans. The giant "seas" may be no more, but His fascinating marine creatures will live on forever.

▲▲▲

You have just come across one of the mammoth blue lakes that God formed on the new earth. Down below the cliff you're standing on, you see a large pod of sea lions basking on the rocks. A trail a hundred yards away leads down to the water's edge, and you notice that the trail is dotted with small, blue and white crabs. You must take a closer look at these creatures on your way to the sea lions. As you start down the path, you pick up one of the crabs, knowing that it won't try to pinch you. Hurting is foreign to this world now, just as it is to the entire universe. A small group of people also examine the crabs along a distant trail up ahead. Not only are you safe from the crabs, but the crabs are safe from careless humans. You and the others only want to look at them and learn more about God's creativity.

You carry your crab down the winding trail which is lined with numerous palm trees. The sand along the path is warm between your toes, and it glistens a gold-speckled white. On the opposite shore, you see thousands of dolphins jumping out over the sparkling, blue water, with a few playful seals and a large group of people swimming among them.

As you approach the sea lions, five or six of them hobble over to see you. They bark loudly as if competing for your attention. You set the crab down, and one of the sea lions curiously follows after it. Other sea lions are having a ball diving into the water, and it looks so refreshing that you walk out to the edge of the rocks and jump right in.

As you splash through the surface, the underwater scenery just explodes with color. The water here is about 50 feet deep, and it is just as light and clear at the bottom as it is near the surface. Fish of countless varieties swim past while the sea lions chase each other. The bright coral formations below are breathtaking, and you quickly swim on down to take a closer look.

Three or four eels stick their heads out of their holes, and you confidently reach out and pet them. One exits its hole and swims past a playful, red octopus, who scurries along the bright coral reef, changing colors as he goes and settling into a bright orange hue with multiple black rings. Several gorgeous blue sharks now catch your eye as they glide peacefully over the top of the reef. You turn east and scan the distance. In the old earth, a distant view underwater would be a contradiction in terms, but here you marvel at how far you can see with perfect clarity. This is the narrowest part of the lake, and your view extends all the way to the eastern shore: several miles off, you estimate. There you again spot the group of people you saw earlier, swimming with the dolphins.

To the north lies the Colossal Reef - the most famous part of these waters. It is the largest coral reef in this hemisphere, towering over everything in sight, like a colorful band of underwater skyscrapers. It must be well over a thousand feet tall and stretches out for miles. This magnificent living structure is just teeming with marine life. The octopus, sea urchin, squid, jellyfish, giant clam, sea turtle, barracuda, starfish and innumerable other creatures have made this their home. Thick schools of vibrant fish flow in all directions, some forming giant, living spirals. Hundreds of people can be seen swimming all about the reef on every level. Even at these depths, the distant light from the Holy City permeates every square inch, clear down to the bright, sandy lake floor, far below.

As you swim closer, you begin to recognize some of the people. A few of them are marine enthusiasts, and they can almost always be found exploring the underwater depths. Some of them have made this their chosen scientific field of study. It is amazing what they have learned. You've attended several of their presentations in the past and always enjoy learning from their vast knowledge of this field. A handful of them you met during various house-raising projects; some have even been to your home. All have come to witness the majestic handiwork of the Creator.

Three sea lions from the shore have kept up with you, and one of them examines a giant school of luminescent jellyfish up near the surface. His idea is a good one, and soon you find yourself encompassed by a pulsating cloud of these strange but beautiful, glowing creatures.

Eventually, the cloud drifts across the top of the reef to the other side, where you notice a giant humpback whale heading toward the surface. You must examine this masterpiece up close, so you head toward the mammoth creature, sea lions still in tow.

With several mighty swoops of that giant tail, the whale launches himself out of the water, breaches 50 feet in the air right in front of you, and crashes back down into the water. It's exhilarating to witness such a sight live, up close, and with absolutely no fear of danger.

Swimming along beside him, you grab one of his massive fins and follow him up out of the water as he breaches again. The fresh air blasting your wet skin is exhilarating and together you and the whale plunge back in for more. This time you grab the whale's tail and hang on for the ride of your life! Two of the sea lions are still with you, and they now seem to be racing with the whale.

Ultimately the whale takes you near a cove where you let go and watch him as he heads back out into the crystal-clear depths. As you turn to face the cove, you spot a narrow, dark shape in the distance, rising out of the water. *Is this what you think it is?* Your guess is confirmed as it reaches its full height. A giant, gray dorsal fin slices through the water, spawning a rippling wake as it heads directly toward you. You quickly judge the distance between yourself and the shore in relation to the speed of the shark closing in on you. You wonder if you should even *try* to race it back to shore. You do, and your heart pounds as every muscle strains on your takeoff. *You can do this.* The dorsal fin turns to intercept your path, and you continually check its position between strokes as you churn across the surface. You've become quite an accomplished swimmer, easily breaking world records on old earth, but this creature was *designed* for it!

There are people on the distant beach, and you see that several are now standing and pointing toward you. Two of them run out into the water and quickly start swimming your way. You turn again to note the shark's coordinates, but too late! The Great White is upon you, and he lunges right into you, shoving you beneath the surface. Your mouth opens, but the water muffles the noise. As you rise to the surface again, the sound freely pierces the air, and your laughter can be heard all the way back to shore. The shark has circled back and again bumps against you, only this time, you grab its dorsal fin and slap its back, playfully. This is your favorite shark, and it's totally ridiculous how much attention this guy craves. To you, it's hilarious.

The two swimmers from the beach now glide up to the commotion. One says she figured it was this shark, even from a distance. His fin is quite unique, and he's known for frequenting this area. She dives below the surface and scratches that famous white underbelly. The other swimmer smiles and says he could tell you were trying to race the shark and he wanted to come and witness the giant fish overtake you up close. You're still catching your breath from laughing at the ultra-predictable shark, who acts like an overgrown seal, constantly trying to swim with the humans. The two swimmers latch onto the shark as he takes them back out into the depths. You call out after them, reminding them to be careful with that guy. He can get a little rough sometimes. You smile and shake your head in amusement at your favorite shark of all.

It's time to swim on into the cove where the water is shallow again. A handful of stingrays glide past, and the bright reflection of the water's surface dances off their backs. These creatures look as though they are flying through the water and you feel right at home as you soar freely among them. You reach out and feel one of their "wings." Its skin is velvety smooth. What an amazing variety of creatures God has made!

On the shore of the cove, you spot several of your friends enjoying a drink together at a tropical refreshment stand one of them set up years ago. The water here is gradually shallow enough for walking, and they call you over as you come up onto the beach. One persistent sea lion has followed you for your entire journey, and he waddles onto the shore with you. Your friends not only hand you a refreshing coconut smoothie, but they toss your whiskered buddy a handful of fruit which immediately disappears. You sit back and enjoy the gorgeous view with your friends as the lofty palm trees wave quietly overhead in the tropical breeze. You begin to discuss some of your discoveries, and several questions arise that you want to bring to the Father. After this drink, the entire group will go before His throne and thank Him again for the beautiful world He made for you. Then you will present your questions about some of His amazing creatures.

A crab scampers over your toes as you take another sip of your drink. You forgot how much you loved fresh coconut. And you forgot how much fun it was to spend the day exploring the depths and learning even more about the endless varieties of marine life. Throughout all eternity you can experience the works of the Master Designer and His "wonders in the deep." And ever before you, there always will be even more wonders to discover.

Thought Questions:

1. What is your main takeaway from this chapter? Why is it your main takeaway?

2. What has been your favorite experience with underwater life? What are some of your favorite fresh- or saltwater creatures? Which would you find it most fascinating to fearlessly swim with?

3. What was the point of God's straightforward words to Job about His monstrous creations of the deep, among other things (Job 38-41)? And what does this rebuke tell you about God's character?

4. Before the Flood covered the earth, sea creatures lived in smaller bodies of water. What does the rainbow after the Flood tell you about God's use of symbols in His promises? What are other examples of God doing this? What symbols in Scripture are promises for you?

5. What did you learn about God's will for you in this chapter? What do you feel He's impressing you to start doing differently this week to walk more closely with Him?

HEAVENLY MUSIC

"Make a joyful noise unto the Lord, all ye lands. Serve the Lord with gladness: come before his presence with singing."

-PSALM 100:1-2

W E LIVE IN a world that often creates myths and clichés about things that are not well understood. You may be surprised to learn that despite what you've heard, the Great Wall of China cannot be seen from space, Viking helmets never had horns, swimming after eating doesn't create cramps (sorry Mom), alcohol won't keep you warm, swallowed gum doesn't take seven years to digest, and bats (my favorite creatures) are not blind.

THREE-STRINGED HARP ON A CLOUD?

It should be no surprise, then, that clichés about Heaven have become quite popular as well. The most widespread being the image of the halo-capped, winged saint sitting on a cloud and strumming a three-stringed harp. Again, it's no wonder so many people would rather live for this world than for the world to come. If the cliché were even close to reality, then heaven *would* be boring. Imagine spending all your days looking over the edge of a cloud and having only the sound of an occasional harp string to break the monotony. The devil knows that this scenario has no appeal and continually propagates such misconceptions to keep us from desiring to ever live there. When we are tempted to instead seek the allurements of this world, we would do well to remember that "Faith is the substance of things hoped for, the evidence of things not seen" (Heb. 11:1).

In reality, the harp you receive will be unlike anything you've ever seen or played. The sound it produces will be more beautiful than anything you can imagine. Now multiply that sound times everyone in the great multitude of the redeemed and blend it with the glorious orchestra of the innumerable angels. If you've ever had chills at the singing of the national anthem or the playing of a powerful composition, you've only begun to experience a fraction of what the music in heaven will be like. All will be blessed with the ability to play their harps, and there will undoubtedly be countless other instruments available as well.

OUR MUSICAL MIND

So why is music such a huge part of our lives, anyway? Few things can elevate the mood like music. All humans have experienced this, believers and non-believers alike. The dog may be man's best animal friend, but music has proven to be a far more constant companion in our trials and triumphs of life. Consider weddings, graduations, funerals, parties, restaurants, driving, retail stores, movie scores, laying out by the beach or pool. Music is always there. Cultures are defined by their music. American music, which encompasses the globe, is an amalgamation of many older types of music, from cultures around the world. Imagine what new sounds will be created when music from cultures across the *galaxies* are blended.

The angels also love music, and in the Scriptures, they seem to be constantly singing (see Rev. 5:8-13; 7:11; Ps. 103:20; 148:2; Job 38:7; Luke 2:13-14). And why do they sing? They love to express themselves, just like we do. They sing about God and the boundless joys of heaven. And what do humans sing about today? Love. Women. Men. The pleasures of the world. Life's trials. We sing and write about what matters most to us. God designed music as a beautiful avenue through which we can express our innermost feelings. As Christian recording artist Jennifer LaMountain puts it "God has created each one of us with a musical mind." He invented music and also the chemicals in our brains that respond to music. Can you imagine what was going through God's mind when He first invented music? How the notes would be strung together, stimulating an emotional effect on us all, including angels? His sole purpose was the positive effect of that feeling you get. There's something about music that affects us in ways nothing else can. The sense of hearing - God even made *it* pleasurable. It seems clear that our pleasure was deeply important to God when He designed our bodies.

But as with most blessings, many have put the creation ahead of is Creator, and have turned to music *instead of* God, just as King Saul did when he needed a lift (1 Sam. 16). We want the *feeling* God's invention of music evokes, without the *fellowship* with its Creator. We listen to lyrics that draw our minds to impure thoughts, rather than to elevating themes that enhance our walk with God. But the more we get to know God today, the more our minds will be recalibrated to enjoy the right kind of music. Believe me, as one who once frequented rock concerts and felt I couldn't live without such music on a daily basis. The principle with music or food or physical attraction is always the same: Love the Creator more than the creation, and both will become more fulfilling. "Delight thyself also in the Lord and He shall give thee the desires of thine heart" (Ps. 37:4).

Hollywood composer Gary Guttman once wrote, "Probably the single most important mantra for any composer - at any level - is that music is merely 12 notes." Humans have created a seemingly endless collection of songs from only 12 notes: what the western world calls the chromatic scale (Eastern music has a slight variation of this). A transformed, heavenly mind would be able to individually compose countless new songs from those same notes; but what would such a mind be able to do with, say 20 notes? Or 100? What about a million notes, with a million new instruments on which to play those notes? If God wanted to, He could continually create new notes for all eternity, and thus the possibilities would be inexhaustible.

When a famous musician's life is cut short, fans often mourn not just the loss of life, but the great songs that will now never be written. One day there will be countless songs, well-known throughout the universe, that you will have personally penned over the eons. But if you opt out of the Kingdom, those moving songs will never be written. It's worth saying once again: Heaven - *eternally* - will not be the same without you.

The music in heaven will be an entirely new experience for the redeemed. As they join in song and praise with the angels, their hearts will be lifted to an even higher plane. They can sing as loud as they want, and nobody (including you) misses a note or sings out of key. History's largest choir will flood the streets of the Holy City with the beautiful sound of their voices and the melodious strumming of those illustrious, glittering harps.

▲ ▲ ▲

You have taken your place among the great choir of the redeemed. Although you've participated many times, you never cease to be amazed by the vastness of this assembly. It is a special time: a time to meet friends and to lift both voices and instruments, uniting in one majestic anthem after another. These songs are sung with more enthusiasm than any church services in the old earth, yet they lack the discordant clamor and irreverence which had marked some assemblies. New songs are constantly being written, and as each one is introduced, you're convinced *this is the best one ever.* Then when you go back and sing a previous melody, you decide that maybe *that* one was actually the best.

Today you've been given the chance to introduce your latest song. It's been a while since you've written one, but recently as you and some friends were visiting on a favorite island, a tune struck you, which then developed into a song. You shared the initial few notes with the group, who then made some suggestions. Later, you fleshed out the song back at your writing room in your estate. Today the song is ready.

One of the things you've enjoyed most since your journey to heaven has been songwriting. In the old earth, you had absolutely no songwriting talents. You dabbled in poetry a bit in school, but to arrange notes into a catchy tune was beyond your abilities. You always had a real admiration for songwriters and an insatiable love of music. Finally, as you have gradually grown into the real you, this dream has become a reality. You've formed several bands over the eons and co-written various songs with friends. You've even collaborated with angels on occasion, and your guardian has been particularly helpful in this regard; your personalities blend as well as the songs you craft together. And wildly unique musical instruments sit alongside a collection of non-musical creations in your "Invention Room," where you like to design and prototype all sorts of new gadgets and products, some of which have already blessed other worlds.

You always enjoy running into people who know your music or hear them singing one of your songs. Just the other day you were browsing a tiny specialty shop on the City's third floor for some parts for a new project when you heard a familiar tune. It was a song you wrote long ago, which has become very well-known. Someone on the next aisle over was humming it, and as you rounded the corner to see who it was, he looked up and immediately recognized you, although you didn't know him. He quickly shook your hand and excitedly stated that he knew you were the one who wrote that song and that he had seen you sing it at this same neighborhood's concert hall, shortly after you first came out with it. He said it was one of his favorites. It was increasingly rare to meet a City resident you didn't know, so this encounter was a double blessing. You shook his hand and thanked him, then complimented him on the liberties he had taken with the arrangement in his humming. He laughed and told you that he actually preferred arranging to composing and the two of you decided that it would be fun to write a song together, combining your special skills.

As you look around the vast assembly now, you know he is somewhere out there, and you're eager to get his feedback on today's song when you get together to write your next one. Today's performance will be right after the next singer, which is a friend that you knew in the old earth since childhood. She walks to the throne of God and the Lamb and bows in reverence as silence fills the assembly. Although she speaks to God in words just above a whisper, the acoustics are designed so that all can clearly hear. She tenderly explains that this song came to her while walking with Jesus through the City gates one day. His smile radiates as He hears her story. This is His precious daughter, and this song will be special to His heart.

You smile as you watch your longtime friend - once so shy, timid, and somewhat clumsy, now beautiful and graceful - preparing to perform for the Majesty of the universe. She is so dear to your heart. How grateful you are that through both of you receiving Christ, your relationship with her could continue in Paradise.

She lifts her golden harp and breaks the silence. You and the great multitude listen with pleasure and will join her on the second stanza. The song is beautiful, and you prepare to join the melody. The solo explodes into an enormous orchestration of sounds that electrify the air. Several million cello-type instruments add depth to the masterpiece, while the flutes and other pipes cover the high end. Trumpets give the song a royal tone as the harps of the redeemed control the melody. Voices from all assembled drift up from the planet as the headquarters of the universe overflows with this awesome song. Ecstasy fills your soul as praises to God become louder and more powerful. You never want this song to end, and the music seems to course right through your veins.

But finally, that last high note is reached, and the mighty orchestra and choir bring the song to a close. Praise to God fills the city as Jesus stands beside your friend and holds her tight against His broad chest. Everything she has, He has given her. All of her musical abilities are gifts from Him. And yet He is greatly appreciative of her expression of love.

As you step out of your place and begin to make your way down one of the silver aisles, you decide to give her your own hug on her way back to her seat. Praises to God continue to rise from the lofty walls of the assembly as your paths meet. Harp still in hand, she throws her arms around you as you embrace this dear friend.

She makes her way up the aisle as you approach the Throne. You bow reverently and then proceed to tell the story of your own song about God's creativity. A song describing how much you have enjoyed exploring His wonderful designs and marveled at His creative genius. The delighted expressions of the Father and Son reveal how much your story means to them.

You then strike the first note of your latest composition. Within moments the entire city - all of the redeemed and all of the angels - will burst forth with the song that you wrote: a song that can only begin to express how you truly feel.

Thought Questions:

1. What is your main takeaway from this chapter? Why is it your main takeaway?

2. What are some examples where music has been used to send the wrong messages? When has music positively affected you? What are your favorite songs about God and why?

3. What does the fact that God invented music for our joy and pleasure tell you about His character? What does the fact that angels are constantly singing about God tell you about Him?

4. Overcomers will sing "the song of Moses...and of the Lamb" (Rev. 15:3) forever. What does this mean and what does it tell you about God's promises?

5. What did you learn about God's will for you in this chapter? What do you feel He's impressing you to start doing differently this week to walk more closely with Him?

WHITEWATER

"There is a river, the streams whereof shall make glad the city of God"

-PSALM 46:4

WHITEWATER RAFTING IS one of the most exhilarating, fun things you can do in the summer. It's also a great way to get out and view God's creation. When I was growing up in Tennessee, every summer we would take visitors to a river called the Hiwassee. It was a blast to go down this river in either a raft or more commonly, inner tubes. The Hiwassee was not quite as rough as other rivers in the area, or inner tubes wouldn't have been allowed. But it did have plenty of whitewater, and we enjoyed the calm parts almost as much as the rough. There were several drawbacks, however, that we won't encounter in the new earth.

For one thing, we had to drive quite a distance just to get to this river. Secondly, we had to pay for the experience. Also, the water was perpetually freezing cold - even in the middle of July - and those first few minutes were always agonizing. Relief only came when the biting chill on our skin ultimately morphed to numbness, and we were finally incapable of feeling anything except for the occasional jutting rock, slamming into our unprotected backsides protruding down through the giant, floating rubber doughnuts. Then there was the inevitable burnt skin from four hours of sun and washed off sunscreen. And finally, the sores that invariably popped up above our elbows from hours of trying to steer our tubes toward the best rapids. I'm glad God has a better way!

▲ ▲ ▲

You just jumped into one of the enormous rivers that flow out of the New Jerusalem from the Throne of God. These rivers frequently branch out and span the far ends of the earth. This part of the river is teeming with people who, like yourself, are enjoying the flowing ride. The water is the perfect temperature, and you have no need to change into a bathing suit. The robe of light that covers you functions perfectly in any imaginable environment.

Cheerful laughter is all around you, and you smile as you see a couple of guys copy each other trying various floating positions. With each fork in the river, groups drift apart, going their separate ways. Some are headed to their country homes. Others are destined for parts of the earth where they are undertaking diverse group projects. Still others are headed out to various giant lakes to view the marine life. And some, like yourself, are simply charting new courses along the river that they've never experienced before.

In the past you've eagerly joined large groups as they make their way down the river, chatting with friends old and new along the way. Today you feel like going it alone so you can focus on nothing but nature. Up ahead is the familiar channel that heads toward your country home. You drift right on past it, for you have only begun to explore, and have plenty of time to enjoy the flowing ride.

You guide yourself into a channel you've never been down before, and it winds its way through a lush, hilly landscape. At times the water turns white, and you enjoy the thrilling ride as you safely plunge through the foam without a raft or tube. It is impossible for you to be injured in any way.

The hills passing by give way to farmland and as you drift along, you see that it's harvest time for one farm known for its delicious sweet corn. Large and small groups of people are combing through the stalks. The harvest here has become somewhat of a community event in these parts, as it's open for locals to come and help themselves to the crop. These harvest events are always accompanied by plenty of music, booths, and activities for folks to come and spend some time together. People from different parts of the globe sometimes travel here, as well. Most of the farms operate like this. The farmers usually specialize in a particular crop they're interested in (although some grow a wide variety), and then offer the crop to anyone who would like to come and join the harvest. But they almost always make it a social event, as well. It's not uncommon to see various artistic signs in town inviting everyone to come by on particular dates when the harvest is ripe. Last year's potato harvest in another region was particularly fun. You remember that you loved all forms of potatoes in the old earth, but the dozens of delicious things these people could do with potatoes blew all that away. You had taken several of their potato entrée recipes, and you're now thinking about making one of the dishes when you get back home. In fact, it's making you hungry just thinking about it. You wonder what little eating stops there are along this river as the water carries you on ahead, leaving the cornfields behind. You'll keep an eye out, but for now, it's time to enjoy the water.

You quickly dip your head below the surface to take in this bright, underwater world. A half-dozen acrobatic otters playfully swim by in the crystal-clear depths, and you laugh as you watch their antics. They dip and dive around you, always eager to see humans who float by these parts. The riverbed down here is gorgeous! And so bright. You spot the submerged base of a large beaver hut up ahead and think of the last time you explored one from underneath. You have several beaver families on your property, and they've actually been quite helpful diverting a few of your rivers for you and turning one creek into a lake. Two younger beavers exit the underwater passageway of the hut and start adjusting the logs along its base as you float on by. A beaver's work is never done.

As you rise through the shimmering surface, you see that this part of the river is edged with countless vibrant wildflowers splashed with yellow and blue. They shine brilliantly as they wave gently in the warm breeze. Rounding the riverbend, you see a little stand by the river's edge that the landowner must have built. It's a tiny thing with a small front porch and stools for river riders who might want to stop by for a bite. A man and a woman occupy two of the stools, snacking on something and chatting with the lady behind the counter. This pleasant woman spots you drifting by and warmly greets you. She has a basket full of something and invites you to try her blueberry-date snacks she has perfected, freshly made this morning. The two at the counter tell you how great they taste. You've heard of these before but didn't know they were on this branch of the river. They sound delicious, so you put your hands up as if to catch one while floating by. She smiles and shakes her head, tossing one to you. You both chuckle as you barely catch it, and she then throws you another, and another, and another, in rapid succession, causing you to lunge further and further in the water to reach them. She giggles at your successful catches, and you laugh too, as you pop one of the goodies into your mouth, amazed by the luscious flavor. She apparently reads your approval by your expression, and you give her thumbs up, your mouth too full to speak as you drift around the next bend.

You notice, as you glance back upstream, two of the otters still bobbing along behind you, and you toss each of them one of the treats, which they promptly make disappear. You're starting to wonder if these clever creatures had more in mind than just playing with you, considering the snack hut so close by.

The river is now passing through a prairie, and the tall, green grass stretches out forever. There's not a soul in sight. These stretches of river are always the most peaceful and they give you a chance to really gather your thoughts and count your blessings. You lean all the way back and float on your back as the river widens and slows along this section. A flock of geese intersects your path overhead in that famous V formation. An occasional honk breaks the silence as your eyes follow them into the horizon.

Now a distant, growing darkness is overtaking the fading V and is headed your way. You've seen this before. But never like this. If you didn't know better, you'd say this was a giant storm cloud rolling in rapidly. But this cloud is living. The blackness grows as it approaches, and you lean up in the smooth water again to watch the show. This is going to be good. You see the front edge of the living, dark cloud, but still don't see its back end on the horizon as the sky continues to blacken under the growing blanket of darkness. They're now directly overhead. Bats. Millions of them. This colony is one of the largest you've seen flooding the sky. It is truly an amazing sight. You can't help but think of your own land and a certain fox bat that befriended you years ago. Your appreciation of bats has grown immensely since you left old earth, and you are simply fascinated by them. You watch in amazement as the colony cloud rolls by overhead and just admire these flying mammals. The river gradually moves you out from under the massive cloud long before the back end ever crosses the river. You lean back again and rest the back of your head in your clasped hands as you relax and take in the beautiful sky. You could do this for hours.

Finally, the water speeds up again, and it's time to do some more exploring. Another quick dive into the river and you swim down to the bottom, examining some of the scattered specks and nuggets of gold that immediately caught your eye. No need for staking a claim; they're available for all. You decide two nuggets are plenty, as a memento of this joyful river trip.

Now back to the surface and you discover that during your time in the bright depths you've drifted into a forest. Dozens of black bears frolic along the river's edge, and a couple of them even dive in playfully when they spot you. You grab onto the back of one, and he takes you for a quick ride across the bubbly channel before crawling out on the opposite side as you dismount, splashing back into the river.

Soon you exit the forest, where another surprise awaits you. A hundred-story waterfall looms ahead, and you are instantly filled not with terror, but joyful anticipation of the thrilling plummet over its edge. You brace yourself for what gravity is about to do with the thousand tons of water that envelop you, and you decide to undertake this thrill ride with your head underwater, viewing it all from this spectacular vantage point. You thrill as you drift over its edge and everything seems in slow motion as the now-vertical river plunges through the air toward the earth! The impact into the crystal pool below drives you down near the bottom, where you observe a family of large brown turtles shuffling their way across the bright, sandy floor, the golden light from the surface dancing across their beautiful shells.

As the current pulls you further downstream, you enjoy some more whitewater before the river finally settles back into a quiet calm. You again float on your back as you just relax and let the stream take you where it will. You see a beautiful valley down below and wonder what surprises are in store for you there. You will soon find out, for your journey has just begun.

Thought Questions:

1. What is your main takeaway from this chapter? Why is it your main takeaway?

2. What are your favorite water activities? What are your best memories involving water or whitewater? Why do so many humans find the sound of various types of flowing water relaxing?
3. The River of Life finds its source in God's Throne. What does this tell you about God's character?
4. Jesus calls Himself the water of life and says whoever takes of this water will never thirst again. What does this tell you about God's promises?
5. What did you learn about God's will for you in this chapter? What do you feel He's impressing you to start doing differently this week to walk more closely with Him?

WITH WINGS AS EAGLES

"But they that wait upon the Lord shall renew their strength; they shall mount up with wings as eagles; they shall run, and not be weary; and they shall walk, and not faint."

-ISAIAH 40:31

THE DESIRE TO fly has been an inherent part of humanity throughout the ages. Ancient drawings and writings reveal that mankind has always contemplated various ways to achieve this seemingly elusive dream.

WHEN BIG BESSIE FLIES

I dreamed of flying when I was a kid (still do). In fact, when I was seven years old and roaming the gullies of Cayce, Mississippi with my good pal Rhonda Thorne, we decided we would accomplish this feat. Our plan was to build a wooden box, just big enough for the two of us, and then tie enough balloons to the box to lift us into the clouds! We even picked out a name for this contraption: "Big Bessie" (yes, it sounds more like an old cow than a flying machine, but we were kids out in the country, mind you). We daydreamed of how jealous our friends would be when we gracefully drifted right over our school in Memphis and waved to our earthbound classmates. Such trivial details, like how we'd steer the thing for the 30-mile trip or regulate our ascent before continuing into the stratosphere or falling to our deaths if some of the balloons happened to break didn't matter to us. We just wanted to fly! We'd deal with the laws of physics as we broke them. Needless to say, Big Bessie never got built. Our guardian angels (and the next childhood distraction) saw to that.

TWO BICYCLE REPAIRMEN SHOCK THE WORLD

After thousands of years and innumerable failures, human beings finally did get their first real taste of flight in a place called Kitty Hawk. On December 17, 1903, the world marveled and cheered at the achievement of two bicycle repairmen, brothers Wilbur and Orville Wright. The long-awaited dream of human flight was then and henceforth a reality. The following label text was displayed with the original Wright Flyer after it was acquired by the Smithsonian Institution in 1948:

> By Original Scientific Research the Wright Brothers Discovered the Principles of Human Flight. As Inventors, Builders, and Flyers, They Further Developed the Aeroplane, Taught Men to Fly, and Opened the Era of Aviation.

They "taught men to fly" by their research and experimentation, which bore fruit in the first successful self-propelled flying machine. Do you suppose God will do any less in the new earth?

Bible writers themselves showed an interest in flight. King David once declared, "Oh, that I had wings like a dove! for then would I fly away, and be at rest" (Ps. 55:6). And in the Proverbs of wisdom, we hear of three things described as "too wonderful for me." The first one listed is: "The way of an eagle in the air" (Prov. 30:18-19). Most of us would agree. It's hard for any of us to look up at an eagle soaring freely and peacefully above the trees and not wonder what such an experience would be like. Technology is now making this a reality without a plane. On YouTube you can see a working model of what the inventor, Zapata calls a "Flyboard Air." Not much bigger than a skateboard, this device can be seen zipping above a lake at over 80 mph. And my friend James Beldin recently introduced me to a Hoverbike Scorpion 3, which is a cross between a motorcycle and a drone. I've also been skydiving, which is thrilling, and I think the wingsuits come the closest to flying like Superman of anything humans have invented. We love to fly, and God knows this.

"Delight thyself also in the Lord; and he shall give thee the desires of thine heart" (Ps. 37:4).

Imagine getting to heaven and watching angels fly over the walls of the Holy City. You ask Jesus if you could fly up and join them, and He says that such activities you can never experience. You must take the stairs if you want to get there. Here is the One who said that "with God all things are possible" (Mark 10:27), and now He is limiting you and telling you that this desire of yours is asking too much? Not likely. The Lord will indeed give us the "desires of our hearts" because "the desire of the righteous is only good" (Prov. 11:23), and "no good thing will He withhold from them that walk uprightly" (Ps. 84:11). But God will go much further than the Wright brothers ever could. He won't limit us to the primitive, bulky framework of an aircraft. Such confining activities would prove utterly boring to us in a universe that holds such limitless possibilities. Granting humans the freedom of solitary flight will not be impossible for Him, and He obviously feels that wings are good enough for angels.

The apostle Paul, under the inspiration of the Holy Spirit, assures us that when Jesus returns in the clouds of glory, we will indeed be caught up to meet the resurrected saints in the air as we rise toward Jesus (1 Thess. 4:16-17). This will be the first of many flights for the redeemed. If Christ is able to make us airborne then, surely, He can do so later.

Once when confronted by the Sadducees over what they considered to be difficulties in the concept of a resurrection and life in heaven, Jesus stated that the redeemed will be "as the angels of God in heaven" (Matt. 22:30). Notice He didn't say that they would "become angels," just that they would be "as," in other words "like" the angels. He was, in this passage, referring to marriage and not our physical attributes. Nevertheless, it leaves us to wonder what similarities there will be between these winged ones and ourselves.

It would do us well to once again remember Paul's statement that "eye hath not seen, nor ear heard, neither have entered into the heart of man, the things which God hath prepared for them that love him" (1 Cor. 2:9). No matter what you imagine "wings" to be, they will be entirely different, beyond our present comprehension. No matter what joys and activities you can picture right now, God will not only match but surpass them a thousand times over (see Eph. 3:20). Will we be able to fly in heaven? The Wright brothers made it happen in this old world. As for heaven, we know with certainty that "with God all things are possible."

▲ ▲ ▲

An eagle appears in the top of a giant redwood tree. You have frequently seen this eagle here and have even given her a name. You decide to ascend to the top of this enormous tree and see the bird up close again. Although climbing is an option, and you, in fact, enjoy climbing trees, you decide you'd rather fly this time. Your guardian angel stands beside you, and he apparently was thinking the same thing, for he stretches out his wings and takes off directly upward. Just for fun, you take off by gliding a foot above the ground at a tremendous speed before ascending. Slowly your altitude rises as you bank toward the east, ultimately spinning around and soaring back toward the tree.

Your guardian angel is nearly at the nest, as he looks back motioning for you to join him. A few more flaps of your wings and you are just above the top branches, looking for a spot to rest your feet. You see a space between the limbs that can accommodate you, and you gently lower yourself into that spot. The eagle sits calmly in her nest as you touch down beside her. You stroke her feathery head and she seems to enjoy it. True to character, she rubs her head against your hand, wanting more and more. You laugh as she moves her head to your other hand.

Now you coax her out of the tree by standing up again and shuffling further out onto the giant, sprawling limb that supports you. She knows what this means; you've done this dozens of times before. Following your lead, she comes out of her nest and hops over to the limb beside you and the angel. You look out over the horizon. Nothing but a sea of green treetops for miles and miles; it is a peaceful sight. You are eager to dip in and out of the foliage in a flight that you know will be thrilling. After that, you will fly to your house and show your eagle friend some new trees you recently added to your land to see if the expert approves.

Launching off the limb, you clear all of the branches and let yourself plunge toward the ground. The free-fall is exhilarating as you let gravity do its work, nearing terminal velocity while dodging countless oncoming branches! As you barrel toward the forest floor, you spring open your wings at the last second, shifting your trajectory just yards off the ground at well over a hundred miles an hour. Leveling out your flight, you now begin one of your favorite flying exercises. The woods are thick with trees, and you quickly maneuver yourself from left to right between them at this incredible speed. Left, right, left, left, right: the trees zip by in flashes. You add a little more excitement to the ride by increasing your altitude among the out-stretched branches above. This creates the need to dart up and down as well as side to side, and you feel as though you're blazing through the world's biggest obstacle course. No video game or extreme sport on old earth ever compared to this ride. Ultimately you pull a final barrel-role as you burst up through the leafy sea of treetops, into the blue expanse above.

Now above the forest, you fall back into line with the angel and the eagle. The angel grins and shakes his head at you - knowing how much you enjoy your extreme forest flights - as you glide up next to the eagle and stroke her outstretched wings. In the distance, you see where the forest ends, and a sprawling meadow begins. This meadow is the land inherited by one of your friends, and you glide down to get a closer look and see if you can spot her down below.

Sure enough, she's out in her orchard, picking fruit. You descend even lower, and she waves, always happy to see a friend. You shout that you'll be back in a little while, then dart upward, just missing her rooftop.

A few more miles of hills, valleys, and rivers pass beneath you until you see another friend's land. This friend has spotted you first, however, and he's already taking off toward you. Your paths meet on your way down, and you fly side by side for a while. You invite him to come to your place for a visit, and he takes you up on the offer and chuckles at the sight of the eagle following you overhead. He recalls from recent flights how she can't resist joining you whenever you decide to traverse the skies.

Nearing your own land, you see several angels flying westward down below, and you exchange waves as you intersect their trail. You wonder if they are headed to the throne of God. Just the thought of that place excites you, and you suggest to your two companions that the three of you go there after showing the eagle her new trees. They readily agree as you see your home on the horizon.

You ask the others to lead the eagle to the new trees you identify in the distance, and then you bank toward your house. You have something for your two friends that you think they'll appreciate. Hovering over your balcony, you gently land upon its husky rail. You hop down and open the large doors to your upper room. Like your main room in the city, it isn't called a "bedroom," for in this land you never sleep, nor grow weary. But this room is still a favorite spot to come and relax, taking a reflective break from the endless activities. On one of your shelves sit two glowing, blue stones that you found on your last expedition. They seem to be shining even brighter than before, but perhaps it's your imagination. You quickly pull them off the shelf and head back out the doors, jumping over the rail of the balcony.

The eagle seems to have already taken to your new trees, as she sits perched atop one of their branches. She calls out in that famous eagle cry and you know she likes what she has found. Your two friends are standing at the base of the new trees. You glide over and gently touch down beside them.

Eagerly you hand your friends the stones, and they respond with surprised delight. Service is what this universe is all about. You love giving gifts to your friends because it really is more fun to give than to receive. The angels have told you that they were amazed at how slow humans were to grasp this truth in the old earth. The unconverted mind indeed could not grasp it. But in the universe of God, it is as natural as breathing.

As your friends express their gratitude, you suggest that the three of you go and thank the Creator of the stones right now for such an amazing and beautiful design. After all, He made the stones; all you did was find them. And besides, you've got a lot of questions for Him about the physics involved in these amazing gems. Your friends agree, and the three of you spread your wings and ascend in the direction of the Holy City. Behind you, a tiny, dark, eagle-shaped spot on the horizon closes the gap as she cannot resist joining your flights. And this flight is your favorite one of all: the flight that leads to the throne of your Father.

Thought Questions:

1. What is your main takeaway from this chapter? Why is it your main takeaway?

2. What has been your favorite airborne experience, and what would you still like to try if you could? What close calls have you experienced? Would you rather have the power to fly or be invisible, and what childhood flying fantasy do you remember?

3. What does Malachi 4:2's description of Christ as "the Sun of righteousness" rising with "healing in His wings" tell you about His character?

4. What does our opening text, Isaiah 40:31 (wait upon the Lord/*wings as eagles*) mean to you, in a spiritual, (not flying) sense today? What does it tell you about God's promises?

5. What did you learn about God's will for you in this chapter? What do you feel He's impressing you to start doing differently this week to walk more closely with Him?

WHEN WE ALL
GET TOGETHER

"For as the new heavens and the new earth, which I
will make, shall remain before me, saith the Lord, so
shall your seed and your name remain. And it shall
come to pass, that from one new moon to another, and
from one sabbath to another, shall all flesh come to
worship before me, saith the Lord."

- ISAIAH 66:22-23

THERE IS SOMETHING special about getting together with friends and loved ones. Humans were created to take pleasure in fellowship, and God Himself declared that it wasn't good for a person to be alone (Gen. 2:18). We enjoy not only small gatherings but larger get-togethers like family reunions, work parties, school reunions, church functions, and of course, notable public events. But what would it be like if such a gathering were filled with hundreds of your closest friends? Imagine if everyone you met there was a person you simply cherished - someone you loved being around and with whom you had lots of great memories. Now imagine if it weren't hundreds of friends, but rather thousands, or even *millions* of them.

MASSIVE GATHERINGS

God promises us that in the new earth all flesh will come and worship before Him. Can you even imagine such an event? All flesh - all people, all of the redeemed - will come together in one place and worship the Lord. What a scene that will be: "After this I beheld, and, lo, a great multitude which no man could number, of all nations, and kindreds, and people, and tongues, stood before the throne, and before the Lamb, clothed with white robes and palms in their hands" (Rev. 7:9).

Consider the crowds at football games. The largest stadiums in the U.S. are typically college football stadiums that hold just over 100,000 fans (Michigan Stadium - home of the Michigan Wolverines - is currently the largest at 107,601). Worldwide, it is surpassed only by North Korea's Rungrado "May Day" Stadium, which tops the list at 114,000 and covers an incredible 51 acres. That's a lot of people, but even that stadium is dwarfed by the largest sporting venue in the world, the Indianapolis Motor Speedway, which has a permanent seating capacity of over 235,000 (infield seating raises that capacity to approximately 400,000). While these numbers are impressive, consider the records for the largest gatherings of humans in history. Quite a few events have garnered over 5 million attendees, including "World Youth Day" in the Philippines (1995) and the Chicago Cubs World Series Parade (2016). But the record for the largest number of people ever assembled in a single gathering goes to the Kumbh Mela pilgrimage in India (2013), which topped the charts at an astonishing 30 million people!

But that impressive record, which happened only once in the old earth, will be shattered *every week* in the new earth, "from one Sabbath to another." Every Sabbath, week after week, will be another opportunity for every one of the redeemed to gather together and worship their King. Not one will be absent. Everyone from Adam to those alive at the Second Coming will be present in that congregation. The new "moon" spoken of here is simply the Hebrew term *chôdesh*, which means "month." In other words, from one Sabbath to the next, month after month, for as long as God's throne exists, everyone in the Kingdom will come to worship Him. And as these weekly gatherings continue, your number of friends will multiply, since you will be meeting more people all the time. Your love for the Lord will also increase so each meeting will be more eagerly anticipated than the last.

The Sabbath is the day that will host these great gatherings. It is an eternal sign to remind all humanity of the One who made planet earth. Way back at the beginning of our world's history, God decided to end His week of creating in an interesting way:

"And on the seventh day God ended his work which he had made; and rested on the seventh day from all his work which he had made" (Gen. 2:2).

God obviously doesn't need physical rest like you and I do; He is omnipotent. He simply ceased the act of working and took in all that He had made, which He declared to be "good." Sin had not yet entered into the human family, and God was pleased with every perfect thing that had just come forth from His hand. Adam and Eve actually witnessed God enjoying this rest, for they were able to hold face-to-face communion with Him on a daily basis. This rest day came the day after they had been created, so they no doubt had lots of questions for the Lord at that time.

They then watched God do something *to that day* that was quite extraordinary. He actually made it holy.

"And God blessed the seventh day, and sanctified it: because that in it he had rested from all his work which God created and made," "For in six days the Lord made heaven and earth, the sea, and all that in them is, and rested the seventh day: wherefore the Lord blessed the sabbath day, and hallowed it" (Gen. 2:3; Ex. 20:11).

The day was sanctified, blessed, and hallowed by God Himself because He had rested on that day. It will forever point back to the genesis of our planet and race. In a world bombarded with theories of big bangs and apish ancestors, it is reassuring to be reminded that there is indeed a loving God who, in fact, created us all; we did not get here descending from a primordial soup that randomly and eventually became you and me. God knew theories would arise to discredit His work as Creator and cause humankind to forget where they came from, so He specifically instructed us to always "Remember" (Ex. 20:8-11) the day He sanctified as an antidote to these various theories.

In the new earth, the redeemed will forever remember and honor this fact by their attendance at these global gatherings.

"All the ends of the world shall **remember** and turn unto the Lord: and all the kindreds of the nations shall worship before thee" (Ps. 22:27).

And what a worship time it will be! There we won't have to listen to the truth through a mere human instrument; the Lord Himself will "teach us of His ways" (Isa. 2:2-3). The mysteries and depths of the love involved in the Plan of Salvation will continually be more clearly revealed. To be in that multitude is worth more than all the temporal things of this world combined. May the Lord help us to decide today, that by His grace we will give ourselves 100% to Him and ultimately praise His name forever upon the Mount of Congregation, from one Sabbath to the next, just as He promised.

The Sabbath has come. It is time to head out to the great meeting at the throne of God. You look forward to this day every week, and today is no exception. Last week's event was even better than the week before, which was better than the week before that. These weekly gatherings are continually becoming more of a blessing to you. As the mysteries of God's infinite love and intellect unfold before you, the new information only enhances what you previously knew. Thus it has been for the last 10,000 years of your life, and thus it will always be.

You're in your country home this morning, and although you have various means of mobility, you feel like walking to the great assembly today. You look forward to friends you'll inevitably meet along the journey. Before descending your front stairs, you stop to take in the beauty of God's creation. You never tire of looking at the trees and flowers as they sway in the gentle breeze. Thousands of bright orange butterflies flutter across the meadow from petal to petal. Recently there were vivid blue ones, and before that, bright yellow ones dotted the land. Typically, dozens of hues appear together to decorate the scene with a medley of colors. You walk down the stairs as a slightly fragrant breeze flows around you. The sky's canvas above is splashed with a royal blue. Your mind races as you think about today's meeting with the King.

A curious deer approaches you, and you reach out to touch her head. She's not the least bit frightened by you, but timid by nature. Her fur is soft and smooth, and she enjoys the attention. You stroke her neck a few times before she wanders over to the pond for a drink. Continuing down the path in front of your home, you think about all of the others who are making this same weekly pilgrimage right now. You break forth into one of your favorite songs as you contemplate this magnificent world you call home. You love music, and you can almost hear the instruments that normally back you up on this tune, whenever you and your pals perform this song downtown.

You travel several miles before entering your neighbor's land. In the distance, you see that he is just leaving his home, but he spots you and gestures for you to come over to where he's standing. You notice that he's looking up at something in a small eucalyptus tree and you break into a trot as your curiosity grows. He smiles as you approach and points toward the small tree. At first, you see nothing, but then you realize that among the branches sits a furry koala bear, nearly camouflaged by the foliage. Your friend explains that he's never seen this little guy before. With no cares of frightening him, the two of you approach the tree and reach up to pet his velvety fur. Your neighbor offers him a special eucalyptus "cake," comprised entirely of a wide variety of eucalyptus leaves, which is a favorite of other koalas on his land. He started making these special treats years ago, and they've been a hit ever since. The koala gently takes it, as your friend promises to bring him more treats when he returns from the New Jerusalem as if the koala doesn't have plenty of food already. You bid the furry creature farewell and together continue your journey to the Holy City.

Eventually, you reach another home, but its occupant has already left. At the next house, however, a dear friend of yours is still inside and just ready to leave. She answers the door and is delighted to see you. She says she would love to join you, and the three of you proceed down the front steps where she then leads you through her rose garden. The aroma is wonderful, and you comment on how great her flowers are looking. Next, you follow her across a grey, stone bridge over a small creek and then head off into the woods toward the New Jerusalem.

This forest is nothing like the woods of old earth. Not dark and gloomy, but rather light and cheerful. The nightingale, the robin, the thrush, the sparrow, all lend their voices to the forest air, filling it with cheerful songs. You walk along the edge of a bubbling stream that you know leads to a roaring waterfall, which you can faintly hear already.

Your guide begins humming a familiar tune as you see patches of the waterfall in the distance through the trees. She has picked a song which was penned by King David long ago: "This is the day which the Lord hath made; we will rejoice and be glad in it!" (Ps. 118:24). The song epitomizes your feelings: the Sabbath – the day the Lord has made - truly is a wonderful blessing.

Soon all three of you are glorifying God in perfect harmony as the humming turns to singing. Praises to God are not only pleasing to the ear, but they raise your joy to an even higher plane in ways you don't fully understand. You and your friends have walked this trail a thousand times on the way to see the King and each time, you discover something new about this place. The trail winds around behind the waterfall, and you continue your tune as the cool mist gently settles onto your skin. The song takes on a unique echoey tone as it fills the cavernous chamber behind the waterfall. You exit the other side, and your eye catches a small, but dazzling rainbow that appears in the mist from the falls. Below the rainbow, thousands of bright red, yellow, and blue fish fill the crystal pool. The light from God's throne that blankets the planet sparkles off the top of the water and shimmers against the rocks behind you.

You ultimately exit the woods where you get your first glimpse of the distant Holy City. Although still hundreds of miles away, its towering jasper walls shine forth above the remote foothills. With your enhanced faculties and ability to fly, you can run, soar or even think your way to any point on the earth within a few minutes. A journey that would have taken months in the old earth is now accomplished during an enjoyable outing with your friends.

Just outside the woods, you are joined by yet another friend who almost always waits for you in the exact same spot. He sits on the grass, leaning against a giant oak tree flanked by several white and scarlet azalea bushes. He remains seated and smiles as he joins in at the very close of your song. As the three of you approach him, the chorus ends, and he stretches out his hand for you to lift him up. You chuckle and give him a heartier-than-he-expected yank, and he springs forward to greet you, laughing. He says he can't wait to hear what Christ has to say this week, and the four of you begin to discuss all of the amazing things you learned last week from the great Teacher.

Your journey over the various landscapes swells your little group from four to several dozen before you know it. Every one of these people is dear to you, and the chemistry between all is strong. No one will ever be an outsider in this land. The selfishness that divided people on old earth like negativity toward race or class or gender doesn't exist here and would be as out of place as the devil himself. You love the diversity of God's creation, and you celebrate the unity that love always creates.

Upon reaching the rolling foothills that lead to the East Wall of the city, you see that numerous groups like yours are merging and forming larger and larger groups. These gorgeous, rolling hills are covered with wildflowers of every type, which, as perfect as they are, seem to get even brighter and more beautiful the closer you get to your glorious destination. More songs are sung and as the multitude grows you begin to see a few people whose faces aren't yet familiar to you. Such people are becoming less and less common as you are constantly making new friends, especially at these weekly gatherings. This is exciting, and you seek out one of them and invite her to join your group as you advance toward the City. In the old earth you were not quite as bold when it came to meeting new people, but here you just love it. She tells you her name and joins your group of friends.

The features of the New Jerusalem are becoming more defined as you ascend its closest hills. It fills you with just as much awe now as it did the first time you saw it thousands of years ago - maybe even more so. The most exciting part is the fact that God Himself sits within those walls. The Father and Son reside at the top of this enormous metropolis.

The growing mass of people seems to be electrified by the fabulous view as scores of them eagerly break into a trot. Several burst out in praise with a song about the city and its Builder, and soon thousands upon thousands of voices have united in harmonious exaltation. The light from the throne that bathes the earth simply floods these foothills, and you quickly join those who now run toward its Source. The great hill is getting steeper as you near the jasper walls, but you don't grow weary in this land. As you make your way up the tremendous incline, you stop for a moment and turn to look around you. The bottom of the hill is covered with advancing worshippers clothed in white. What a sight! Up ahead and above you are more of God's children and beyond them the base of the city's great eastern wall which stretches for hundreds of miles to the north and south, and hundreds of miles straight into the sky. All around you, as far as the eye can see, people are ascending the great slope. The hill is just loaded with countless souls, all seeking the same goal: to be with their Savior. The God they so persistently sought in the old earth they now have the privilege of seeking here. And just as the Lord promised, those who seek, indeed find.

Some people wait along the steep slope for companions beneath the branches of the hillside trees. You recognize one woman who smiles as you pass by. You met her a few hundred years ago at one of these assemblies, and she has been a dear friend ever since. Far ahead, up the steep incline, you see a man leaving one of the trees and walking down a few steps to greet his friend. They embrace and turn to start their climb again. The city wall towers up ahead, and the enormous pearl gate invites all to share the glories within. Looking up the side of the wall from here has always been one of your favorite views for some reason. That glimmering surface rising straight up from the earth as far as the eye can see; that immense center gate ablaze in pearly white;

the glory from the very throne of God illuminating the entire massive structure; everything about this view just captivates your senses. You always tried to picture it, even read about it in books back on earth, but the reality before you puts all of that to shame.

The center gate on this Eastern Wall bears Benjamin's name and it, like the other 11, is attended by a tall angel who shines like the sun. He welcomes you with a loving smile as you pass through the ever-open portal.

Inside the city, you and three of your friends walk along main street which is bustling with people. All are heading toward the throne of the Father and the Lamb to worship as one united family. All retrieve their amazing harps from their city homes within these walls. All faces shine even brighter now as they near the Source and Origin of all glory, just as Moses' face did after being in God's presence (Ex. 34:29-33).

You and your friends are ascending a great, sapphire staircase. Through its sky-blue, transparent steps, you can still see the hustle and bustle below. People and angels are flanking the River of Life, which passes just beneath you as it flows from a giant waterfall to the west. Your soul feels perfectly at home here, and you and one of your closest relatives have decided that after today's worship, the two of you will stop by your home here and have a nice visit.

Now you enter the Great Congregation. The light in this place, shining from the throne of God and reflecting off the robes and faces of the redeemed, is awe-inspiring. You are now standing at the very brightest spot in the entire universe. The One who upholds the worlds and controls the movement of the tiniest particles of the atom sits before you on that massive throne. The One who can create living personalities from nothingness by the power of His voice, you are now seeing face-to-face. The Son of God and His Father both sit on the throne and all their children now bow in reverence and adoration.

Upon rising, you and the others quickly find your seats, as a massive cherubim orchestra begins performing its most recent masterpiece with its wide variety of instruments. Worship cannot start until all of the redeemed are present, and the Lord knows if even one saint is missing; each soul is priceless to His heart. But attendance isn't a problem here. All His children long to be in His presence. Just as they loved God and fellowship with each other in old earth, so they love it here. Just as they didn't forsake assembling for weekly worship in old earth (Heb. 10:25; 4:9; Acts 2:42), so they don't forsake it here.

As the great multitude grows, so does anticipation. The Lord scans the sea of faces, and it is clear by His expression that His joy is complete. Nothing delights Him more than being with His children.

Finally, the last of the redeemed come in and find their places. The orchestra concludes its opus as a hush settles over the "multitude that no man can number." And though you've experienced this many times before, you still marvel that so many beings can be so utterly silent. Reverence is completely natural in the presence of Holy Omnipotence. The Lord then motions the angels to play a particular song that always starts the meeting. The orchestra joyfully begins, and each musician in the great multitude knows exactly where to join in, which they do at their designated time. The music floods every inch of that great City, resonating out into the farthest reaches of the universe. You never realized in the old earth just how wonderful singing and playing an instrument really could be. Sure, you liked the idea, but it was nothing, nothing like this. Here it lifts your spirits like few things can.

Now the Lord does something that no one in old earth ever witnessed. The Inventor of music actually begins to sing to you! The prophet Zephaniah is there, and he sees the words of his own prophecy fulfilled to the letter: "He will rejoice over thee with joy...He will joy over thee with singing" (Zeph. 3:17). In that song lies the power of creation itself, for His very words formed the earth - twice now. His song surpasses anything human or angel can produce. The arrangement of both melody and lyrics has an invigorating effect on the soul that can be found nowhere else. Hearing Daddy sing makes up for all of the trials on earth. For you, *this* is indeed "heaven."

The song ends, and the Lord begins to speak to the assembly. His deep voice bestows many blessings on you and expounds upon things that had challenged even the most advanced minds. Every word breathes life into the soul. Everything about your Father is admirable to you. His kingly features are beyond handsome. His voice: sweeter than the richest music.

You glory in His presence and bask in His light. Never in the old earth, when you thought of heaven, could you possibly imagine that your greatest pastime amidst the limitless possibilities of the universe would be simply dwelling in the presence of God. To the unconverted, it always sounded so boring. The carnal mind could never grasp the truth, for spiritual things are spiritually discerned (1 Cor. 2:14). But by the grace of the Holy Spirit, you know the truth. You know that you are where you are because Jesus gave all for you and asked you to simply believe and surrender, receiving Him. The words of God continue to fill your soul, and you never want to leave this place. This truly is the day that He has made. Forever you will rejoice and be glad in it!

Thought Questions:

1. What is your main takeaway from this chapter? Why is it your main takeaway?

2. What are your best memories of church fellowship? Why do you think God tells us not to forsake the assembling of ourselves together (Heb. 10:25) and why do humans need each other, especially for church? Why do you suppose God said to "Remember" the Sabbath (Ex. 20:8)?

3. What does God rejoicing over you with singing tell you about His character?

4. You and "all flesh" will worship before God every Sabbath in the new earth for eternity. What does this tell you about God's promises?

5. What did you learn about God's will for you in this chapter? What do you feel He's impressing you to start doing differently this week to walk more closely with Him?

TOURISM

"*Through faith we understand that the worlds were
framed by the word of God*"

- HEBREWS 11:3

"*The works of the Lord are great, sought out of all
them that have pleasure therein.*"

- PSALM 111:2

MY WIFE RECENTLY bought a decorative plaque that says: "I would rather own a little and see the world than own the world and see little of it." Millions would agree with this sentiment. For thousands of years, people have enjoyed visiting distant lands. Not just to see the various landscapes and buildings, but usually to absorb the rich details of the local culture as well.

If you were to win a trip to Paris, you wouldn't just hang out at the Eiffel Tower the entire time. You'd also want to explore the amazing art collection at the Louvre or take a tour of the Notre-Dame Cathedral or the Luxembourg Palace, or maybe spend a day shopping along the endless blocks of sidewalk stores and cafés. You'd also most likely seek out a restaurant that captures the "flavor" of Paris, at least once while you were there. You'd probably even buy a souvenir or two to remind you of the trip.

Whether it's Paris, Moscow, Hong Kong, Tahiti, Martha's Vineyard, or even places like the quaint little tourist traps along historic Route 66, we humans have a thing for checking out all we can about any place we find fascinating. But even the most exotic destinations fall short of what God has in store for us.

OTHER WORLDS?

At this point, we should make one thing clear: the Bible doesn't say "And ye shall visit other worlds." Such a belief is not listed among the basic, fundamental doctrines of Christianity. The Bible doesn't specifically say that there is life on other planets, although it confirms the fact that there is life outside of this world - angels traveling to and from heaven for one thing. Before we proceed with this chapter, I'd like to clarify that I do *not* believe in aliens or extraterrestrial creatures as they are portrayed by Hollywood. Such grotesque, villainous beings are not in harmony with Scripture. They, in fact, cast shadows of doubt upon the Bible and the mission of Christ in coming to this world. These creatures, without exception, seem to have no knowledge of a Savior named Jesus, who the Bible says created all things (see John 1:3; Col. 1:16-17; Heb. 11:3). But let's be real. Science fiction writers know that science fiction is just that: fiction. In fact, it's hard to look at the aliens and monsters portrayed in the 1950s without snickering, and wondering *Was anyone actually* scared *watching this stuff back then?*

Most likely, it is to prevent just such inevitable wild speculations that the Bible remains somewhat vague on this subject (just look at all the sensational theories that have developed about the Antichrist and the Mark of the Beast, for example).

Outside of our world, all creatures under heaven worship and adore the Father, Son, and Holy Spirit. They do not spy on humans from spaceships nor devise plans to take over the earth with their superior technology. Cherubim (Gen. 3:24), Seraphim (Isa. 6:2), and other heavenly hosts all work in harmony with God in His plan to save the inhabitants of this world. The exception to this, of course, being Satan and the evil angels, who are spirits and not spaceship pilots (although many believe these demons are behind some of the paranormal/alien incidents around the world). These demons are not aliens from other planets; they are fallen angels who once lived in heaven itself (Rev. 12:7-9; Luke 10:18).

The issue of whether there is intelligent life on other worlds has been debated among Christians for generations. Some pastors insist that there is, while others are not convinced. In this book, we will consider the possibility of intelligent, heavenly beings existing on planets, perhaps on the other side of heaven. Remember that with God all things are possible.

BOUNDLESS UNIVERSE

So, if the Bible - while not ruling out the possibility - doesn't specifically say that there *is* life on other planets, why think about it? Well, let's do a little math here. Scientists have evidence for over 200 billion suns in our Milky Way galaxy alone (some estimates go up to 400 billion). Our own sun has *nine planets circling it (*In 2006, the International Astronomical Union downgraded Pluto to a "dwarf planet," as opposed to a "real planet," bringing the total down to eight, until evidence for a "Planet Nine" was revealed on January 20, 2016. It is 10 times the mass of Earth and 5,000 times the mass of Pluto.). Researchers also revealed, in 2012, that each sun in the Milky Way has, on average, 1.6 planets orbiting it. So, with the 200 billion figure for suns, that would put the total number of planets in the Milky Way at around 320 billion. But let's cut this down to an unrealistically conservative estimate and see what we come up with. Even if scientists were wrong and there were only *one* planet for every 200 suns, there would still be *over one billion planets* in this galaxy alone.

But how many galaxies are there? Four can be seen from earth with the naked eye. Ours, of course; then there is the Andromeda Galaxy (a.k.a. M31, containing approximately one trillion stars), visible from the northern hemisphere. Stargazers in the southern hemisphere can see two others: the Small and Large Magellanic Clouds (three billion and 30 billion stars, respectively). These three other galaxies would, of course, multiply the potential number of planets significantly. But these are just the galaxies visible to the naked eye.

With the aid of powerful telescopes, astronomers have discovered and named a multitude of galaxies, and at the time of the first printing of this book (1999), it was believed that there were at least 50 billion of them out there. Shortly thereafter, the Hubble Telescope uncovered evidence for a new total of up to 200 billion galaxies. Then in October of 2016, scientists declared that there were actually more like 10 times that amount, placing the estimate at around two trillion galaxies. Remember that our galaxy alone has an estimated 320 billion planets within its borders. The math at this point becomes, pardon the word, astronomical. Add to that the fact that these are just the galaxies of which we are aware. What else is out there, beyond the scope of our instruments? This universe is simply loaded with planets, all created by God. With that in mind, consider the following words:

"For thus saith the Lord that created the heavens; God himself that formed the earth and made it; he hath established it, he created it not in vain, **he formed it to be inhabited**" (Isa. 45:18).

Then we are told in Hebrews 11:3 and 1:1-2 that "the **worlds were framed** by the word of God," and "God...hath in these last days spoken unto us by his Son, whom he hath appointed heir of all things, by whom he also **made the worlds**."

God said He does not form worlds in vain; He creates them to be inhabited. In His foresight, He knew that fallen man would one day reach the surface of the other planets in our tiny solar system. Therefore, He left them barren, confining the destructive, polluting influence of sin to planet earth alone. But in the great galaxies beyond, the worlds serve a purpose. It would seem a bit out of character for God to tell us when we get to heaven, "Yes, I went through the trouble of creating trillions of orbiting planets out in the vast expanses of My universe, but there's nothing on any of them. They're just empty balls of dust, taking up space." Can you imagine exploring the outer reaches of God's universe with nothing but dead planets to see?

In Job 38:4-7 we are told that at the completion of earth's creation "the morning stars sang together, and all the sons of God shouted for joy." Angels are sometimes referred to as "stars" in the Bible (see Rev. 12:3-4,9). But who are the "sons of God"? We know that Jesus is the one, true Son of God, so that phrase cannot be taken to mean others equal to Him.

Scripture tells us that anyone who is born again and created anew in Christ has become a "son of God" (John 3:3,6; 1 John 3:1-2; Gen. 6:1-4). But more specifically, the Bible refers to Adam as "the son of God" in Luke 3:38. Adam was given dominion over planet Earth and would have retained that position had he not fallen into transgression (Gen. 1:26; 1 Cor. 15:22). This act brought death and thus prevented him from being present at a great cosmic meeting when the "sons of God [like Adam had been] came to present themselves before the Lord" (Job 1:6). He, as the head of planet Earth, the "son of God" representing our world, left a vacancy at this meeting. But the vacancy was quickly filled by another who had no invitation.

"...and Satan came also among them. And the Lord said unto Satan, Whence comest thou? Then Satan answered the Lord, and said, From going to and fro in the earth, and from walking up and down in it" (verses 6-7).

God knew full well where Satan had been, but this was asked for the sake of the others in the assembly. Neither from heaven, nor from the other worlds did he come, but from the one fallen planet called Earth: the very planet for which God's beloved Son was to die. Christ's parable of the one lost sheep among the hundred signifies, in one sense, the sole dark spot - our planet - among the innumerable worlds (Matt. 18:12).

God loves variety. Each of these distant worlds probably has its own culture, with each city or village being unique as well, subcultures within a culture. Imagine all of the free restaurants, historic landmarks and local "atmosphere" that these millions of places have to offer. They're just waiting for you to check them out.

And there is another reason universal tourism is probable. The Cross of Christ will be our science and our song for all eternity. Of all the countless beings in this universe, only those from planet Earth have experienced redemption by the blood of the Lamb. Jesus loves all of His created beings, of course. But He *died* for you; for you and the inhabitants of planet Earth, He died. As stated above, we are the one lost sheep the Good Shepherd went out to find and save. No other planet has required His death to save its inhabitants from sin. Yet it is not our planet alone that will benefit. The lesson wrought out in the Plan of Salvation is a lesson for God's entire unfallen universe. They too needed to see beyond any shadow of a doubt that Satan's way was wrong, and that God did indeed know best. They needed to witness the thoroughly selfless love that was manifested in the gift of the Son, and the thoroughly self*ish* act of Satan inspiring the inhabitants of Earth to turn on and kill their Creator. One of our greatest joys in the New Earth and in traveling to worlds afar will be telling the inhabitants of those planets what it was like to be saved from the Fall by the Son of God. The twofold activity of studying the Cross and sharing our testimony will bring us a deeper fulfillment than anything else in the next life. Shouldn't the same be true in this life? It can be.

This chapter was not written to "prove" anything. It merely presents ideas for contemplation. I hope you are blessed by this brief, extremely limited view of some of the potential secrets of the universe which are "past finding out" (Job 9:10).

▲ ▲ ▲

You have been planning this trip for quite some time. It was arranged so that you and three of your friends could all travel together. With an infinite number of things to explore and do, it was necessary to plan ahead.

Two of your friends arrive at the front door of your country home together. You invite them in and offer them each a tasty, cool drink, produced from your own vineyard and orchard. You know that one of them prefers grape juice and the other loves your special cherry-vanilla smoothies. You then pour yourself a new banana-peanut butter shake you've been working on (which smells delicious), and with drinks in hand, the three of you head up to your palm-laden west balcony as you wait for the third friend. At first, you discuss an additional lake that you've considered developing on your land, but inevitably the conversation turns to Jesus. Love for Him is the one thing that all inhabitants of the universe have in common; they never tire of talking about Him.

Now in the distance, you spot an approaching traveler, rising out of the hilly horizon on horseback. The conversation ceases as the three of you gaze at the advancing rider, whose midnight black horse now gallops along the stretch of your road that curves around the lake. You tell them it must be your third friend, and as the horse approaches and slows to a trot, you see that your guess was right. Your friend introduces you to his husky stallion, whose jet-black coat shimmers in the light. This is one beautiful creature, and as your friend dismounts, he explains that the horse had been following him around his land lately, after lingering behind a migrating herd. He says this is the fastest horse he's ridden in over three thousand years of training horses. The gentle steed wanders over to the lake for a drink as your friend stands beside your favorite palm, looking up to the balcony. His eager smile broadens as he rubs his hands together jovially and asks if you're all ready for the trip of a lifetime. This is the ultra-extrovert of your group, and he's the one who originally hatched the idea of the four of you undertaking this adventure together. He's already been to several of your planned destinations, but a few of them he's only heard about from enthusiastic friends.

Although you have a long list of worlds you plan on visiting, you don't have to rush to get them all in. In the old earth it seemed there was never enough time to really get to know the local culture whenever you traveled anywhere. Now you can spend as much time as you want at each destination with no deadlines to worry about and no bosses texting you from work with "pressing" issues, wondering when you're coming back. No "Paid Time Off" to calculate and no vacation budget to adhere to as your excursions quickly pile up. Your worries long ago vanished as you realized that eternity lies always before you and you plan on enjoying every minute of it.

You tell him you'll be right down, as the three of you head back into your estate, eagerly discussing all that you've heard about the distant cultures awaiting you. On the ground floor, you toss a special treat to your favorite tiger (who thinks he owns the place) as your friends head out the door. You tell him to keep an eye on the place while you're gone as if there is anything that could actually go wrong. He starts to roar but is instantly sidetracked, chasing the tumbling treat into the corner like a giant, striped kitten. You smile and shake your head as you watch him tackle the treat, then circle his favorite rug and plop down, satisfied with his catch, protruding out of either side of his mouth.

Your equestrian friend is leaning against the palm tree with one hand and munching on a mango with the other. He wipes his mouth and tells you that the rumors are true: yours *are* the best mangos outside of the City. He then asks if the three of you are ready to go, but before you can answer he glances up into the distant treetops and whistles loudly as he throws the half-eaten mango into the air. *Way* into the air. The ballistics involved easily break old earth throwing records many times over. You think back to how odd and wonderful it felt when you first experimented with your own enhanced capabilities. You still enjoy skipping stones from the beachfront side of your massive lake all the way to the opposite shore with incredible accuracy.

As the mango projectile becomes a speck overhead, he calls out the name of your favorite black fruit bat, a large "flying fox," hanging from the top of a distant tree. The dark bat responds immediately, letting go of his grip and unfurling those magnificent black wings that launch him up toward the mango's trajectory. When you first built the house, you trained a gregarious crow this trick and then wondered if a bat could learn. Bats don't normally catch fruit in the air, but this one eventually caught on over the years, gripping it with his teeth like a dog with a ball and impressing onlookers below. Your necks are all craning as the megabat quickly and easily intercepts the mango in mid-flight. You're not sure if it's the taste of the fruit or the fun of the catch, but for some reason, this creature just loves doing that. Indulging his habit has become a regular ritual of all your friends now when they come and visit. Your friend then turns to you, satisfied with the bat's success and now, ready to depart, says, "Let's do this."

Eight wings quickly unfold and propel the four of you into the blue expanse above. Such freedom you could only dream of in the old earth. You really love to fly! And the view of your sprawling land from up here is awesome. A few barrel-rolls and freefalls are in order as your gang performs multiple air stunts that skydivers and wingsuit flyers of old earth would envy. Your bat friend, the half-eaten mango still in his mouth, dives with you, attracting another black fox bat, which emerges from the treetops below. You've never seen this bat before, but that's not uncommon; creatures of countless species pass through your land all the time. The newer bat seems a bit confused, trying to navigate human dives and rolls, but your favorite bat knows exactly what to do. Eventually, you level off and are flanked by the two bats as you near the outer border of the forest below. Their cute, doglike faces make you wonder how anyone in old earth could have been afraid of these amazing creatures. What a thrill to now share a flight with them!

As you gradually ascend, the bats finally peel off and soar back down toward the earth, leaving just the four of you on your trajectory off the planet. You ultimately leave the atmosphere behind and begin your trek into outer space. Your wings, like those of the angels, are capable of operating even outside the realm of the earthly atmosphere.

You arrive at your first stop, three galaxies away, just in time for lunch. This village is known for its delicious use of a famous food that grows only in this world and in this particular region. All of your friends who have tasted it over the past 30,000 years have said that if you go there "you've just *gotta* try it!" You've discovered a delightful little café on the edge of town that serves this famous dish. They bring the delicacy out to the four of you and your taste buds are not disappointed. Words can't describe the scrumptious flavor that fills your mouth. You compliment the chef for the fabulous meal, and he promptly gives all the glory to God for creating and growing the food in the first place.

A quintet arrives at your table and delights you with beautiful songs about the local culture and their love for the Creator. The next few songs are performed in the particular genre of music that is indigenous to that world but has, over time, spread to other galaxies that you've visited over the millennia. It is their "sound," and you've always wanted to visit the birthplace of the genre. The last song is the one that is synonymous with this place - its name is even in the song - and it's the one visitors most look forward to hearing. Large, colorful birds add their sound to the music, and soon you and your three friends are singing along as well. Joy fills the room as all stop eating for a moment to join in on that famous last line, always sung slowly and loudly for a grand finale effect. The final note is a high one, and all cheer and praise God as the song ends.

Although there is absolutely no charge for any of this, you have brought along some small gifts of gratitude. The chef gratefully receives them on your way out and tells the four of you that he looks forward to seeing you again in the future. You have all made new friends, and with your perfect memories, if you return here in 100 billion years, your friendships would still be as fresh as if you had never left this little café, even if the look of the town were to become altered over time.

In the streets, some of the locals are offering you various gifts from their village. Not because they want something in return, but because they're filled with the love of God, and enjoy nothing more than sharing what they have with the many tourists who visit this place from countless other galaxies. You and your friends gladly accept these small gifts. In particular, you notice one souvenir that you immediately realize would go perfectly in one of your rooms; you know just where to put it.

It's finally time to go, and you're eager to get to your next stop: a world which has planned an event to hear the four of you speak about how Jesus changed your lives. You bid your farewells to the local villagers and again raise your wings for departure. A hymn of praise to the Lord wafts up from the streets as you ascend into the skies. Although the sweet chorus fades, the further you get from the town, you know your memories never will.

The inhabitants of the next planet have arranged for your visit and have broadcast your appointed time of arrival. News has spread throughout the population, and they're eager to hear you speak. This planet has a reddish hue from a distance, but as you approach and slow your flight, the scarlet seems to fade, and the green of a lush landscape fills your vision. You have been given a specific place to land, and you descend in eager anticipation.

The roof of the designated resort is just below you as you and your friends expand your wings to ease your landing. This is a patio-type roof, complete with sidewalks, trees, and a shimmering blue, fountain-fed pool. Thousands of onlookers surround the base of the building as you gently touch down on its roof. These holy people are eager to hear your personal story of how Christ changed your life. They know the history of the great controversy between Christ and

Satan, but they never tire of hearing personal testimonies from each descendant of the Eden couple.

Although you were nervous about public speaking in the old earth, you and your friends are perfectly at ease addressing this vast crowd before you. The Holy Spirit resides within you, and He is inspiring you as you speak. You use no microphone or speakers, yet the multitude below can hear you perfectly.

It seems as though you have only begun to speak of His love and life-changing grace when you realize that a block of time has passed, equivalent to two Earth hours. The joy of telling that story reconfirms the fact that time really does fly when you are having fun.

At this point, you take questions from the audience. Answering each question enhances your appreciation for the plan of redemption, and you are again filled with amazement that the Creator of all this died for you. You pause for a moment as emotions of love and gratitude flood your soul. One of your friends then senses your emotional state, and she steps up to embrace you lovingly. Christ's love has the same effect on all of you. You finish your answer, and your friend then speaks for a while, radiant with joy as she tells her own story.

After your three friends have shared their testimonies, the people invite you on a tour of their ancient city. This place is known for its incredible architecture, and you've been eager to see it for yourselves. You've seen trillions of buildings on billions of planets, and yet each one is so unique and beautiful that you're always ready to see more. Your knowledge of architecture is continually increasing, and you plan to use this new knowledge in future ventures.

Soon you are walking across an enormous swinging bridge that connects the two tallest skyscrapers on the planet. The building you approach is over a thousand stories high and was constructed a million years before the creation of Earth, yet it looks brand new. Its arches and pillars give it a look unlike any of the high-rises in old earth. You've never seen thousand-story pillars before.

Your guide, who designs the interiors and themes of resorts as a profession, gladly takes you from building to building, explaining their ever-increasing knowledge of architecture. You visit the Ruby Manor with its dazzling, opaque, red walls, the Giant Fire Dome, constructed of one massive sheet of fire, and an extraordinary structure actually made of compressed air. It is nearly invisible, yet strong as steel.

One of the buildings near a tropical beach has what looks like a waterfall that flows out of all four sides near the top and splashes down over the ever-widening sides until it lands in a pool, bright as the sun, around the base of the structure.

Following your guide's lead, the four of you jump off the edge of the neighboring building and fly down to get a closer view of this pool. As you land, you realize that this is not a waterfall at all, but rather a diamond-fall.

You scoop up the precious gems in your hand. Although these jewels are commonplace in the New Jerusalem, you are still impressed with their beauty. A new crowd is gathering, and they invite all of you to sit by the falls and enjoy a cool drink made fresh from the local fruit. For years they have enjoyed many of the songs you have written, and now they wonder if they could hear a few firsthand. They ultimately hand your group a variety of instruments which you gladly accept. With the roar of the diamond-fall in the background and the gorgeous beach before you, the four of you then start in on one of your older, more famous ballads of praise, followed by a few newer ones they've never heard before.

Several hours pass and you end with one of your most famous songs on this planet, then return the instruments to your appreciative hosts. As the crowd disperses, the sun begins to dip into the watery horizon, spilling its gold all across the gentle waves, turning the rows of over-water bungalows into silhouettes. Your friends agree with you that next time you come here, you should stay in those bungalows with the fabulous, unique views. This world has three moons, and two of them are rising over the water, invading a golden-orange sky.

With some of the locals sharing the discussion, you try to decide which place to see next. There's the Annual Global Parade at one particular world and the Ice Metropolis at another. One solar system is about to have a planet-alignment celebration, complete with shooting star displays. Someone suggests the moon of one planet that is famous for its incredible lightning shows. These grand spectacles are continually active on the moon's dark side. And then, of course, there's that quaint little village on another world that your aunt said was comprised of the most unique network of treehouses she had ever seen.

Ultimately you agree that your next stop should be the Labyrinth: a world which has utilized the planet's insides by creating a vast maze of underground tunnels, rivers, stadiums, and cities. These interconnecting passageways - with openings ranging from several miles across to only a few feet - crisscross their way to the very core of the planet. Sheets of magnifying, reflective glass are positioned so that the light from their sun is actually channeled into the depths of the Labyrinth and back out the opposite side. You've been told that because of this, as it rotates, the shadowed side of it appears to be covered with scattered flames. There are also the famous scavenger hunts throughout the planet: a favorite activity among the tourists. Another friend of yours, who is currently researching the reptile species of a desert planet (his specialty) has contacted you and says he would like to meet you there as well. You look forward to seeing him, since it's been a long time, and you'd like to catch up on old times with him.

As you rise to leave, you turn to your guide and ask him if he would like to come and visit you sometime in the new earth. His eyes light up, and he readily accepts the offer. You have added yet another precious soul to your ever-growing circle of friends.

Sharing a few final hugs with your new friends, you say your good-byes. The four of you then ascend into the atmosphere and fly off toward the sunset. You will surely visit your new friends again.

As you contemplate the cosmos, you are amazed by the endless variety of worlds that still await your exploration. It would clearly take an eternity to see all of the things this universe has to offer. But you and your friends aren't worried. After all, that's exactly how long you have.

Thought Questions:

1. What is your main takeaway from this chapter? Why is it your main takeaway?

2. What is the most unique place you have ever visited? Why do humans like to travel so much? What else have you imagined might be out there on other worlds? Why do you think beings on other worlds are almost always portrayed as hideous gray creatures who don't know God?
3. What does Christ's parable of the one lost sheep in Matt. 18:12 tell you about God's character regarding this tiny, rebellious planet?

4. Adam was called a "son of God." In Job 1:6 the "sons of God" came to present themselves before God. What does 1 John 3:1-2 (*we can be sons and daughters of God*) tell you about His promises?

5. What did you learn about God's will for you in this chapter? What do you feel He's impressing you to start doing differently this week to walk more closely with Him?

A WALK WITH JESUS

*"For the Lamb which is in the midst of the throne shall
feed them, and shall lead them unto living waters"*

-REVELATION 7:17

I'VE ALWAYS LIKED how one child described the translation of Enoch
from earth to heaven after Enoch "walked with God" for years. He
put it this way: "Enoch walked with God so much that one day God
said to him 'Enoch, we're closer to My house than yours now. Why
don't you just come home with Me?'"

Enoch walked with God in the Old Testament, and the disciples
walked with God in the New. Have you ever wondered what it would
have been like to live, and walk, and talk with Jesus just as His disciples did all those years ago in Palestine? I mean, to move beyond what
we read about Him in the Bible and actually interact with Him on a
daily basis as a friend. Eating with Him, discussing social issues with
Him, watching His expression as He interacted with the animals and
the children and even with the Pharisees as they tried to entrap Him.
Considering who He is, it must have been an amazing experience.

Jesus told His disciples that it was beneficial for them that He should go to the Father because if He left them, He would send the Holy Spirit, and through the Spirit, He could then be with them constantly (see John 16:7; Matt. 28:20). Think about what He was saying right there. What He means is, you and I have access to Him right now, just as they did. Do you believe it?

We already mentioned that Enoch (who lived before the Flood) "walked with God" (Gen. 5:24). According to the Newberry Bible, the Hebrew word for "walk" here, means to walk *habitually*. In other words, this was normal and consistent behavior for Enoch. It was a fulfilling habit. Even though Jesus was not physically there in person, walking beside him, Enoch, nevertheless "walked with God." And so can you and I. And then, of course, the really good part...

And "God took Him" (verse 24). As the little boy said, God and Enoch were so comfortable walking together that God just invited him home.

Noah also "walked with God" (Gen. 6:9). And similar language is used with Abraham (Gen. 17:1-2) as well as Zacharias and Elizabeth (Luke 1:5-6). But what does it really mean to walk with the Lord when we can't even see Him? How did Enoch and the rest of these believers do it? How can we do it?

"He that saith he abideth in him ought himself also to walk, even as he walked" (1 John 2:6).

To walk with Christ, then, is to abide in Him. Okay, so how do we do *that*?

"If ye keep my commandments, ye shall abide in my love; even as I have kept my Father's commandments, and abide in his love" (John 15:10).

To abide in Him is a mindset, not just a one-time choice. The thesaurus includes the words "continue, remain, persist" among its synonyms. It is to submit fully to His will and obey Him in His strength; it is to be crucified with Him. Our will is to be lost completely in His will, trusting that He always knows what is best for us, without exception. Christ calls us to live by "every word that proceedeth out of the mouth of God" (Matt. 4:4). This cannot be done in your own strength, but God promises that it is He that "worketh in you both to will and to do of his good pleasure" (Phil. 2:13). Again, do you believe it?

Jesus has a great hope and promise for you, which He expressed in the world's most famous prayer: "Thy will be done on earth, as it is in heaven" (Matt. 6:10). To have the Father's will done on earth, in the lives of human beings, as it is done in heaven by the holy angels, is the plan Christ has for all of us. It is His promise to you and me. He says that He will do it *in us* if we receive Him.

When it comes to the will and law of God, we are told "His commandments are not grievous" (1 John 5:3). In fact, James calls it "the perfect law of **liberty**" (James 1:25). And David declared, "I will walk at **liberty**: for I seek thy precepts," "Blessed are the undefiled in the way, who walk in the law of the Lord" (Ps. 119:45,1).

Walking with Christ means allowing Him to continually strengthen us to accept *all* of that "good, and acceptable, and perfect will of God" (Rom. 12:2). It is a mindset change from our old, carnal mind (Rom. 8:5-10) to the "mind of Christ" (Philip. 2:5; 1 Cor. 2:16). When we find ourselves rationalizing away any portion of what the Word of God tells us, we can know that we are no longer walking with Jesus.

"Can two walk together, except they be agreed?" (Amos 3:3).

Blessed is the person who takes the leap of faith - even a "mustard seed" sized leap (Matt. 17:20) - and begins to personally experience the freedom and joy that comes from submitting to the will of our Creator, no matter how crucifying it is at first to the selfish, carnal mind. The will of God is the only path to true happiness. Andrew

Murray, that great Christian author of the 19th century, called God's will "our dwelling place" (and I highly recommend his book of the same name). When one is surrendered to the providence of God in all things, there comes a peace in knowing that nothing can touch you outside of the will of your loving heavenly Father.

Jesus experienced this on the grandest scale in the Garden of Gethsemane. The Father's will said *Go to the Cross*. In contrast, Christ's human nature said *Let this cup pass from Me*. But then the Savior added, "Nevertheless, not as I will, but as thou wilt," "if this cup may not pass away from me, except I drink it, thy will be done" (Matt. 26:39,42). Those last four words are the key. Nothing on earth was more important to Jesus than the will of the Father. Why? Because if He allowed the will of the Father to direct Him, everything else would fall right into place (even if it didn't seem like it at the moment). It is because of His decisiveness on this point that you and I even have the opportunity to talk and read about such things as heaven. Every breath we take is because of His faithfulness here. Following Christ by making the Father's will our top priority, and doing so through the grace that gives us "the mind of Christ" (1 Cor. 2:16), is the one sure way to keep from falling into spiritual darkness.

"He that followeth me shall not walk in darkness, but shall have the light of life" (John 8:12). These promises seem almost too good to be true, but the Kingdom of God is made up of citizens who live by faith in God's Word and not feelings (Hab. 2:4; Rom. 1:17; Gal. 3:11; Heb. 10:38), They live by the evidence of things *not seen* (Heb. 11:1).

Letting Christ into our hearts fully, with no reservations whatsoever, is the only way we can ever have this mind of Christ and actually experience for ourselves His continual submission to the perfect will of the Father that He lived out years ago.

May God grant us the wisdom to make that decision today, and may we always be listening for His voice in the Scriptures as it says to us, "This is the way, walk ye in it" (Isa. 30:21). Those who make such a decision will, by the grace of God, keep their garments clean. And to such Christ has promised, "they shall walk with me in white" (Rev. 3:4).

▲ ▲ ▲

It is your quiet time alone with Him. You and Jesus are walking together along a quiet stretch of the massive River of Life. You are on the top level of the New Jerusalem, with a backdrop of the gorgeous green curvature of the earth in the distance. You look forward to this time more than anything else. Endless are the activities to occupy the mind and challenge the intellect. Infinite is the universe, just waiting to be further explored. But these simple walks with Jesus appeal more to your emotions and intellect than any of those things ever could. Your friendship with Him runs deeper than any other relationship you have ever known, eclipsing even your closest kinship in old earth.

As you walk together beside the river, Jesus expounds on how He, the Father, and the Holy Spirit were as One from eternal ages past (Matt. 28:19; Micah 5:2). The idea that this Man walking beside you never had a beginning is too great for even your perfect, new mind to comprehend. As a created being, the only thing you can relate to is a starting point for everything. Even your guardian angel was spoken into existence thousands of years ago. The way Christ explains it makes more sense than any explanation you have ever heard, and with each of these encounters the concept seems to be getting clearer. He knows exactly how much to reveal at each particular stage of your increasing mental development and capacity. His patient smile exhibits the constant and deep love that He feels specifically for you. Although He loves all of the redeemed equally, each one has a special place in His heart that only they can fill.

Together, as you descend a resplendent marble staircase along the riverbank that leads to a transparent, crystal arch bridge, the conversation turns to the Plan of Salvation. The Savior reveals different aspects of how the Great Plan was devised. Deity did not intend for the human race to fall into sin, but they foresaw it and met the emergency with an agreement. The moment the guilty couple was to face the penalty of death, the Son would step in and shield them from the wages of their transgression (Rev. 13:8).

At the bottom of the stairs, you ask the Jesus why the law could not have simply been changed so that the wages of sin would not be death, but rather a lesser punishment to teach the guilty pair a lesson and simultaneously spare the Savior's life. Christ smiles and explains that the Word that goes forth from the mouth of God cannot be changed (see Ps. 89:34; 119:89; Mic. 3:6; Isa. 40:8). If it could, then God would cease to be God, for His Word would lose its power (see Isa. 55:11). It would then appear as though God did not know the future in that particular case and had to change His mind to cover for this oversight. Rather than let the unchangeable penalty fall upon the guilty race, Jesus chose to take their place. The requirements of the law were holy, just, and good (Rom. 7:12), and only the life of One who was equally holy could be adequate as a substitute.

You stop at the base of the glistening arch bridge that spans the River of Life. That giant expanse of crystal clear water flows peacefully before you. Before crossing the bridge, you take a quick detour as Jesus leads you down to the river's edge and invites you to partake once again of the refreshing, cool water that you have enjoyed so many times before. He is fulfilling Revelation 7:17 and giving you the living water. This river flows directly from the throne of God, the Source of all life. You have experienced many wonderful foods and drinks since coming to this place, but none refresh you quite like the quenching water from this river.

As you partake of the water, your mind returns to the great Sacrifice that made this drink possible. The thought re-emerges that your Friend didn't just step in to save Adam and Eve at the Fall, but to save you personally. He loves you so much, He would have done the same thing if you were the only one who had ever sinned. He would have died for just you. Sometimes in the old earth, it was hard to believe that He could love you on such an intimate level. It seemed at times that His sacrifice was an impersonal event that happened two thousand years earlier. Doubts were occasionally creeping into your mind regarding just where you fit into His plan. But as you look into His face, radiant with benevolence and love, you realize just how unfounded were your doubts. This glorious habitation of the human race will for all eternity be a testimony of just how much He cared for you. But the greatest testimony and the Savior's greatest glory are the everlasting nail prints in His hands and feet, and the spear mark in His side. It is in perfect harmony with His character to have these scars upon Himself as the only trace of the one and only rebellious planet's sinful history.

You fall upon the Savior's broad chest and hold Him tightly. On the old earth you were never known for your emotional displays, but in His presence, you just can't help yourself. John 3:16, the world's most famous text, is a living reality this very moment.

The Redeemer leads you back up the riverbank and onto the bridge, where the two of you proceed across the River of Life. You have lots of other questions for Him that only He can answer. The King of kings and Lord of lords, the Savior and Redeemer of mankind, has given you His personal attention. You cherish the thought as you watch the crystal waters flow peacefully beneath you. Oh, how you love these walks.

Thought Questions:

1. What is your main takeaway from this chapter? Why is it your main takeaway?

2. What do you admire most about Jesus? What do you look forward to telling Him face-to-face when you can physically walk with Him one day? And why does Christ describe His "law of liberty" as "not grievous" as we walk with Him today, despite the struggles?

3. What does the fact that Christ was willing to come to this earth and become a human, like you (Heb. 2:17), grow up like you (Luke 2:52), get tired like you (John 4:6) and be tempted like you (Luke 4:2; Heb. 4:15) tell you about His character?

4. How does the promise in Isaiah 30:21, that God's voice will reveal to you the path to walk *now*, tie in with Rev. 3:4, that you will *one day* "walk with Me [Christ] in white"?

5. What did you learn about God's will for you in this chapter? What do you feel He's impressing you to start doing differently this week to walk more closely with Him?

STRANGE FIRE

*"For, behold, the day cometh, that shall burn as an
oven; and all the proud, yea, and all that do wickedly,
shall be stubble: and the day that cometh shall burn
them up, saith the Lord of hosts, that it shall leave
them neither root nor branch."*

-MALACHI 4:1

WHEN DISCUSSING THE eternal realities of heaven and the new earth, the question eventually arises: What about the lost? Where will they be and what will they be doing throughout the billions of millennia? Will they be dead or burning? Controversies over this subject have possibly kept more people away from the Christian religion than any other issue. Perhaps you have your own doubts about starting a relationship with a God who would burn people in hell. A Hindu friend of mine once told me "I could never be a Christian because I could never serve a god who tortures people forever." Renowned scholar, evangelical leader and Anglican priest John Stott (and one of *Time* magazine's 100 most influential people in the world) stated: "Emotionally, I find the concept [of eternal conscious torment] intolerable and do not understand how people can live with it without either cauterizing their feelings or cracking under the strain." Stott believed in hell, but also that God would destroy both body and soul there (Matt. 10:28), rather than burning them without end. Let's see what the Bible really says about this.

WHAT THE BIBLE SAYS

That there *is* a place and event called hell is quite clear in the Scriptures. But many Christians are confused about what actually happens in this place. As previously stated, some believe that the lost will be burned up like stubble, leaving neither root nor branch, while others teach that the torment and suffering will go on and on throughout the ceaseless ages. Without a doubt, this confusion stems from the wording of certain Bible passages. The subject of hell, like many subjects in the Bible, involves verses that, on the surface, seem to contradict each other. Before we look at these particular texts, let's consider how God Himself is affected by the act of punishing the lost.

"Have I any pleasure at all that the wicked should die? saith the Lord God: and not that he should return from his ways, and live?" "For I have no pleasure in the death of him that dieth, saith the Lord God: wherefore turn yourselves, and live ye" (Ezek. 18:23,32).

And God describes His "wroth" "determined upon the whole earth" as His "strange work" and His "strange act" (Isa. 28:21-22). It is both strange and painful for the Life-giver to put an end to any of His own children. He hates the act; it wounds His heart. But does He inflict pain on His children for all eternity? That is what we need to know. Jesus said in John 17:3 that it was vital to our salvation that

— 251 —

we "know" just who God is. Is the God we pray to every day the same God portrayed as an all-powerful One who will plunge His own creatures into agony without end?

First, let's look at a few texts that support the belief in a punishment that does indeed end. In the 37th chapter of the Psalms we find four verses that shed some light on the subject:

"For yet a little while, and the wicked **shall not be**; yea, thou shalt diligently consider his place, and it shall not be," "But the wicked shall perish, and the enemies of the Lord shall be as the fat of lambs: they shall consume away; **into smoke shall they consume away**," "I have seen the wicked in great power, and spreading himself like a green bay tree. Yet he passed away, and, lo, he was not: yea, I sought him, but he could not be found" (Ps. 37:10,20,35-36).

In Isaiah 47:14 we read: "Behold they [the wicked] shall be **as stubble**; the fire shall burn them; they shall not deliver themselves from the power of the flame: there shall not be a coal to warm at, nor fire to sit before it." Here we see that they are so utterly consumed that there won't even be a coal or fire left smoldering.

WHEN IS HELL?

But when does the Bible say that this fire takes place? When do the wicked become like stubble and turn into smoke, leaving neither root nor branch, or a coal to warm at? The Bible makes it clear that the devil himself will be thrown into hell and burned in the lake of fire (Rev. 20:10). He and his demonic evil spirits - fallen angels - will suffer *right along with* the lost human beings. And yet what does the Bible say about these evil spirits? "And the angels which kept not their first estate [Heaven], but left their own habitation, He [God] hath

reserved in everlasting chains under darkness **unto** the judgment of the great day" (Jude 6; see also 2 Pet. 2:4).

These angels are **reserved** *until* the judgment of the "great day," which is, of course, still future (Revelation 20). The Bible gives further evidence that the fire which destroys the wicked is yet future through a number of passages. First of all, consider the fact that "Our God is a consuming fire" (Heb. 12:29). It is *in the presence of God's holiness* that the fire does its job. God loves the sinner but hates sin (Rom. 5:8, Heb. 1:8-9), and sin is consumed in His presence, so if we keep clinging to our sin, we are consumed with it. But if we let Christ cleanse us *from* sin and cover us, then those sins will have been dealt with *before* judgment (Matt. 1:21) and we can safely stand "before the throne of God" and see Him "face-to-face" (Rev. 7:15; 1 Cor. 13:12). Notice the focus is being in His presence.

"As smoke is driven away, so drive them away: as wax melteth before the fire, so let the wicked perish **at the presence of God**" (Ps. 68:2). "[The wicked] shall be tormented with fire and brimstone **in the presence of the holy angels**, and **in the presence of the Lamb**" (Rev. 14:10).

UTTERLY CONSUMED

The clearest text in the Bible describing the destruction of the wicked is found in Revelation 20. This chapter describes the end of the "thousand years" (verse 7), often referred to by Christians as "the Millennium." At the end of the Millennium, Satan rallies the wicked who "live not again until the thousand years were finished" (verse 5). The Bible describes these people as "the rest" who had no part in the "first resurrection" (verse 5), which occurred at the *beginning* of the Millennium (as described in Chapter One of this book). Now Satan leads this group whose number is "as the sand of the sea" against the New Jerusalem, that "beloved city." Then the Bible gives us that clear text: "And fire came down from God out of heaven and **devoured them**" (verse 9). The language is quite clear here; it *devours* them.

"Let the sinners be **consumed out of the earth**, and let the wicked **be no more**" (Ps. 104:35).

"Wait on the Lord, and keep his way, and he shall exalt thee to inherit the land: when the wicked **are cut off**, thou shalt see it" (Ps. 37:34). Chapter 10, "Behold All Things New," picks up right after this event where the wicked are "cut off" and "devoured" by the fire. The fire that destroys the wicked cleanses the old earth and makes everything new again before the redeemed "inherit the land." Notice that at our conversion, we are baptized first with the *water* at church and then with the *fire* of the Holy Spirit. The earth was likewise cleansed first with the *water* of the flood and someday again with the *fire* of God.

"And ye shall tread down the wicked; for **they shall be ashes** under the soles of your feet in the day that I shall do this, saith the Lord of hosts" (Mal. 4:3). Ultimately "ashes," not writhing, burning souls. This seems pretty clear.

"NOT QUENCHED" AND "FOREVER"?

So where, then, does all of the confusion come from? In a few texts that use phrases like "everlasting punishment" (Matt. 25:46), "fire that never shall be quenched" (Mark 9:43), and "tormented day and night for ever and ever" (Rev. 20:10). Let's prayerfully look at these texts.

The punishment is indeed "everlasting." There is no hope of a resurrection *ever* for those who are lost and consumed by the fire.

Notice the phrase uses the noun punish*ment* (result) and not the verb punish*ing* (action). This punishment is described as "the blackness of darkness forever" (Jude 13; see also 2 Pet. 2:17).

So then, the punish*ing* is fire, as bright and hot as the sun, which leaves only ashes in the presence of the Lamb. The eternal punish*ment* is the complete opposite – the blackness of *darkness* forever. This eternal darkness is the same state of non-existence they had before being conceived by their parents and given life by God. This is the "second death" (Rev. 20:14), the final death.

But what about the "fire that never shall be quenched"? The word "quench" means "to put out." No one will put this fire out. It will do its work of consumption and then *go* out, leaving neither root nor branch, only ashes, which don't burn. If you've ever stayed up late by a campfire, you've inevitably been faced with the decision: "Should we just let the fire burn itself out, or should we quench it before we go to bed?" Only you can quench it; the fire doesn't quench itself. And what is left in the morning? Ashes. This same principle holds true with what firefighters have learned about forest fires. Years ago, they would try to quench them as soon as possible but have since learned to let some fires burn themselves out since occasional fires can actually be good for the cycle of life in the forest. In these cases, they choose not to quench them.

The Bible itself gives us another example of a fire that was not to be quenched. In Jeremiah 17:27 we read God's warning that if His people in Jerusalem disobeyed, then He would "kindle a fire in the gates thereof, and it shall devour the palaces of Jerusalem, and it shall not be quenched." This prophecy was fulfilled in 70 A.D. when Titus destroyed the city with a fire that the Jews could not quench. It destroyed the whole city but is obviously not still burning today.

And finally, what about that daunting phrase "tormented day and night for ever and ever"? The Greek word rendered "ever" here is *aion,* which can literally be translated "an age." The same word is used in Christ's statement that the great harvest (the Second Coming) will be at the "end of this world" - the end of the *aion*, or age (see Matt. 13:39). The word can mean either a *specific time frame* **or** *forever*, depending on its usage in the text. So then, one may legitimately ask: How are we to know which definition to use in this troubling text about the torment of the wicked? In light of all the other texts we have studied, the answer should be clear. The wicked will be burned until the end of an *aion*. The end of the present "age" is when fire covers the earth, and this world is re-created before our eyes (see 2 Pet. 3:10-13; Rev. 21:1,5).

God doesn't reserve a volcanic chasm in His presence where all of the lost will fill the air with their bloodcurdling shrieks of agony for all eternity (imagine the effect this would have on those weekly Sabbath gatherings of the redeemed in His presence, promised in Isa. 66:22-23). No, according to the Bible, the cities of Sodom and Gomorrah are "set forth as an example," of what will happen to the wicked, "suffering the vengeance of **eternal** fire" (Jude 7). Are Sodom and Gomorrah still burning today from their "eternal fire"? No. The fire *did its job* and went out (see also 2 Pet. 2:6).

PARABLE PUZZLE: WATER ON LAZARUS' TONGUE?

There has also been confusion surrounding the parable of the rich man and Lazarus (Luke 16:19-31), but Christ never intended for all of the symbolism in the story to be taken literally (the dead going directly to Abraham's bosom; the saved being able to converse with the lost as they writhe in pain; merely a drop of water on the tongue requested by one whose entire body was blistering in the flames, etc.). Christ was not giving a discourse on the specifics of hell, but rather teaching some very important lessons for both the Jews in His day and all future believers about prioritizing our spiritual life above this temporary life, while we still have time to do so.

GOD'S CHARACTER

Think it through. We are talking about the very *character* of our Savior here. If God were to actually plunge His own lost children into unfathomable agony without end, He would become, without competition, the cruelest being that ever lived. The monstrous dictators that have come and gone in our world would look like Cub Scout bullies by comparison.

Countless seeking souls have avoided or abandoned the Christian faith because of just such unbiblical representations of God. They cannot bring themselves to love an all-powerful being who feels He has a right to actually torture human beings - that He brought into existence - to torture them for all eternity, as retribution for few decades (or less) of sin. And how can we blame them for distrusting such a god? The good news is that although justice is coming for the wicked, all suffering will finally come to an end. Our loving, tenderhearted God Himself would be living an eternal hell if He had to inflict or even be aware of such endless agony. Never again would His benevolent heart find happiness as He lived with the knowledge that multitudes were suffering, with *no hope of relief* - ever. Can you fathom it? Have you prayed about it? According to Scripture, both the body *and the soul* will be consumed by the flames. The Bible is quite clear on this point:

"The **soul** that sinneth it shall **die**."

-EZEKIEL 18:20

"[God] is able to **destroy both soul and body** in hell."

- MATTHEW 10:28

"For the day of the Lord is near upon all the heathen: as thou hast done, it shall be done unto thee: thy reward shall return upon thine own head....and **they shall be as though they had not been**."

- OBADIAH 1:15-16

HELL AND MR. FUDGE

More and more Bible scholars and pastors of various denominations are discovering and embracing the truth about the fate of the lost. The critically-acclaimed, award-winning 2012 film *Hell and Mr. Fudge* tells the true story of Evangelical pastor Edward Fudge's journey from a proponent of eternal torment to a believer in *The Fire That Consumes* the wicked until they are no more (the title of his exhaustive book on the subject). *Christianity Today* has called Fudge's book "the standard reference on the subject." But above all earthly books, God He has given us the Bible so that we may see from His Word that such boundless cruelty is out of harmony with His character.

There are two, opposing ditches that we must avoid when discussing God's holy character, and the devil constantly tries to lead us into either of them: the first portrays God as a pushover who gives us His law, but then treats it as a mere list of suggestions, and isn't really concerned when we decide that we know best and choose to sin (which is "the transgression of the law - 1 John 3:4). In other words, there are no real consequences for our sin, and He doesn't mean what He says. In this error, a warped view of mercy is pushed so far that any semblance of justice disappears.

The opposite and equally dangerous ditch portrays God as a tyrant, who pushes a warped view of justice so far that there is no semblance of mercy, and who metes out unlimited pain and unending suffering to millions who don't submit to His authority during their brief stint on earth. Reader, the Creator is neither of these caricatures, and as you study God's Word daily, you will get to know Him so well that both ditches will gradually fade into oblivion. God is our "heavenly Father," who has the will and fortitude to run the universe perfectly and the grace and love to give His fallen children a path to redemption through His Son's sacrifice at Calvary. Thank God He chose to use all of His power for good, demonstrating both justice and mercy. And thank God the following scenario is one that will fortunately **never, *ever* take place in the earth made new.**

▲ ▲ ▲

(Adults, please read this section through on your own before deciding whether to share it with younger listeners)

You are on your way to see Jesus. Your heart thrills over the love and grace that He has shown you. You speed up your pace because you are eager to ask Him more questions about the eternal mysteries of Redemption. Studying His love and the miracle of the Plan of Salvation is the favorite subject of the ransomed, and you break into a run up the giant, golden staircase, skipping steps in joyful anticipation.

At the top of the ascent, you enter the Great Throne Room where the Redeemer sits in all His glory beside the Father. You bow in loving reverence and then rise to converse with your best Friend.

He tells you that He wants you to walk with Him as you talk. The King rises and steps down to meet you. His tall figure leads you out of the Throne Room, and the two of you pause at the top of the towering, golden staircase. The view from up here is breathtaking. You are multiple times higher than the tallest skyscrapers in the old earth, and yet you have no fear of heights whatsoever. You are in the presence of the Life-giver, and nothing can harm you now. But from this height, you also see something from which you have averted your eyes in previous visits to the Throne. From here you can see that unusual lake that few talk about in this land. It is the one thing in the entire universe that can tap unfamiliar emotions that you thought were long ago banished from human experience. Dark emotions that you would prefer to avoid in this blissful utopia. But the enticing pull of curiosity under the law of free will invariably takes effect when you visit here. Christ is obviously aware of your emotional plight as He offers that for the sake of transparency you should take a closer look at what is going on down at "the lake." As you descend the stairs, Jesus tells you that together you will now view the Justice of His Righteousness. He warns you that this will not be a pretty sight but reassures you that your own fate is eternally secure. You wonder if you are ready to take this closer look as curiosity gradually gives way to dread.

Walking together along the ground now, you start to notice an awful stench. The smell is putrefying and gaining strength as you continue down this unfamiliar path. The ominous wails and shrieks grow louder as you approach the giant, smoking chasm. The reek of burning human flesh stings the insides of your nostrils. Violent plumes of black smoke ascend from the pit, and for the first time, you can see frantic movement within the molten brimstone below.

As you hold your nose and step up to the edge of the cliff, a relative of yours - a very close relative - recognizes you. Her terror-filled eyes meet yours as she bellows out your old name and begs you to dip your finger in some water and then put it on the tip of her tongue. Your heart is torn, and you instinctively open your mouth to call out to her, not even sure what you could possibly say in response. But before you can make a sound, she sinks beneath the boiling surface of the flaming lake. Horrified, you look to Jesus who seems devastated by the scene. You ask Him if your relative has suffered enough. After all, she has been in this flaming torture chamber even longer than her entire life on old earth, without even one second of relief! The punishment seems more than sufficient to you. But the Creator declares that no, there is never to be any rest for your loved one. Never. A tear trickles down the Savior's cheek as He scans the fiery horizon. He will never transport this torture chamber to a remote corner of the universe, for the wicked are tormented in the presence of the Lamb, as His own Word declared. The distant flames are now overheating your own skin and you slowly back away from the smoky edge of the chasm.

As your relative comes back up to the surface, she releases yet another gargling shriek of agony. You quickly avert your eyes as you hear your name screamed out once more amid the uproar of the hopeless. You can't take this. It's too much.

You try again to convince the loving Savior that maybe it would be best to put this woman and these other poor souls out of their misery. But Jesus again shakes His head, declaring that the wages of sin is not death, as Paul said in Romans 6:23, but eternal life - an eternal life of ever-increasing torture beyond your wildest, nightmarish imagination. You mind races as you frantically cite Matthew 10:28 about the Father destroying both body and soul in hell and Jesus explains that the word "destroy" is really referring to an ongoing torture with no real destruction. Nothing is actually destroyed.

Slowly you turn from the scene as tears slide down your own cheeks in this land where you thought God promised to wipe away all tears and there would be no more of the pain or sorrow now displayed before your eyes. Rev. 21:4 seemed pretty distinct on these points.

What *other* shocking disappointments await you in this new environment? You're no longer in the mood to ask Jesus your questions about Calvary, for these images have burned their impressions upon your mind and dampened your mood for now. Perhaps things will get better later on. Somehow.

Ultimately you find yourself contemplating this scene in your favorite chair back at your comfortable estate with all its amenities. Suddenly the chair doesn't feel so comfortable. How can you ever enjoy this peace and quiet, these joyful relationships and activities, or even fellowship with the Lord, when you know that your loved one is at that very moment - no matter what the moment - suffering pain beyond comprehension? Your pet tiger strolls up to you and rubs his large head against your knee, sensing your gloom. You force a smile and reach out to rub his neck, but happiness is shrouded by the memory of your loved one in that pit. It then dawns on you that the fate of this tiger is actually better than that of your loved one. In fact, the fate of the insects that crawl along the forest floor outside actually have it better than she does. Your stomach churns as you contemplate it further and you just want it to go away. You want everything to go away. But maybe it will get better over time, you think, as a glimmer of hope starts to flicker in your confused mind.

Time passes, and eventually your nagging thoughts compel you to once more visit the horrible chasm that is ever in the presence of the Lamb, who continually oversees the lake from His Throne, miles overhead. You cringe as several flaming souls suddenly roar out for help before being sucked back down by the white-hot liquid. As your darting eyes scan the lake of brimstone, you hope that your loved one doesn't see you. Then something touches your shoulder and you swirl around to see what it is. Your nerves are on edge, but a bit of relief settles over you as you see the loving face of Jesus, there to comfort you. Again, you plead with Him to put these poor, suffering folks out of their misery and make them like they were before they were born: "as if they had not been." After all, it has now been *two thousand years*, and not even the oldest human in this lake of fire lived long enough to warrant this kind of punishment. But alas, Jesus again shakes His head and says that their punishment has only begun, and justice must be served. This is exactly what these people deserve; in fact, they deserve much, much more, which is coming. These two thousand years of non-stop agony are but a split second compared to the eons of torture that lie before them. You begin to wonder just how a lowly, created being like yourself acquired more love and mercy than the infinitely loving and merciful Creator - the source of all love.

A gargling, screaming voice calls out your name. Your relative has spotted you, and she reaches up for help, arms dripping with flames. Again, you turn to Jesus, but He reluctantly shakes His head No, before you can speak. Thoughts about your Savior slowly creep into your mind that you quickly dismiss for fear that they will grow. Somehow you must be wrong about all this because He is always right...*Right?*...

Time has passed, and you are again in your opulent estate contemplating just what you can do to save your poor loved one. It's all you think about anymore. What if you gave back all of the heavenly blessings Jesus bestowed upon you? What if you traded places with the lost woman? Perhaps you could pray for a thousand years, and at the end of the thousand years, your prayers would be answered. What if you got millions of other redeemed ones - and even the angels - to join you in your endeavor! Yes, yes, maybe that's it! A strange chuckle escapes your lips as you force the thought that maybe this scheme will work. You're beginning to doubt your own sanity. The fate of the lost has taken over your mind, and nothing seems pleasurable anymore. It is consuming you, just as surely as the flames of God are consuming the wicked - never ending, never destroying, just an ever-growing, constant force.

Ultimately you find yourself for a third time with Jesus at the edge of the monstrous, hideous pit. *200 million years* have now passed, and the shrieks and wails have only grown louder. Without even the hope of relief by losing consciousness, these poor souls have been suffering every second since you came into Paradise. In fact, they've been suffering from the moment that they died, since you now realize that death is really just a passage into eternal life. So if Satan and his angels were busy on earth during the Bible stories, and "reserved" for hell at a future time, you have another question: Why did millions of these start suffering while Satan and his demons were allowed the enjoyment of tempting and even inhabiting humans? Why did the demons' own punishment and suffering start *after* the punishment of the humans, when they had been so much guiltier than humans and had fallen long before them?

You're suddenly jarred back to the present by a familiar blood-curdling scream. It's your loved one, and she's spotted you. She realizes Christ won't stop the agony, so she continually cries out to you in hopeless desperation. She's still in the same horrifying condition, and as she wails and cries out your old name, you wonder how any being could withstand such continual blistering agony for so long. Only God's power must be keeping the poor woman alive, for only God can give life. But now the Live-giver is using His powers to prolong the suffering. He is keeping the consciousness alert and the pain sensors active so that the keen torment can never subside - not even for one second. And all for what, you wonder? What lesson is to be gained from such endless suffering? That God's way is right? That sin is to be avoided? These lessons were learned during the span of old earth's miserable history and at the price of Calvary. All have seen the foolishness and great cost of sin. All finally realized that God's way was best and that He always had your best interest in mind. The grand irony of this eternal chasm of terror is that it is the *one and only* thing that is actually causing the inhabitants of the universe to now question those previous conclusions - to doubt God's benevolence toward His creatures and His right to govern. Lucifer's argument from the beginning was that he, not God, should rule, since God's governing obviously had room for improvement, regarding the well-being of His subjects. Christ had called this rebellious angel "the father of lies," but was it possible that rather than spreading lies, this covering cherub was onto something? That perhaps he knew something about God's character that the King would rather keep secret?

And yet, the heart of Jesus seems to be ripped right from Him, too. This place where all tears were to be wiped away now only creates and perpetuates more tears - far more than you ever experienced in old earth, even under your most severe trials. Your knees finally buckle, and you fall and weep bitterly for these people, grasping fistfuls of grass and craving more than anything in the universe that *you* were in charge and not God. Did you actually just think that? Yes, yes you did. And you cannot drive the thought from your unhinged mind. But it's an impossible wish. If only you could somehow convince this Being that enough is enough! You look up at the Savior, tears flowing down your cheeks, and cry out that you can't stand it anymore. This is the closest you have ever come to yelling at Christ as you beg Him to just put them all out of their misery. Take back all of the gifts, if it will help - the mansions, the land, everything you've inherited. Do anything with these countless rewards, but just please, PLEASE stop the suffering!

But once more the Sustainer of all life insists that justice has not yet been served. His universe runs on love and fairness, and it would not be fair for them to suffer anything less than immeasurable and constant agony for all the ceaseless ages of eternity. He starts to share His rationale for why He must keep them alive and suffering forever as you turn your face from Him and helplessly, frantically crawl back to the chasm's edge and stare back down into the molten torture chamber. You aren't even listening, you are so overcome with pity for your fellow human beings and rage over the situation. It now dawns on you that yes, you are indeed more merciful than this God who stands behind you. With no other choices, you finally turn to Him and on your knees cry out that if He won't put them out of their misery, then please, please, please, put you out of *yours!* You see that Jesus Himself is also miserable and will be for all eternity. You can no longer endure living in His new earth. You hate it here. To go on any longer would not be heaven for you, but rather a living hell. Although the flames do not engulf you, you realize that mentally, emotionally you are doomed to share in the fate of the lost and suffer ever-increasing pain in the strange fire without end.

▲ ▲ ▲

Reader, believe on the authority of God's Word that the scenario you just witnessed will never, ever take place. Let us always remember that it is Satan who enjoys inflicting pain and watching suffering, not our Lord. And Satan loves attributing to God his own evil traits. The heavenly Father loves you more than any earthly father ever could. Although justice will be served in the destruction of the wicked, never forget that "**He retaineth not his anger <u>for ever</u>, because he <u>delighteth</u> in mercy**" (Mic. 7:18).

Thought Questions:

1. What is your main takeaway from this chapter? Why is it your main takeaway?

2. Why do you think there has been so much confusion surrounding the fate of the lost? Why is Satan often portrayed controlling hell and burning lost souls? What are the two definitions of the Greek word "*aion*," and how do these definitions affect meaning?

3. What does God's decision to destroy both body and soul in hell/the lake of fire, rather than torturing them without end tell you about His character? And why is even this act called His "strange work"?

4. In the end, Satan and his demons, who have caused you so much pain, sorrow, and suffering, will ultimately lose the war and be devoured in the lake of fire that is prepared for them. God wins. His children win. What does this tell you about God's promises?

5. What did you learn about God's will for you in this chapter? What do you feel He's impressing you to start doing differently this week to walk more closely with Him?

THE CROSS

"Saying with a loud voice, Worthy is the Lamb that was slain to receive power, and riches, and wisdom, and strength, and honour, and glory, and blessing."

-REVELATION 5:12

"For I determined not to know any thing among you, save Jesus Christ, and him crucified."

-1 CORINTHIANS 2:2

IF YOU WERE to study just ONE Bible topic and nothing else for a year, what would it be? **What do you think would be the most beneficial to you, in every way?** Heaven? Bible prophecy? Old Testament stories? Church outreach? Worship styles? The Ten Commandments? Of course, God is clear that all of these matter, and we should be studying all of them. I pose this question, not to downplay the others (I've written and re-written a book about Heaven, so you know I'm not downplaying that); I pose the question because the most important subject is probably one of the least understood and least appreciated: the Cross of Christ. Bear with me, here, because I'm convinced that if you really start looking into it, the Holy Spirit will enlighten your mind and make "Jesus Christ and Him crucified" your favorite theme of study.

THE POWER OF THE CROSS

What is it that makes the inheritance of the meek possible? What reveals the love of God more than anything else? What exhibits His perfect justice and hatred for sin most clearly? What is it that makes the cleansing from sin possible? And what is it that supplies us with the power to overcome sin? The answer to all of these questions can be nothing else but the Cross of Christ. This is why Paul openly declared that he was determined to know nothing except "Jesus and Him crucified." But do we naturally feel this way about the Cross? Does the unconverted person even see all that is involved in it?

"For the preaching of the cross is to them that perish foolishness; but unto us which are saved it is the power of God," "But the natural man receiveth not the things of the Spirit of God: for they are foolishness unto him: neither can he know them, because they are spiritually discerned" (1 Cor. 1:18; 2:14).

The "natural man" is the person who has yet to be converted. Many call themselves "Christian," but this title is no guarantee of conversion. After more than three years of training him, Jesus said to Peter, "When thou art converted, strengthen thy brethren" (Luke 22:32). Without true conversion, the power of the Cross quickly shrinks down into a dead theory or scholarly doctrine to learn once and look at again every Easter or so.

It would be well for us to contemplate the life and death of Jesus every day of our lives. Just to spend some thoughtful time allowing the Holy Spirit to make the Sacrifice real to us so that it is no longer "foolishness" or a lifeless doctrine. When we begin to do this, the Cross then becomes what it was meant to be: "the power of God."

And *how* is it the power of God to the converted soul? How can it give us victory over sin? The more the Holy Spirit impresses our minds with the suffering our sins caused Jesus, the more eager we will be to put those sins away, by the grace of God. We have all heard the Proverb "The fear of the Lord is the beginning of wisdom" (Prov. 9:10), but what exactly is meant by "the fear of the Lord"? Part of it is a holy reverence for Him, but the Bible gives us another definition as well: "The fear of the Lord is to hate evil" (Prov. 8:13). Nothing can make us hate evil so much as Calvary. Seeing the innocent and willing Sacrifice on the Cross is the world's greatest antidote for a life diseased with sin. Until we allow the Holy Spirit to impress this great truth upon our minds, we will "continue in sin, that grace may abound" (something that "God forbids" - Rom. 6:1) and "crucify...the Son of God afresh, and put him to an open shame" (Heb. 6:6).

But should we stay away from Jesus until we *feel* repentance for sin? Not at all. We must come to Jesus *for* this repentance just as surely as we need Him for pardon. Christ is described in the Bible as the One who is able to "**give** repentance to Israel, and forgiveness of sins" (Acts 5:31). Jesus *gives us* the ability to repent. It is a gift, there for the asking. We cannot change our own hearts (Jer. 13:23), we cannot change our motives (Jer. 17:9), but we can freely come to Him and ask Him to change them for us (Ezek. 36:26-27; Ps. 51:10). Then He gives us the gift of repentance, followed by the forgiveness of sins.

And how does the Cross bring about the cleansing we so desperately need? By the "precious blood" of the Lamb that was shed.

"Forasmuch as ye know that ye were not redeemed with corruptible things, as silver and gold...But with the precious blood of Christ, as of a lamb without blemish and without spot," "and without shedding of blood there is no remission," but "it is not possible that the blood of bulls and of goats should take away sins" (1 Pet. 1:18-19; Heb. 9:22; 10:4)

His blood is the only substance in the entire universe capable of cleansing your record of sin. Why? Because "the life of the flesh is in the blood" (Lev. 17:11). His very life must cover your life if you are to be found "faultless" (Jude 24) in the Judgment. "For we must all appear before the judgment seat of Christ" (2 Cor. 5:10). As Jesus, our High Priest, administers His own blood on our sinful record, the record itself is changed to reflect His perfect record (see Hebrews, chapter 9 and Isa. 1:18).

Had He failed even once while on this earth and slipped into a sin of any kind, all hope for you and me would have vanished. There would have then been no blood found in the universe that could cover our sinful record. But praise God, Jesus did come off victorious, and He did set His face toward the Cross, no matter how strongly temptation beckoned Him to turn back. It is because of His death on the Cross that this blood is now available to be placed over your spotted record.

The Cross also reveals to us the immutability of God's law and His Word. Could the law have been changed, the Son of God need not have died. He could have simply remained at His Father's side on the Throne of the universe and altered the law to meet the emergency. But God's justice is equaled only by His mercy. Sin had to come to an end, and the definition of sin is "the transgression of the law" (1 John 3:4). Rather than let the punishment fall upon the transgressors of the law, Christ took our place. The very real pain that Jesus suffered upon the Cross was not just the nails piercing His hands and feet, but rather the sins of the world - your sins and mine - upon His very soul. This brought separation between Him and the Father, for sin always separates the soul from God (Isa. 59:2).

Justice and mercy met face-to-face in the Sacrifice on the Cross. "Mercy and truth are met together; righteousness and peace have kissed each other" (Ps. 85:10).

Just as clearly as the Cross reveals God's hatred for sin, it reveals His love for the sinner. When faced with the choice to let sinful mankind perish and retain His loving Son at His side, or let His beloved Son go down to the cold, dark world and experience the wrath of justice *in place of* mankind, He chose to send His Son. Considering His decision, it's quite amazing that anyone could doubt such love. What more could He do? Often when we fall into sin, we conjure up pictures of a God who leans back in His throne with His mighty arms folded, reluctant to offer forgiveness. But this is all a carnal delusion. If God so loved the world that He gave His only Son to die in your place, would He not also be eager to pardon you after a fall? "Like a father pitieth his children, so the Lord pitieth them that fear him," "because he delighteth in mercy" (Ps. 103:13; Mic. 7:18).

It is God who is there to lift you up when you fall. He is the One who reaches out His hand, pulls you out of the muck, and cleans you off. More patient than any earthly parent could be with a child is your Heavenly Father with you. The Cross reveals this more than anything else can.

And finally, how does the Cross give us access to heaven? First of all, it gives us power over death, the great barrier that sin erected over a rebellious planet.

"And if Christ be not raised, your faith is vain; ye are yet in your sins. Then they also which are fallen asleep in Christ are perished... For since by man came death, by man came also the resurrection of the dead. For as in Adam all die, even so in Christ shall all be made alive. But every man in his own order: Christ the firstfruits; afterward they that are Christ's at his coming...The last enemy that shall be destroyed is death" (1 Cor. 15:17-18,22,23,26).

Christ's death on Calvary and His resurrection from the tomb revealed the power that unlocked the mysterious forces of death. "Forasmuch then as the children are partakers of the flesh and blood, he also himself likewise took part of the same; that **through death** he might destroy him that had the power of death, that is, the devil" (Heb. 2:14).

"I am he that liveth, and was dead; and, behold, I am alive for evermore, Amen; and have the keys of hell and of death" (Rev. 1:18).

Jesus' sinless life made Him the spotless and therefore worthy and acceptable Sacrifice on Calvary. By His resurrection (the result of His sinless life) He broke the curse of sin and made possible the resurrection of all who have received Him. It is because of His perfect Sacrifice that at His Second Coming multitudes will declare as they come forth from their graves, "O death, where is thy sting? O grave, where is thy victory?" (1 Cor. 15:55). Death will, in that day, be "swallowed up in victory" (verse 54) - the victory that Christ gained on the Cross.

And there is another way that the Cross gives us access to heaven. The prophet John had a vision of the future, where a "great multitude" stood before the throne of God, wearing white robes (Rev. 7:9). They still refer to Jesus as "the Lamb" (verse 10), signifying their association with His great Sacrifice. This great multitude is described as those who "have washed their robes, and made them white in the blood of the Lamb. Therefore they are before the throne of God" (verses 14-15). Notice the wording: "*therefore* they are before the throne." Because they have washed their robes in Christ's blood, they not only receive forgiveness, not only receive empowerment, but they also gain access to the very throne of God in heaven. Had they not had this robe of Christ's righteousness - supplied by His cleansing blood - they would have been consumed with their sinful record in the presence of a Holy God, who indeed is a "consuming fire" (Heb. 12:29; see also Matt. 22:11-13).

"Blessed are they that do his commandments, that they might have right to the tree of life, and may enter in through the gates into the city" (Rev. 22:14).

To "do his commandments" is possible only through the blood of the Lamb shed on Calvary's Cross. "And they overcame him [the devil] by the blood of the Lamb" (Rev. 12:11). They did not overcome by their own efforts, in their own strength, with their own righteousness. It was by the blood of the Lamb that they were able to gain the victory and inherit eternal life in the New Jerusalem. The only way they were enabled to have His strength, was to die to self and *the strength of self*. "For ye are dead, and your life is hid with Christ in God" (Col. 3:3). His blood not only covered their record of sin, but it empowered them to die to self and let Him live out His perfect life through them (Col. 1:27; Gal. 2:20). Consider it: Jesus, through His blood, obeys the Father *in us*.

THE CROSS AND THE MIRROR OF HIS LAW

Does the keeping of the commandments, then, save anybody? No, "For by grace are ye saved through faith; and that not of yourselves: it is the gift of God: Not of works, lest any man should boast" (Eph. 2:8-9). The Commandments are the world's biggest and most accurate spiritual mirror. Not only do they protect us like a guardrail beside a cliff and provide a great blessing, but they reveal to us our true spiritual condition so that none might deceive themselves into a false sense of security apart from Christ. There are two you should never try to deceive: God, because you can't, and yourself, because you can. This mirror, then, can keep us from self-delusion, if we experience it as described below:

"But be ye doers of the word, and not hearers only, deceiving your own selves. For if any be a hearer of the word, and not a doer, he is like unto a man beholding his natural face in a glass [a mirror]: For he beholdeth himself, and goeth his way, and straightway forgetteth what manner of man he was. But whoso looketh into the perfect law of liberty, and continueth therein, he being not a forgetful hearer, but a doer of the work, this man shall be blessed in his deed" (James 1:22-25).

"And hereby do we know that we know him, if we keep his commandments. He that saith, I know him, and keepeth not his commandments, is a liar, and the truth is not in him," "By this we know that we love the children of God, when we love God, and keep his commandments. For this is the love of God, the we keep his commandments: and his commandments are not grievous," "And he that keepeth his commandments dwelleth in Him, and He in him. And hereby we know that He abideth in us, by the Spirit which He hath given us." (1 John 2:3-4; 5:2-3; 3:24).

The law saves no one; Jesus saves us. But since the fall of humanity, our carnal minds needed the law to be written out so that we would know the one, true path to follow, and to be aware of whether or not the Savior truly "abideth in us."

"Therefore by the deeds of the law there shall no flesh be justified in his sight: for by the law is the knowledge of sin," "Nay, I had not known sin, but by the law" (Rom. 3:20; 7:7).

Without the law, we would have no idea what sin is and would not be aware of how much we need the Savior to forgive, cleanse and empower us. The law shows us what sin *is*. The Cross shows us what sin *did*. As we look upon these two, we begin to grasp our true condition, and we run to the only One who can save us.

The Cross of Calvary brought to an end the whole sacrificial system that pointed ahead to Jesus, "nailing it to his cross" (Col. 2:14). But thank God His eternal, moral law, written with His own finger, endures forever (see Ex. 31:18; Ps. 111:7-8; Luke 16:17; Matt. 5:17-19). We are not left in darkness to be "carried about with every wind of doctrine" (Eph. 4:14); we have God's unchanging Word as a guide: "a lamp unto my feet, and a light unto my path" (Ps. 119:105).

THE FOOT OF THE CROSS

Reader, have you come to the Cross and dwelt at the foot of it? Perhaps that concept seems odd or even corny to you at this point. Think of it this way: Have you considered the enormous price that was paid on your behalf? Perhaps you have never given your heart to Jesus and are learning about Him for the first time. Perhaps you have been a Christian for years but had no idea of the limitless power of the Cross; you really *can* have victory over those inherited or cultivated sins. Maybe you are realizing for the first time what the biblical definition of sin is - the transgression of God's law - and you want to come again to Jesus and have Him make things right. You might be one who once enjoyed deep fellowship with the Lord, but have drifted far from Him on your prodigal journey; you know the path you should be on but have deliberately chosen a course of sin and self. You don't hate God, you just don't find Him that interesting anymore. Whatever your condition, no matter how dark your past, it is not too dark for the Savior to read and to cleanse. He waits for you even now as you read these words. He specializes in giving new starts, providing clean slates. He wants to free you from whatever is holding you back and show you who the *real* you is, the one He created you to be. Let nothing, nothing stand in your way of coming to the Savior now, just as you are, and letting Him give you the peace of total forgiveness, which surpasses all understanding.

The Cross was devised in a Master Plan by the Father and Son so that you could share in the pleasures of heaven and the joy of fellowship with your Creator. Believe that in God's mind heaven will not be the same without you. He tells us that He thinks about you constantly and that those thoughts are of peace and are more than can be numbered (Jer. 29:11; Ps. 139:17-18). In the Father's great house are many mansions, many "rooms," created for all of His children. One was designed especially for you. One has your name written over its door - a physical door just as real as the book you now hold in your hands. It is no fantasy, no Christian daydream.

DON'T WAIT

Don't wait until you feel "good enough" to come to the Cross, or you'll never come. The blood available there is the *only* thing that can ever take away your sins and transform your life, so waiting to get better is pointless, a tactical delusion of the devil. Neither wait until you feel like you love Him. Always remember that repentance and love, as well as a change of heart, come from God alone; they are not inherent traits of your soul. Romans 5:5 tells us that "the love of God is shed abroad in our hearts by the Holy Ghost which is given unto us." The ability to love the Lord is itself a gift from God because God IS Love (1 John 4:16). Give yourself to Jesus today, based upon the truths in His Word, and the repentance and love will come. God promises they will. The feelings that we so often rely upon as a guide will then take their true place, as the *result* of our decision, not the *deciding factor*.

Remember that emotions are like fire: a wonderful servant, but a horrible master. Think about it.

As you come to the Lord in prayer, believe that God is always working; He never ceases (see Ps. 121:4). The repairs that need to be made on your heart and soul will be underway at that very moment, though you will not feel them. The love of God will be shed abroad in your heart that very hour, though you will not immediately sense it. Trust in the Lord, and let Him do His work.

Then the Cross will begin to appear in its true power. The Great Sacrifice, Who hung upon it in your place, will be seen in a whole new light. The truths which, to your mind, were either new, unfamiliar information or an old love which had waxed cold, will shine forth in a newly discovered luster. Jesus Himself will cease to be merely a figure in history, whom you know so little about, and will become the "Sun of righteousness," rising in your heart "with healing in His wings" (Mal. 4:2). Then you will have the "peace that passeth all understanding" (Phil. 4:7), and Jesus will find a resting place in your soul. True life will finally begin and eternity will be yours, shared with the Man who was wounded for your transgressions and bruised for your iniquities, the Man by whose bloody stripes from a whip you are finally healed (Isa. 53:5).

▲ ▲ ▲

The world is watching. Inside the New Jerusalem stand the redeemed of all ages, clothed in white and shining "as the stars" (Dan. 12:3) as they reflect the glory of Christ. Outside the city, arrayed against it for battle, stand the rejectors of God's mercy: those who hardened their hearts against the tender promptings of the Holy Spirit. Their numbers are "as the sand of the sea" (Rev. 20:8-9). Sin is about to be eradicated from the universe. Those whose sins have not been placed upon Christ and cleansed by the blood of the Lamb will share in the fate of their iniquity.

But before the end is to come "the earth shall be filled with the **knowledge** of the **glory** of the Lord, as the waters cover the sea" (Hab. 2:14). The glory of the Lord is His character (see Exodus 33 & 34), His perfect benevolence, combined with His perfect hatred for sin. In order for the whole earth to be filled with a knowledge of such, they must first see it as it was most clearly manifested: in the Cross of Christ. The only way that "every tongue should confess that Jesus Christ is Lord" (Phil. 2:11) across the planet, is if a view of the Great Sacrifice on Calvary is given.

There, above the City, for all to see in panoramic view, is the visual story of the great controversy between Christ and Satan. The closing scenes of the Savior's life are now presented before all. Although it demonstrates the deepest love and grace in the clearest possible fashion, it spawns polar opposite effects in the hearts of the countless viewers. While the cosmic display engenders the warmest affections within those inside the city, these same scenes evoke thoughts of judgment and guilt to those outside the city. You, like the billions of others at this moment, cannot turn your eyes from the spectacle. All are transfixed on this momentous scene of truth, starkly contrasting the countless lies of the past, propagated by man and demon. All of the greatest human philosophies are forgotten in light of the divine scene. The so-called human search for meaning is now clearly defined for all to see - it is, and always was, to simply be a part of the heavenly family. The value of each precious soul is settled once and for all: their lives were worth the priceless death of the Creator, to save them from eternal loss and separation from God.

All are now witnessing Christ's anguish in the darkness of the Garden of Gethsemane. The weight of the sins of the world is pressing down upon Him. He knows where His path is rapidly leading, and He must decide now whether or not to go through with it amid all of Satan's whispered suggestions. He takes a few more labored steps and then falls to the ground in prayer. Beads of sweat mixed with blood are forming across His forehead, signifying the anguish of soul that is now His. Separation from the Father: never before experienced by this Man who has been one with the Father from eternal ages past. How tempting it would now be to depart from the unappreciative, rebellious planet and return to the Father's side, retaining the throne and authority that are rightfully His. How just it would be to let the guilty race pay the penalty which each has brought upon themselves. To turn back now and let the punishment fall upon mankind would be no miscarriage of justice. It would simply be the fair and deserved consequences, called for by the law of God: "The wages of sin is death" (Rom. 6:23).

The Son pleads with the Father to find *another* way, if it is possible, to save the guilty race. He does not plead that perhaps the fallen world should *perish so that He can avoid* the Cross; His selfless interest in their salvation remains steadfast. But the thought of separation from His eternal Father is horrifying. "If it be possible" to *save the people* He loves so much, in any other way, He asks that such a way be implemented. But no such way is found. The Son of God hears no alternate plan flowing down from the throne in heaven. Only silence greets His prayer. The Word that has already gone forth from the mouth of God does not return to Him void but accomplishes that which He purposes (Isa. 55:11). It cannot be changed; no second option materializes. Sin must bring forth death (James 1:15).

Three times the Savior petitions the Father with the same prayer. Three times He hears no encouraging utterance that the cup of guilt can pass from Him. As you watch the scene, you are fully cognizant that the decision is made for you. If *you* are to be saved, then the

Redeemer must accept the cup and press on toward the penalty. His thoughts are on *you* as He makes up His mind. Although surrounded by billions, you are transfixed by the scene and aware of no one except your Savior, choosing to go forward and pay your price. To your grateful soul, His choice now seems to have been made not for the sake of the multitudes, but rather for you personally. The magnitude of the thought that the King of the universe, the one through whom all things were made, gave Himself for *you*, is overwhelming. And yet the decision has been made. Jesus lifts Himself off the ground, ultimately accepting the fact that there is but one course to follow if you are to be saved. Come what may, and whatever torment is brought to His own soul, you are worth it to Him. His face is set toward the Cross, and there is no turning back now.

In the distance, Judas and the bloodthirsty crowd appear as Jesus rouses His sleeping disciples. He had truly been alone through His agonizing, prayerful ordeal. The comfort of a friend, the joint prayers of His companions, would have lessened the pain and loneliness of His trying hour. But alas, "I have trodden the winepress alone, and of the people there was none with me" (Isa. 63:3).

Upon seeing the approaching mob, several of the disciples brace themselves for the conflict. After the initial flash of glory which surrounds the Savior finally fades, Judas is emboldened to step forward and greet Jesus with a customary kiss. The one who, for more than three years, was in the presence of Love itself, now betrays the Savior for 30 pieces of silver. What depths can the human mind sink to, when continuing down the path of sin!

Recognizing the kiss as their designated sign, the angry horde quickly moves in to bind the hands that had helped and healed so many. With one snap of His fingers, Jesus could, even now, wipe out every man in that throng. He could command angel warriors to instantly destroy the mob (Matt. 26:53). But He knows that everything that happens henceforth is the Father's will, making possible your freedom from the penalty.

Seeing his Master's hands so easily bound, the ever compulsive Peter becomes indignant and draws his sword, lashing out at the high priest's servant and cutting off his ear. Consistent with His character, Jesus calmly releases His tightly bound hands and heals this malicious servant's ear. What must be done, must be done, and resistance is not in the Father's Plan. The Savior then returns His hands to the bewildered throng as Peter and the others flee for their lives, forsaking their Lord, as predicted in Scripture (Zech. 13:7). The crowd once more secures Jesus' hands, and they hurry Him out of the garden like a common criminal.

You watch as Jesus is brought before the various authorities, each sending Him to yet another, none standing up to the injustice of it all. You cringe as you see numerous officers strike the Savior's face with glee and treat Him with contempt. You witness Peter adamantly deny that he ever knew Jesus, and you know that by your own course of action you had done likewise on more than one occasion.

Ultimately Christ is brought for a second time to a Roman Governor named Pilate. Pilate places Jesus and a criminal named Barabbas before an angry crowd, which is then faced with a decision. He asks the Jews to choose which man he should release and which he should therefore condemn. This is, in essence, the same choice you had faced throughout your lifetime. In your daily walk with Christ, decisions arose which ultimately amounted to: Do you choose Jesus or the world? No one can deflect and choose both (Matt. 6:24).

Now the decision of the crowd comes bellowing forth: "Away with this man, and release unto us Barabbas!" And when asked what to do with Jesus? "Crucify Him! Crucify Him!" Angels watch in amazement as the chant ascends to heaven. The One who came to save the world is now being rejected by it. Christ indeed had to die, for this was the Plan of Salvation. He would inevitably be betrayed and sent to His death, for it was written that it would be so; "but woe unto that man by whom the Son of man is betrayed!" (Mark 14:21). The "mystery of iniquity" (2 Thess. 2:7) reached its apex with the irrational decision to reject and destroy the Son of Man. Satan's true character was revealed to the watching universe at that historic moment years ago, and again in this moment as it is replayed in panoramic view for the entire human race to witness.

Although openly finding no fault in Christ, and initially trying to reason with the mob, Pilate ultimately sees that they are militantly determined, so he foolishly attempts to appease them. Here he demonstrates the universal principle that small compromises with sin do not alleviate a problem, but always somehow make things worse. The vacillating politician abandons justice, allowing the innocent Jesus to be chastised for no just reason. Already wearied from a sleepless night, and covered with wounds from spiteful hands, Jesus is taken into "the hall, called Praetorium." The whole band of Roman soldiers then gathers around Him, and you witness these infidels drape Him in a purple robe and twist a jagged crown of thorns together, which they then pound onto His tender head. Thorns, the very symbol of sin itself, placed mockingly upon the head of the sinless One. Again the thought comes to you that with the raising of an eyebrow, Jesus could immediately lay His abusers into the dust. But for you and the prospect of your eternal happiness, the Redeemer does not do this. He accepts their cruel treatment, their violent scourging of His flesh until it is torn and bleeding profusely from the lacerating whip. Your heart aches as you witness Jesus take the continual blows, determined to do whatever it takes to clear the way for your salvation. Now the soldiers begin to bow down sarcastically and salute Him, shouting, "Hail, King of the Jews!"

You then notice, unseen by His tormentors, several angels of God, faithfully recording every word and deed. Little do these mockers realize that "God shall bring every work into judgment, with every secret thing, whether it be good, or whether it be evil," and "every idle word that men shall speak, they shall give account thereof in the day of judgment" (Eccles. 12:14; Matt. 12:36).

Pilate now makes one, final attempt to set Jesus free and has Christ brought forward, bleeding and wearing the robe and crown of thorns. Hoping that this humiliating scene will soften the hearts of the crowd, too late he discovers that his unjust compromise has only emboldened the frenzied mob. They realize that this leader will cave if pushed hard enough and push hard they do until Pilate ultimately grants their fiendish wish.

The scene changes and now the dreadful sentence begins, much to the delight of the crowd: the Savior will finally be crucified. You watch as the cross, which had been prepared for Barabbas, is thrown upon His bruised and bleeding shoulders and He is made to carry the burden. The penalty that should be yours is borne instead by your worthy Substitute. He marches forward, already badly wounded for your transgressions and bruised for your iniquities. He is determined that the Father should now lay on Him all of your iniquity, all of your sin, and let the full force of the sentence fall squarely upon Him. Let Him be brought, in your place, as a Lamb to the slaughter.

But now the Savior's humanity, exhausted from severe water, food and sleep deprivation, and debilitated by the cruel scourging, falls beneath the weight of the cross. Providentially, among the crowd is a strong man named Simon, who is compelled to go and support the cross to its dark destiny. Others in the crowd - particularly a group of women - now begin to weep for Jesus. He turns and consoles them, even as His death sentence is being carried out. He is constantly thinking of others, even in the most brutal circumstances.

Finally, the mob reaches a hill called Calvary. You watch as the cross is laid on the hard ground and Jesus is roughly stretched out on top of it. His thoughts are on you. You realize that the prospect of your eternal salvation through what He is now enduring is what keeps Him going. It was "for the joy that was set before him" of seeing you in His Kingdom, that He "endured the cross" (Heb. 12:2).

Large, cruel nails are brought forth and are driven through the willing hands of Jesus. "Behold, I have graven thee upon the palms of my hands" (Isa. 49:16). As the nails pierce His skin and the blood begins to flow, you are engraved there. You are worth *everything* to Him, and forever the scars on those hands testify to this fact. Next, His feet are pierced and the magnitude of this moment with its eternal consequences washes over you. You now witness Jesus being lifted up, the cross slamming roughly into its channel as His pain intensifies.

"And I, if I be lifted up from the earth, will draw all men unto me" (John 12:32).

This prophecy is now fulfilled in your sight as all men, all human beings, are drawn to the scene, captivated by the enormity of just how costly that Sacrifice was. This "drawing" had already been working on the hearts of all, by the Holy Spirit, throughout their lives. Both the saved and the lost fully realize that nothing more could have been done to save them.

For hours He lingers on the Cross. The crowd's mockery continues, with the lone voice of a crucified thief expressing faith during those final hours (Luke 23:42). Satan himself is there, pressing his sophistries upon the dying Savior's wearied mind. Here is temptation in the highest degree. If the deceiver can win here, the battle is over. The sun itself is stricken as its Creator's life is being drained, and darkness covers the cross for the space of about three hours. The awful separation is taking place. The separation that the impenitent sinner must face is transpiring in the soul of the Redeemer. This brings about a change in

Him that He has never experienced. You know this because He cries out with a loud voice, "My God, My God, why hast Thou forsaken Me?" You are cognizant of the fact that Christ cannot now see through the portals of the tomb. He fears that the sin which He is now taking upon Himself is so offensive to the Father that the separation must be eternal. And yet He still remains true to His beloved cause. This is the course He is to follow, and although He *feels* forsaken, He trusts in the Father's Plan. He fully believes that His death will ultimately result in your redemption. And He knows that to escape now would most assuredly cost you your salvation. Thus, He endures the Cross. In full view is His love for you.

As Jesus revives to a sense of physical suffering, He quietly says, "I thirst." His thirst is met with the prophetic sponge of vinegar, but even this act of sympathy angers the crowd. They had misinterpreted Christ's words "Eloi, Eloi, lama sabachthani" as a desperate cry for the prophet Elijah. Now they angrily declare with one voice, "Let be, let us see whether Elijah will come to save him!" These pitiless, mocking words are the last ones Jesus hears before His life comes to an end.

Beneath the great panoramic display, the great multitude inside the New Jerusalem and the countless millions outside its walls all stand silently transfixed as the closing moments of the Savior's life pass before them. You now hear the three words that mean eternal victory to your soul. Jesus lifts His wounded, bleeding head toward the sky and declares in the voice of a Conqueror, "It is finished!" The words roll across the earth like peals of loudest thunder. And then He adds, "Father, into Thy hands I commend My spirit!" Completing the work the Father gave Him to do, He bows His head upon His breast, breathes His last, and dies.

Satan is finally unmasked for who he really is: "the father of lies." All see the true character of the enemy of souls in contrast to the perfect love of Christ. Truth is driven home to the conscience of every witness - the same truth that the Holy Spirit had been trying to impress upon humanity since the fall of Adam and Eve.

Although enraged with the outcome, and by no means in love with Jesus, the lost now join the saved in fulfilling a prophecy of God.

"That at the name of Jesus every knee should bow, of things in heaven, and things in earth, and things under the earth; and that every tongue should confess that Jesus Christ is Lord, to the glory of God the Father" (Phil. 2:10-11).

The great multitude of the redeemed bow first, joined by the countless holy angels within the city. Next, the vast sea of the wicked outside the walls, history's largest army and rejectors of God's persistent mercy, bend the knee. The fallen angels quickly follow suit in acknowledging the justice and fairness of Jesus. And finally Satan himself - the father of rebellion, the accuser of the brethren and the enemy of souls - marches down to the gate of the Holy City, gets down on his knees, and declares that Jesus Christ is indeed Lord. In unison with the saved, the wicked declare a phrase so often repeated within the Holy City: "Just and true are thy ways, thou King of saints" (Rev. 15:3). The truth has finally triumphed. The power of the Cross has been plainly revealed. Your best Friend Jesus sits on the throne of the Universe, acknowledged as "just and true" by all.

"That thou mightest be justified when thou speakest, and be clear when thou judgest" (Ps. 51:4).

Christ is indeed justified and cleared in the judgment of the wicked. The Cross demonstrates that there is nothing more He could have done. The eternal loss of the wicked was brought on by themselves in the face of overwhelming evidence of God's love. Each has seen just where their path diverted from the plan that God had laid out for them and where they rejected the promptings of the Holy Spirit

(Eccl. 12:14; Matt. 12:36; 2 Cor. 5:10; Rev. 20:12). Their hardened, rationalizing hearts would find no joy in the peaceful New Jerusalem or the New Earth, where submission to God, obedience to His will, and service to others bring the utmost joy and pleasure. The words of truth that just came from their own lips find no appreciative chord within their hearts. While they acknowledged the overwhelming *evidence* of truth, they know not the Savior and author of truth. And they certainly do not love Him. In the end, God gives every human who has ever lived exactly what they want: either eternal companionship with Him or eternal separation from Him. All either opt into the Kingdom of peace, joy, and service or they opt out of it, returning once again to the state of non-existence they had before they were conceived. Each has made their choice.

The fulfillment of this prophecy is followed by a brief stillness, which covers the planet. For the first time in history, every soul in the universe is thinking the same thing: God's ways are just. He always did have His children's best interest in mind with every instruction He ever gave. His government, His Kingdom, is based on love. Satan's lies are forever exposed, and sin will never raise its ugly head again. Their final acknowledgment of the truth is the last act of the wicked before they angrily surround the city and are consumed by the fire. Sin and its adherents are about to be no more. The entire universe will once again be clean. From then on, the prophecy of the Redeemer's exaltation will be fulfilled, not by lips compelled to speak the truth, but rather by those who *love* the truth and speak from the heart. For all eternity they will have the opportunity to praise, adore and thank Him for all that He did on the Cross. They will sing with boundless love and gratitude, "Worthy is the Lamb that was slain!"

Thought Questions:

1. What is your main takeaway from this chapter? Why is it your main takeaway?

2. What does the Cross mean to you? Why did Jesus have to die? What did His resurrection do for you? Why will the Cross be our science and our song throughout eternity? Why won't we simply learn it all and be done with it?

3. God didn't change His law to meet the emergency of humans sinning. What does this tell you about His character? Jesus took your penalty and paid your price, so you can live. What does this tell you about His character?

4. What does the world's most famous Bible text, John 3:16, mean to you and what does it tell you about God's promises? And what does it mean to fully "believe in Him," in the deepest spiritual sense?

5. What did you learn about God's will for you in this chapter? What do you feel He's impressing you to start doing differently this week to walk more closely with Him?

BEFORE THE JOURNEY

*"But ye, brethren, are not in darkness, that that day
should overtake you as a thief. Ye are all the children
of light, and the children of the day: we are not of the
night nor of darkness. Therefore let us not sleep, as do
others; but let us watch and be sober."*

-1 Thessalonians 5:4-6

*"It is time for thee, Lord, to work: for they have made
void thy law."*

-Psalm 119:126

THIS BOOK HAS been filled with themes of brightness and light
and joy. Even the cover is bright. But the Bible says that before
the eternal brightness in the land of beginning again, a deep darkness
is coming to our world. This has happened at least three times before.
The flood, the days just before Christ, and the "dark ages."

HEARTS FAILING FOR FEAR OF WHAT'S COMING

The Bible describes a time of darkness where things are not business as usual. The things we have relied upon and assume will continue like always, they change. The change is so drastic that all around us will be "Men's hearts failing them for fear, and for looking after those things which are coming on the earth" (Luke 21:26). In other words, worse than you can imagine. It is a time when you cannot rely on the knowledge of others or the relationship that others have with Christ. A time when "they shall wander from sea to sea, and from the north even to the east, they shall run to and fro to seek the word of the Lord, and shall not find it" (Amos 8:12). The parable of the 10 virgins describes this scenario in another way, where five were prepared for the bridegroom to appear (they had their oil) and five were not prepared (they had neglected to get their oil). When the bridegroom (Christ) appeared, it was too late to go and get the oil they needed to be prepared beforehand (Matt. 5:1-13). The oil represents the Holy Spirit (Isa. 61:1; Luke 4:18; Acts 10:38). Is the Holy Spirit living in your life, or have you substituted a *knowledge* of truth for *experiencing* it?

As we look at the world around us, there can be no doubt that we are living in the last days. More and more people are wondering where society is headed as it seems to break down before our eyes. Children are now taking the lives of other children in school shootings. Crime, in general, is on the rise. Natural disasters are intensifying around the globe. An increasing number of nations are acquiring nuclear capabilities. Despite what the politicians promise, we know that things are only going to get worse. In fact, it is only by the grace of God Himself that the human race even still exists. Long ago we would have extinguished ourselves had He not mercifully held back the process of self-destruction.

Nevertheless, the woes of our world continue to increase, and as a result, more and more people are starting to turn to the Word of God for answers. They remember hearing about strange disasters predicted in the book of Revelation. Their minds recall bits and pieces of sermons they heard as they flipped the channels on various Sunday mornings. They wonder, *Is there any truth to these things?* Whether longtime Christian or self-proclaimed atheist, many are beginning to take a second look - a *deeper* look, at Bible prophecy.

Perhaps you are one who has studied prophecy and feel quite secure about the order of predicted events. Maybe your pastor has done a Revelation seminar, and you know all about who the Beast of Revelation 13 is, and can accurately identify the Mark of the Beast. Whether you feel knowledgeable in this area or not, it would do us well to review some things that Scripture has been telling us for thousands of years - things that are soon to take place, probably in this generation.

The Bible offers a blessing for those who actually spend time studying the prophecies of Revelation. "Blessed is he that readeth, and they that hear the words of this prophecy, and keep those things which are written therein: for the time is at hand" (Rev. 1:3). And notice it said the blessing was not just for those who read the words of the prophecies, but who keep them as well.

Maybe you have told yourself, "When I begin to see these things happen, *then* I'll give my heart fully to the Lord." Sound familiar? This is just self-deception. The Bible says: "**Today** if ye will hear his voice, harden not your hearts" (Heb. 3:15). Do you hear His voice today? Then what should you do? Or in this case, *not* do.

We won't go into detail about the specifics of the Beast power, and if you are one who has no idea about such things, then I recommend the Bible studies at the back of this book. In my forthcoming prequel to this book, *Before the Reaping*, I'll be covering these subjects in detail. In the meantime, let's just look at a few simple facts.

The book of Revelation tells us that a Beast power will deceive the people and cause them to make an "image to the beast" (Rev. 13:14-15). Deep inside, we all know that this is not talking about a giant statue in some metropolis of the world which we will all be forced to go and worship. Many Christian prophecy books are filled with James Bond-type scenarios of a coming great villain who will have a giant tattoo machine, which he uses to imprint a conspicuous "666" on the foreheads of nearly eight billion of us. But God says, "Come now, and let us **reason** together" (Isa. 1:18). God has given us enough common sense to know that these sensational speculations are as misguided as the Pharisees' views of the Messiah's role in the first Advent (and their errors led them to crucify Him).

God calls on us in these last days to lay aside all the ideas and predictions of man and turn to His Word as the only true and safe guide. "The grass withereth, the flower fadeth: but the word of our God shall stand forever" (Isa. 40:8).

If we really want to know what's going to happen before Jesus returns, and how we can be ready, we need to take a look at the end of the world, as described by His prophets. Remember, God has promised us, "Surely the Lord God will do nothing, but he revealeth his secrets unto his servants the prophets" (Amos 3:7).

The prophet Isaiah describes the end of this world in detail.

Imagine this scene, which I believe is going to happen soon:

WHAT WILL HAPPEN?

"Behold, the Lord maketh the earth empty, and maketh it waste, and turneth it upside down, and scattereth abroad the inhabitants thereof...The land shall be utterly emptied, and utterly spoiled: for the Lord hath spoken this word. The earth mourneth and fadeth away, the world languisheth and fadeth away, the haughty people of the earth do languish. The earth also is defiled under the inhabitants thereof..."

WHY WILL IT HAPPEN?

"because they have **transgressed** the **laws, changed** the **ordinance, broken** the everlasting **covenant."**

THEREFORE, WHAT?

"Therefore hath the curse devoured the earth, and they that dwell therein are desolate: **therefore** the inhabitants of the earth are burned, and few men left" (Isa. 24:1,3-6, emphasis supplied).

We are saved by grace; this is Christianity 101. We can't add any merit to what Jesus did for us with His blood. But the Bible makes it too clear to miss, that when human beings, in their finite wisdom, attempt to change God's holy law, they are bringing down the curse of God upon themselves. Note, again, the three **reasons** God gives for the final destruction of the earth. The inhabitants have:

1. **"Transgressed the laws."** Do people today transgress God's laws? More so than ever before. Just look around our world and see the stealing, killing, immorality, sacrilege, adultery, and every other sin condemned by God's laws being committed on a wholesale level. Look no further than the Internet,

and the easy access children are given to that doorway to everything. In the Sermon on the Mount, Jesus made it clear that we sin in our minds long before we actually commit the act (see Matt. 5). Pride, self-righteousness, lust, unbelief, impatience, hate, and selfishness in all its forms are still sin, although they don't appear on the evening news. "The Lord looketh on the heart" (1 Sam. 16:7). Even if we break just one of His Commandments, we have, in essence, broken them all (James 2:10).

2. **"Changed the ordinance**." Have humans today tried to change an ordinance of God? Most definitely. This was happening even in Christ's day. He said to the Pharisees, who claimed to be promoting and keeping God's laws, "Thus have ye made the **commandment of God** of none effect **by your tradition**." He also made it clear that they were "teaching for doctrines the **commandments of men**" (Matt. 15:6,9).

This same problem that Christ pointed out, Isaiah said would be taking place just before the end of the world. Have the traditions of this world caused you to forget or neglect God's laws, which He wrote with His own finger, and specifically told us to "Remember" (Ex. 31:18; 20:8)? Traditions are fine as long as they don't replace the Word and will of God. This attempt to alter the Ten Commandments is what we should watch for in these last days.

3. **"Broken the everlasting covenant**." What *is* the everlasting covenant? Let's let the Bible interpret itself.

An angel in Revelation 14 is portrayed proclaiming the "everlasting gospel" to "every nation, and kindred, and tongue, and people" that "dwell on the earth" (Rev. 14:6). The angel that follows proclaims the fall of "Babylon," and the third angel warns the earth of the Beast, his image, and his mark (verses 8-10). So we see that the everlasting gospel (which is really God's covenant with those who have faith in Him) is tied inseparably to this proclamation that *Babylon is fallen* and these warnings about the Beast and his mark. Don't miss that point. Looking at verse 12, we see a picture of those who do not receive this "mark" of the Beast: "Here is the patience of the saints: here are they that **keep the commandments of God**, and the **faith of Jesus.**"

As we take the words of Isaiah's vision of the end and place them beside these final three messages that God is sending to the world, it becomes very clear that the coming Beast power will have only one goal in mind: to somehow make human traditions alter the law of God. This is going on right now all around us, but when pressure comes to enforce these traditions upon people, then we can know that Isaiah 24 is starting to unfold.

WHAT IS THE NEW COVENANT?

Remember, God showed Isaiah that the specific *reason* the earth will be made desolate is *because* the "everlasting covenant" would be broken by humans. The best definition of that covenant will not be found in most "Armageddon" and "Antichrist" books that are circulating today. It is found in the New Testament:

"This is the **covenant** that I will make with them after those days, saith the Lord, **I will put my laws into their hearts, and in their minds will I write them**" (Heb. 10:16).

Reader, please do not allow yourself to be "tossed to and fro, and carried about with every wind of doctrine" (Eph. 4:14). Don't look for a mystery man to arise in the Middle East and take over the world with his tattoo machine. Don't wait for a global attempt to implant a microchip into an unwary population. Don't speculate about the power of some vague supercomputer in Europe that will supposedly enforce the Mark of the Beast. No, look inside your own heart and ask Christ to take control of it. Ask Him to clean out any of the things inside that are not in harmony with His will. Allow Him to write that everlasting covenant within your heart and mind - to put His perfect law there - and you will be safe from the storm that is coming to our world. Ask yourself this, and be honest with yourself: *Is there **anything** that I am doing - even in my spiritual walk with God - that conflicts with His Commandments, and that can be supported by nothing more than the "traditions of men"?* Examine the Ten Commandments prayerfully. Read them through very carefully. The Holy Spirit will guide you as you seek to know His will, for we have been promised that He will lead us "into all truth" (John 16:13).

Before the journey to heaven in that great, fiery cloud, a final test comes to all on planet earth. A global test came in Noah's day. A test came to Shadrach, Meshach, and Abednego; to Job, to Daniel, to Esther and to Abraham. And the Bible says a final test comes to you and me. It tells us that the world will one day focus on issues that will pit man's traditions against the Commandments of God. May God help us to be prepared by knowing both Him and His Word. The following scenario gives a brief glimpse into issues that the Bible says will one day be front and center.

▲ ▲ ▲

You have studied God's unchanging Word, and you know all about last day events. Long have you waited for the fulfillment of these prophecies, for you know that when these things take place, the end "is near, even at the doors" (Matt. 24:33).

You see increasing trouble coming upon the world in crime, pollution, natural disasters, wars, and rumors of wars. The world's attention seems to be focused more and more on finding a solution to the problem. Many who recognize the problem as a *moral* one, mistakenly propose a *legal* solution. Instead of calling on a confused and dying world to turn to God and ask Him for a new heart (Ezek. 36:26), the religious leaders work to influence the government and its laws. The growing number of crises have bound the world into a tighter and tighter snare of apparent helplessness, and those in authority seem to be increasingly willing to resort to drastic measures.

You have seen the civil rights of the people rapidly decrease, and yet, like the Pharisees against Christ, persecution has been promoted in the name of religion. *The end*, it has been reported, *will surely justify the means, for we as a nation must get back to God and regain His favor.* Just as Jesus predicted, they blindly think that they're doing God a favor (John 16:2) as they oppress those who do not see things their way.

This erroneous view of God reaches its climax in the enforcement of laws which dictate the observance of Christian traditions - traditions which cannot be found in the Word of God, but which, as in the days of the Pharisees, have supplanted God's Word. You know that even if these new laws *were* in harmony with Bible standards, the very fact that they are being *forced* on people is contrary to God's principles of free will. You've spent time with Him daily in prayer and Bible study, and you have grown to know Him as a God who wants our service and obedience to be a response of love, not just fear of retribution.

Your favorite news anchor announces that according to expert sources, these new laws will be difficult to enforce and that they really are just a symbolic gesture, sure to be left as a technicality on the law books. But you know better. The Bible has told you where this is headed.

You are amazed at the lack of concern by your fellow believers. Many of them have also known about these events in prophecy, and in fact, have proclaimed them to the world. But for some reason, they have not remained true to the message, and now they brush this news report off as "no big deal." Some of them even support the new measure. You remember the words of Christ that "brother shall deliver up the brother to death, and the father the child: and the children shall rise up against their parents, and cause them to be put to death. And ye shall be hated of all men for my name's sake: but he that endureth to the end shall be saved" (Matt. 10:21-22).

And what brought all of this about? You get out your Bible again and re-read Isaiah 24, Exodus 20, Revelation 13 & 14, and many of the other passages that you've learned. A decision *must* be made. Will you go along with these new laws, or will you stand upon the Word of God? No thoughts of open rebellion come to mind, no plans for stockpiling weapons. These are the tactics of the fearful, and you have implicit faith in the protective power of your Father alone. You have no fear of this world, because "love casteth out fear" (1 John 4:18). Your love for and friendship with God, along with submission to His will, have cast out all fear of anything that can come to you now. Like the three Hebrews facing the fiery furnace, you don't concern yourself so much with your own well-being as with the glorification of your heavenly Father, and the holiness of His will.

A peace that passes all understanding fills your soul as you stand by your daily commitment to put God above everything else. Come what may, and with no retaliation on your part, you rest assured in the providence of your Father. Like Daniel asleep in the lions' den, you have committed your soul into the hands of your Lord. You trust that where to go and what to do will be made plain to you as He sees fit. In prayer, you thank God for the lifesaving truths that have been revealed in His Word. And you know that the only reason you can make this decision to put His will first is because of the strength that He supplies. Had you put off your relationship with Him, this moment would have had a vastly different outcome. Your actions would then be prompted by fear and self-preservation instead of love and trust in God. Thankfully, graciously, the Lord has exercised your faith daily for quite some time now, so that it would be prepared for this final conflict.

An emotional tug of war takes place within you. Your heart is heavy with sorrow for those who have chosen blindness and the traditions of men over God's Word. At the same time, you have peace from the throne of God, and excitement and joy because the end is indeed near. The moment for which you have so long waited is about to take place. Soon you will see Jesus face-to-face and share in His fellowship forever. Soon you will declare with the great multitude of the redeemed those words so long anticipated:

"Lo, this is our God; we have waited for him; and he will save us: this is the Lord; we have waited for him, we will be glad and rejoice in his salvation!" (Isa. 25:9).

Thought Questions:

1. What is your main takeaway from this chapter? Why is it your main takeaway?

2. What is the "new covenant" that God said He would write in our hearts and minds? What are the three reasons and predictions God gives in Isaiah 24:1-6 for destroying the

earth someday? Do you see any ordinance or law of God that humans have tried to change since God wrote them? Why are we safer letting the Bible interpret itself than guessing about what the Mark of the Beast is?

3. What do God's specific teachings, instructions, warnings and predictions in the Bible about final events - and the fact that He does nothing unless He reveals it to us through His prophets - tell you about His character?

4. What do Christ's seven messages in Revelation to those "that overcometh" tell us about His promises? (Rev. 2:7,11,17,26; 3:5,12,21) (see 1 John 5:4-5 and Rev. 21:7 for more insight on this word).

5. What did you learn about God's will for you in this chapter? What do you feel He's impressing you to start doing differently this week to walk more closely with Him?

PLEASURES
FOREVERMORE

"I am come that they might have life, and that they might have it more abundantly."

-JOHN 10:10

"Thou wilt shew me the path of life: in thy presence is fulness of joy; at thy right hand there are pleasures for evermore."

-PSALM 16:11

WHAT DO YOU love to do? I mean really love to do? The original version of this book was read by a broad spectrum of people, so I know that this question will garner a wide range of answers.

Just take a moment and think about the things that really make you happy. There are no right or wrong answers because this is just for you. Perhaps you're reading this book on the beach right now. Is vacationing your passion? Is it reading? Is it movies? Sports? Decorating? Gaming? Shopping? Hanging out with friends? Perhaps partying with friends? Imagine if you won the lottery. What passions would you pursue with virtually unlimited resources at your disposal? Often when we think about heaven and the prospect of living there someday, we contrast it with the things of this world that so easily attract our attention right now. Too quickly we conclude from that snap comparison that the things of this world are much more appealing. They can *really* make us happy. Heaven is just an afterthought.

We mentioned some common things that people pursue, but what about those enticing things that you perhaps keep to yourself but continue to do because they're so addicting. How does heaven compare to these temptations? What alternatives does it offer? The answer will surprise you.

Some people, when discussing a fictitious world overflowing with their favorite vice, declare with a bit of a chuckle "Now *that* would be heaven!" But would it really?

I like how C.S. Lewis described such a common mindset: He summed it up in six simple words:

"WE ARE FAR TOO EASILY PLEASED."

Lewis paints a scenario that describes our situation perfectly:

> "It would seem that Our Lord finds our desires not too strong, but too weak. We are half-hearted creatures, fooling about with drink and sex and ambition when infinite joy is offered us, like an ignorant child who wants to go on making mud pies in a slum because he cannot imagine what is meant by

the offer of a holiday at the sea. We are far too easily pleased."
- C.S. Lewis, The Weight of Glory, and Other Addresses

What are *your* mud pies? Are you far too easily pleased, settling for substitutes, rather than experiencing the real deal? The grand irony is that we pursue happiness in place of God when God is the inventor and the source of all real happiness (Eccles. 2:26). The One we often view as a hindrance to our happiness is, in reality, the only pathway to it. Jonathan Edwards said, "The enjoyment of God is the only happiness with which our souls can be satisfied." He also said everything that brings us happiness here is but a shadow and God is the substance; these are but scattered beams, and God is the sun. Everything you know about pleasure came from something God invented and placed within you.

GOD INVENTED HAPPINESS

Consider for a moment the fact that neither humans nor demons ever truly created any pleasure. The receptors in your brain and body were placed there by God alone. Every addiction and vice stems from something good that was given as a blessing which we perverted and pushed too far or manipulated in an unhealthy way.

It was the Catholic author Bruce Marshall who penned the now-famous quote "The young man who rings the bell at the brothel is unconsciously looking for God." Why? Because pleasure was invented by God. Pain, suffering, jealousy, self-loathing, discontent, emptiness, these are the devil's contributions to the human condition. Like the young man ringing the bell, every soul has a God-given desire for pleasure, including our longing for intimacy. In the Garden of Eden, the Lord declared a truth that now seems obvious: "It is not good" for us to be alone (Gen. 2:18). We desire human companionship. God implanted this holy desire within us. And part of that companionship usually leads to fulfilling what has been called the most obeyed commandment of all time: to "be fruitful and multiply," and fill the earth (Gen. 1:28).

In His wisdom and love, God set parameters for this edict and designed that it should occur within a special bond between husband and wife. It is an attempt to find happiness outside of this bond, pushing past any boundaries, that has led to so much misery, jealousy, and suffering in today's relationships.

And what of music? We looked at music in chapter 18 "Heavenly Music." Music was invented by God. But in the hands of one who assaults the sense of hearing, tapping into emotion, bypassing the sense of reason, and adding lyrics that convey messages of self-absorption or denigration of others, everything changes. Music then becomes another example of how a good thing, without boundaries, can be turned into something harmful.

Even pride, one of the most grievous sins there is, stems from our desire to have value, to know that we matter, to be loved. Yet pushed beyond the God-given framework, this desire soon becomes our driving force and causes us to seek praise and attention, sometimes even by putting others down. It makes us the center of our own world. This was the one that caused Lucifer to fall.

Drug and alcohol abuse and addiction – these, too are merely perversions of something God placed within us. Your remarkable brain is already loaded with natural drugs called neurotransmitters. Dopamine is considered the pleasure drug and serotonin is the "sense of well-being" drug, just to name two. The levels of these drugs and others are normally kept in balance to maintain your best possible state of mind. But manipulate these levels, via caffeine, alcohol, or more serious prescription or illegal drugs and you again break through the healthy guidelines, desiring no limits. The initial stimulation might be what you start to crave or even feel you need, but the body quickly works to bring the neurotransmitter levels back to normal ("homeostasis"); thus, the famous hangover after a night of drinking or the afternoon crash after tanking up on too much morning coffee. It becomes a cycle that millions desire to break, but it is often not so easily done. Meanwhile, the health continues to suffer.

The world is finally catching on to God's natural ways. A health emphasis, once relegated to "fitness freaks," "hippies," and "new-agers" is now given far more credence, even by corporate America. I've noticed the trend, that more and more material on leadership and good decision-making is emphasizing the importance of physical and mental health. Invariably the research points corporate leaders to a natural, healthy lifestyle, more in line with what God set up in the Garden of Eden (although this correlation is never mentioned).

God desires that we both prosper *and* be in good health (3 John 1:2). The mind and the body affect one another, and when we abuse one, we abuse the other. Overtax your brain long enough with harmful stimulants and drugs, and eventually, it will catch up with you. It affects everything you do.

Again, pleasure was invented by God. He just as easily could have designed us to function like plants, where we simply get our nutrition from the soil or maybe from tasteless pellets that are a chore to get down. But instead, He invented taste buds, making eating a pleasure. He made music pleasurable, relationships pleasurable, beauty pleasurable, intimacy pleasurable - an endless variety of things pleasurable. And of course, where there is pleasure, there are emotions.

We mentioned in a previous chapter that emotions are like fire: they make a wonderful servant, but a horrible master. Maintain the fire as it serves you, warming your house, cooking your food or lighting your path, and things are terrific. But let that same fire begin to creep up your living room curtains, and the servant transforms into your worst nightmare of a master, threatening you with destruction.

Too often we allow our emotions to be our master, whether pleasure, fear or places in between and they affect our decision-making. God designed you so that pleasure would be the natural *result* of a choice to obey His principles, not the driving force *behind* our choices.

Now consider the handful of pleasure sensors that you have and then contemplate the fact that God has unlimited resources. He could have given you twice as many or ten times as many senses and pleasure receptors as He did. Can you even begin to imagine what is waiting for you in heaven?

THE FOUNDATION UPON WHICH
PLEASURE IS BUILT

But all pleasure, all real joy, real happiness, real fulfillment, must be built upon a foundation of peace. Without peace, every emotion we seek is merely masking its absence. Without peace, we seek stimulation as a distraction. Instead, start with peace and your sense of well-being becomes more consistent, and every pleasure is magnified.

It is no accident that Jesus is described as the Prince of Peace (Isa. 9:6). No accident that He promises to give us a peace that is unlike what the world tries to give us through the masking attempts we have adopted (John 14:27). No accident that His peace, upon which every other positive emotion is built, is described as the one that passes all understanding (Phil. 4:7). It cannot be described; it must be experienced.

Without Christ, there is no real peace. He invented it, as well. Any peace without Him is the peace "as the world giveth," which is entirely different. It is temporary, constantly requiring more and more from us and never truly satisfying us. It is forsaking the fountain of living water and making our own cisterns that hold no water (Jer. 2:13).

The great truth about pleasure and the abundant supply of it in heaven is that it requires us to get our priorities straight, and as we get to know God, this will happen. These priorities are best summed up in Psalm 37:4: "Delight thyself also in the Lord, and He shall give thee the desires of thine heart." There is the secret to unlimited pleasure. When we delight ourselves in God, then we are safe to receive the endless pleasures that He has waiting for us in heaven. They will no longer be a snare to us, distracting us from God, because we have experienced the fact that He is the highest pleasure of all. Until then, "the desires of thine heart," can often become a snare. This is the secret to the entire Kingdom's success. It is why sin will not rise up the second time. Not only can God be fully trusted to run things, but there is nothing He can create that would ever be more desirable than He is. This is also why the devil creates lies about what heaven will be like; so that we'll never desire it *or* God.

There are two great misconceptions about heaven. On the one hand, there's the idea that its source of joy will be the mansions, the beautiful city, the lion rides, material possessions, and other such things. On the other hand, is the notion, discussed at the beginning of the book, that it will be a boring place, void of all of the "fun" things in life. Those who think of heaven strictly in terms of gold and mansions need to spend more time getting to know God. Those who feel it will be boring need to do their research. The Bible promises that our future home will be a land so full of joy and adventure that it will bring us "pleasures forevermore" (Ps. 16:11).

Our finite minds can't even begin to grasp the countless blessings that await our discovery. What will that first trip from earth to heaven really be like? Will we go directly there, or will we stop and visit distant galaxies along the way? What about the fact that Jesus said He would grant the overcomers to actually sit with Him on His throne (Rev. 3:21)? Have you ever really thought about that promise? Sitting with the Creator and King of the universe on His throne? We certainly don't deserve it, but it is a promise. And He wants His reason to be apparent, that's why He says it in so many ways in Scripture: He wants you to be near Him (John 14:3). He loves you.

Will any new life forms be created after we get to heaven, and if so, imagine the stories you and I can share with them about our experiences in this one dark world. These new beings (should God choose to create them) will have never witnessed the great rebellion, which started eons ago in the heart of a mighty angel: a rebellion in which we have all shared a part. Imagine explaining to them that you were once on the side of that Prince of Darkness but were saved and re-created by the Prince of Peace.

Jesus promises to give every one of the redeemed a "white stone" inscribed with their new name (Rev. 2:17). What do you suppose that white stone looks like? And what is its purpose? We aren't even given enough clues to speculate. What new name has Christ chosen for you? This will be the name of the "real you," that you'll finally become. That V8 "you" that is at your best, as opposed to the 4-cylinder you that is hindered by sin. Jesus also promised to give a "crown of life" to those who "love Him," and are "faithful unto death" (James 1:12; Rev. 2:10; see also 1 Cor. 9:25; 2 Tim. 4:8; 1 Pet. 5:4). In the presence of the King of kings, however, the redeemed will no doubt cast them at the foot of His throne as did the "24 elders" in John's vision (Rev. 4:10). And the song that only the 144,000 can learn (Rev. 14:3), what will it be like to sing that special song? So many things to contemplate. So many things to look forward to.

Physical activity and stimulation will be a constant blessing to the redeemed. The tending of the land will forever provide peaceful contentment and joy. The projects undertaken will exercise and strengthen every physical and mental faculty. Architectural endeavors planned and completed under the blessing of the Creator will perpetually provide new and exciting challenges.

Perhaps you're a thrill seeker who'll try anything. You've never known thrills until you have scaled the peaks of distant worlds that dwarf a thousand Jupiters or plunged down blue sky rivers which cascade from cloud to cloud. You've lived a sheltered life until you've navigated caves which trail to the very core of a world or perched atop a distant sun after riding the crest of a solar flare.

In addition to all of the physical activities, there will be an endless number of studies to engage the mental powers. The human mind was created to derive pleasure from learning and discovering new things. This is why humans invent things. It's why we're fascinated by the latest technological advances. It's why we like watching the national news or researching news on the Internet, and why we love to travel. We are an inquisitive people: constantly seeking, constantly discovering. There's just something about the quest for knowledge, even if only for curiosity's sake, that intrigues the human soul. The innovative projects undertaken, individually and in groups, will create new and exciting challenges to surmount.

Endless are the interests which can be pursued in the world to come. Is music your passion? We haven't even begun to understand all of the facets of this wonderful gift or the intimate ways it affects the human soul. Perhaps astronomy is your thing. The wonders of the universe stretch out eternally before you, awaiting your study. Are cosmic black holes actually what we think they are, and if so, what's it like to explore one? A recent set of pictures from the Hubble telescope revealed, among other things, a vast, cloud-like pillar in space which measured *around 1 trillion miles* from top to bottom. Our entire earth would be just a speck by comparison. The boundless expanse of the universe contains endless secrets for your continual discovery.

Maybe you're enthralled by nature. Even in this old world, there are creatures in the deepest parts of the ocean that have rarely, if ever, been seen by humans. New species are still being discovered on sea and land. In the new earth, what else will we uncover? Firsthand, you'll be able to observe and explore every intricate detail and function of plant and animal life, with the Creator Himself sharing fascinating insights. And what about the molecular elements? Consider all of the incredible advances that have already been made through molecular engineering. One look at the science that was behind the atom bomb and you realize that there are secrets still awaiting us, the discovery of which can unleash a torrent of new energy and power. What other forces are lying dormant out there, just waiting to be tapped? Oppenheimer barely scratched the surface.

THE GREATEST STUDY AND HIGHEST PLEASURE

And yet in spite of how satisfying and enlightening these studies will be in themselves, all sciences will ultimately point the student to the love and power of God. The Creator's name is written upon every tree and flower, upon the lofty mountain and the humble insect, upon the largest planet and tiniest atom. His signature of wisdom can be found on everything which came forth from His hand. As His creative authorship is thus revealed, it will magnify His power to re-create as well. And nowhere was that power more clearly revealed than at Calvary. There mankind, by beholding such selfless love, might be changed into the same image. The science of all sciences is and ever will be the Cross. The Sacrifice on Calvary will be the study that brings forth our deepest fulfillment and highest praise. It is the highest level of knowledge ever to be attained. And yet eternity itself is not long enough to unlock all of its mysteries. As we investigate this glorious truth, we will see that our redemption involved far more than we understood on the surface.

Many Christians today feel that once they've read the crucifixion account in the Bible, they've learned pretty much all there is to know about redemption. They approach it much the same way that a student might read about the death of Abraham Lincoln – just a linear set of facts. They assume that there are no more treasures to be gleaned from the mystery of such infinite condescension on our behalf. But some diligent souls even today have grasped the fact that Calvary continually presents new truths - indeed new layers of truth - to those who are willing to search. How much more will be uncovered by minds changed to perfection at the Second Coming of Christ and continually growing in wisdom?

As the years roll by, your greatest pastime will be hearing of this redemptive love from Jesus Himself. Learning more about the great controversy between Christ and Satan, which brought about the perfect Plan to save your soul, will evoke an overwhelming desire to simply abide in His company. As you thus spend time in His presence, you will discover that it provides the greatest joy in the universe. So it can be today. Our quiet time with Him now can become the best time of the day. Our highest joy can be found in loving Him. We can get to the place where we no longer rush through our personal devotion time, but instead *commune* with Him as our best Friend throughout the day. Those who spend time with Him here and now will be dwelling in His presence then and there. By beholding Him day by day, we will gradually become more like Him in word and deed (2 Cor. 3:18; 1 John 2:6). We will live as He lived, and love as He loved because it will not be merely us, but Christ living in us generating such love (Gal. 2:20; Rom. 5:5).

It is no accident that God describes the "pleasures forevermore" at His "right hand." Guess what else is described in that same spot? Jesus, Himself (Mark 16:19). Of all the pleasures God has in store for you – "Eye hath not seen, nor ear heard, neither have entered into the heart of man" – your relationship with Christ, Himself will be the greatest pleasure of all.

May you come to know by experience the fullness of joy that is found in God's presence today, and for all eternity, at His right hand, share in those pleasures forevermore.

▲ ▲ ▲

It is time for your favorite journey. Billions of glistening trumpets herald the event. The angels themselves wield these horns atop the jasper walls of the Holy City. What is this glorious occasion? The Son of God is going to visit the outer reaches of His universe, and He's taking you with Him. As one who was "redeemed from among men" - alive at the Second Coming and translated to heaven without seeing death - you are among those who "follow the Lamb withersoever he goeth" (Rev. 14:3-4). During the eleventh hour of earth's history, you had shared in the trials of those who lived through the "time of trouble such as never was since there was a nation" (Dan. 12:1). By the blood of the Lamb, you overcame the Beast power and did not receive his mark. Therefore, on these occasions, you and the rest of the 144,000 accompany Christ on His journey. And you sing a special song; "and no man could learn that song but the hundred and forty and four thousand, which were redeemed from the earth" (Rev. 14:3).

Now you and the others in this group begin to sing the "song of Moses the servant of God, and the song of the Lamb" (Rev. 15:3).

True to prophecy, this song can only be sung by you and the others who were translated at the very end. It is a song about your unique experience: a song about the seemingly impossible victory that is available through Christ when He is formed within. This song glorifies Jesus and declares to the endless universe that fallen human beings had no righteousness and no power within themselves and that their only hope was through the life, death, and resurrection of the Savior.

And oh, how you love this song. It swells as earth's last generation streams into the city for the voyage. With each uplifted voice the song moves closer to its climax, yet it will not end until all have arrived for the journey. From near and far they approach the King. Some were already in the city, while others are returning from distant galaxies. All have the majestic chorus on their lips. Every singer has a unique part in this magnificent song. As Jesus listens to the hymn of praise, He can hear if a single voice is missing. His relationship with each one of you is special to Him. Each soul, so precious to His heart. His face reveals His boundless love, surpassing any father's love for his children, as the numbered throng continues to gather around Him.

You wonder where you're going this time, as you wait for the group to assemble. Jesus doesn't map out all of His plans for you, and that's just the way you like it. You know that wherever He takes you, it will be filled with fantastic surprises and new, glorious revelations of His character and omnipotence. In past journeys, you've watched Him create colossal new suns. You've seen quasars ignite at His command, and nebulas called forth from nothingness. You've accompanied Him from world to world across the distant galaxies as He blessed the inhabitants along the way.

Your own life has been blessed in infinite ways since the first day you gave yourself to Him. You've experienced "the mystery which hath been hid from ages and from generations" (Col. 1:26): that mystery being "Christ in you, the hope of glory" (verse 27). To have the Savior living His life in you by the Holy Spirit is the highest honor ever bestowed. Just to be in His presence provides a fullness of joy beyond anything you ever dreamed possible. He is the Life-giver, the sustaining power for everything that exists in the entire universe. In Him, all things consist (Col. 1:17). You admire and love His character. You follow Him wherever He goes.

Here in this place of eternal glory, you have contemplated with endless delight, the magnificence of both creative power and redeeming love. All of your faculties have been enlarged and exercised as you have undertaken new challenges to the intellect and imagination. Spiritual, physical, and mental capacities are continually increasing by the grace of God. The deeper secrets of the sciences, so long hidden from the wisest of earthlings, are now open to your mind as you search the wonders of the universe. Your highest ambitions are reached, and yet with each advance in knowledge new heights are presented and surmounted. Boredom has been forever blotted from existence as the science of God's love and power unfolds before you.

You stand at the center of the universe, beholding the Source of all life. The endless galaxies and solar systems follow their appointed paths circling the great throne of the Infinite One: the one Light that outshines all of the suns combined. In His presence, all else seems to disappear. At times such as these, it's just you and Him, creature and Creator, engulfed by an energy of love that surpasses all understanding. To experience this love is all that matters. To truly know God is indeed eternal life (John 17:3).

The last of the assembly have arrived. The song of Moses and the Lamb reaches its climax, and the final note includes every voice. All kneel in the presence of the Lamb. Silence surrounds the Savior, but soon His powerful, deep voice pronounces a blessing upon the group.

There is power in those words, and your very being is charged with new energy. All rise, eyes glued to Him as He speaks into existence the cloud which will transport you into the great beyond.

A fine, white mist begins to form and slowly swirls around the throng as it grows. The City rumbles below as the power of God gently lifts the entire mass off the glistening surface. An awesome wind churns the air around you. It sounds like a chorus of hurricanes. Chills dance along your spine as you experience the mighty force. You look down, and the cloud is bubbling, yet firm beneath your feet. In the spaces that open and close, you spot patches of the fire that has ignited under its base. The New Jerusalem now shines far beneath you. The cloud accelerates as it enters the outer limits of the atmosphere and now the earth itself begins to shrink in the distance.

These cosmic expeditions always remind you of your first incredible journey with Him so many millennia ago: the journey that rescued you from a dying planet called Earth and ushered you into that "exceeding good land" called Heaven. Although ages upon ages have since rolled by, your memory of that first trip has never dimmed. Your love for the Savior has only grown as your knowledge of Him has increased.

Your eyes gaze upon the One who took your place on Calvary, and you rejoice in the truth of what He did and who He is. The greatest thing about forever is the fact that it will be spent with Him. You wonder in amazement how anyone in the old earth could have doubted such love. How *you* could have ever doubted it. He is everything to you. You have found Him to be just what the Scriptures declared Him to be: "the Chiefest among ten thousand," "the Desire of all nations," and "the One altogether lovely" (Song 5:10,16; Hag. 2:7).

As the massive cloud traverses the cosmos, your anticipation grows. What glorious destination awaits you this time? What fresh displays of creative power will be exhibited on this trip? You take one more glance back as the New Earth fades from view. Only the light of Glory can be seen among the stars. Amidst that light is your real home, your priceless inheritance, the place where Jesus reigns. You actually live in that better land: the land of beginning again. So long spoken of, so long hoped for. Made from the hand of God, it cannot help but be true, lovely and pure. How great is the love that God has for you! For endless ages to come, you will contemplate this love. Throughout all eternity you will think on these things.

Thought Questions:

1. What is your main takeaway from this chapter? Why is it your main takeaway?

2. Why did Jesus say that knowing God is eternal life? Why wouldn't one who doesn't know God or care to know Him find Heaven appealing?

3. God invented pleasure and has pleasures for you at His right hand forevermore. What does this tell you about His character?

4. What do the concepts of "Christ **in you**, the hope of glory," (Col. 1:27) and "God hath given to us eternal life, and this life is **in His Son**," (1 John 5:11) tell you about God's promises of eternal life?

5. What did you learn about God's will for you in this chapter? What do you feel He's impressing you to start doing differently this week to walk more closely with Him?

EPILOGUE

Spending eternity with Jesus is the greatest gift that will ever be offered to you. Nothing is worth forfeiting that experience. "For what is a man profited, if he shall gain the whole world, and lose his own soul? or what shall a man give in exchange for his soul?" (Matt. 16:26).

Appreciation for anything grows with our familiarity with it. This is also true in our relationship with the Lord. Think about eternal realities often. Think about the Cross even more often. Slow down and spend some time at least once a week out in nature, God's glorious creation, examining the works of the Master Designer. If you don't have easy access to such a place, then take some time to enjoy the incredible view that God has given to all parts of the world: look up into the canopy of stars at night and contemplate the Creator of them all. It may seem like a small thing, but it truly makes a difference. In this steel and concrete world, our bond with nature is slowly breaking. A great blessing awaits those who would restore that bond. Many portions of this book were written after morning walks out in nature, where the trees, birds, and flowers brought to mind the eternal springtime of the land that awaits the children of God. It is a real land. Just as real as any place you have ever visited.

HIS THOUGHTS ON YOU

You've spent some significant time now reading and thinking about God and heavenly things. Never forget that the Lord thinks about you, too. His thoughts are on you every day. His love for you, His concern over things that frustrate you, His plans for your life, and all the things He longs to do with you as you spend eternity together: these are the things that fill His mind.

"But I am poor and needy; **yet the Lord thinketh upon me**: thou art my help and my deliverer," "How precious also are thy thoughts unto me, O God! How great is the sum of them!", "Many, O Lord my God, are thy wonderful works which thou hast done, and thy thoughts which are to us-ward: they cannot be reckoned up in order unto thee: **if I would declare and speak of them, they are more than can be numbered**" (Ps. 40:17; 139:17; 40:5).

Let me say again that God's thoughts toward you are more than can be numbered! You are not just a statistic; you are His son, His daughter. He thinks about you constantly. He is thinking of you right now. As was stated at the beginning of this book: God feels that Heaven will not be the same without you. Give yourself to the One who gave Himself for you and begin your eternal relationship with Him now.

WHEN THE ANGEL APPROACHES

Life in this world is temporary; it's all soon to pass away. In comparison to eternity, your life on this planet is but a split second. Your angel will likely approach you one day in the New Jerusalem and tell you that your time in heaven has just equaled your entire lifespan on earth. Yet it won't seem possible. You'll feel as though you just got there. And still, an eternity of increasing joy awaits you. Someone once said that true life begins after the Second Coming; our existence today is really just stepping up to the starting line. Where will you be in a billion years from this moment? Or will you still "be" at all? The choice is yours.

THE THREE VOTES

There are only three votes cast for your eternal destiny. God always votes for you to be in His Kingdom and Satan always votes for you to miss out on the Kingdom. Only you can cast the deciding vote. That vote means surrendering all to your Savior and receiving Him. Satan can never force the will, and God won't. He loved your freedom of choice so much He decided it would be better to have His own Son suffer an ignominious death on the Cross than to take away your free will. Exercise that will by giving yourself to Him today.

RECEIVING HIM

It has been my wish that all who have had enough interest in heaven to read this book would come to a knowledge of the boundless love that was manifested on the Cross of Calvary. I have hoped and prayed that the words on these pages would bring the love of Jesus into clear view for those who may have gotten lost in the fog.

Friend, have you received Him as your Savior? You can do it this very minute - right now. It's not at all too late. You have not "gone too far" for Him to hear and save you. Do you want to get to know Him on an intimate level? You can begin a new, life-changing relationship today. His hand is outstretched just waiting to pull you up out of the mire of sin. Perhaps you once knew the Lord, but the cares of this world, or maybe some painful trials, have pulled you away. Maybe you have failed so many times in your spiritual walk that you are ready to throw in the towel. Do believe He is still on your side. Do trust in the One who longs to forgive and delights in mercy. Come to Him now and determine to spend more time with Him than ever before. He *will* change your heart (Ezek. 36:26). You *will be* a new creature (2 Cor. 5:17). The Creator has promised.

CORAM DEO

Enoch walked with God, as we explored in chapter 23 "A Walk With Jesus." As you spend more time with God, you will find Him continually more attractive and eventually you will experience "Coram Deo" as Enoch did. The Latin term literally means something that takes place before the face of, or in the presence of God. So, one who lives "Coram Deo" is one who goes throughout their day, continually aware of the presence of God. They spend their entire life as though in the presence of God. It's what Andrew Murray called "practicing the presence of God." And why do they do it? Because there's no place that they'd rather be. Where God is, there is heaven. They want heaven now, and they receive it in His presence, moment by moment. They fully understand why Christ said that the Kingdom of God is within you (Luke 17:21). They completely relate to David saying there was no place he would rather be than in God's presence (Ps. 27:4). They know why Paul said prayer to God should be constant (1 Thess. 5:17). And like Moses, they refuse to wait to see God's glory (Ex. 33:18). If you receive Him, you too will decide you can no longer wait for heaven, and you will find yourself satisfied with nothing less than the presence of God. You will live a life of Coram Deo. Heaven will be yours now. The Second Coming will then be Moving Day, to take you to the throne of the one you've been with all along.

May the Lord bless you in your daily walk with Him, and may the God of peace sanctify you wholly so that with the apostle Paul you can proclaim for all eternity "I count all things but loss for the excellency of the knowledge of Christ Jesus my Lord" (Phil. 3:8).

THE MARTIN CWP BIBLE MARKING SYSTEM

Since first telling others about my simple CWP Bible Marking System, which has helped me get a clearer and more intimate picture of God, I've had quite a few people ask me to write it down somewhere so they could start practicing it themselves. The system is very simple. **CWP** stands for: **C** – Character; **W** – Will; **P** – Promise. Here's what that looks like:

You'll need just three things:

-A Bible

-3 Highlighters (yellow, blue and green - a 4th orange, optional)

-A Simple Prayer for guidance and enlightenment

Open your Bible to any part you'd like. You can start at Genesis and work your way through, or you can jump all around - whatever works best for you. I recommend those yearly Bible reading plans that divide the day's reading into selections from the Old Testament, New Testament, and Psalms. The variety makes it easier to stay with it. Hundreds of these plans can be found online for free.

Start reading, and when you come to a text or section of text that describes the **CHARACTER** OF GOD, highlight that in **YELLOW**.

A section of text that reveals GOD's **WILL** for your life (instructions, commandments, counsel), highlight in **BLUE**.

A section of text that is a **PROMISE** of GOD, highlight in **GREEN**.

Yellow = God's character
Blue = God's will for you
Green = God's promises

That's it! Nothing complicated. There will sometimes be overlap in these categories. Just select the color that you feel is the closest match for what those words mean to you.

Here's what the most famous text in the Bible would look like:

JOHN 3:16

"For God so **loved the world** that He **gave His only begotten Son** (God's Character – **Yellow**), that whosoever **believeth in Him** (God's Will for you – **Blue**) should **not perish but have everlasting life.**" (God's Promise – **Green**)

NOTE: You may want to have an ORANGE highlighter handy to mark interesting passages or facts you want to remember, which don't necessarily fall into one of the above three categories (I find red highlighters are often too dark). **Also, look for highlighters that mention no- or low-bleed, or "Bible markers," made for a Bible's thin pages. Gel or "dry" markers are a good option, as well. Experiment until you find the best markers for you.**

You will find that the Bible comes alive once again for you (even those ultra-familiar passages that you've heard or read so many times they seem to have lost their impact). It totally changed my walk with God. Try it and see what it can do for you.

You will gradually discover that spending time in God's Word, searching for revelations of His character, His will, and His promises is more fulfilling than TV, the Internet, movies, gaming, social media, or any of the other things that have consumed so much of our time. For lack of a better word, your time with God will become addicting!

Enjoy! Share with others!

FOR FURTHER STUDY

For good Bible studies, it's hard to beat the classic reference website **BibleSchools.com**, which has one of the widest varieties of Bible studies available in over 40 languages. Everything from basic intro studies, to studies focusing on the four gospels, to studies specifically for Jews exploring Christianity, to studies written *by* Christian native people *for* native people. They also have kids' Bible studies and topic search features.

WORLD'S BEST TAMALE PIE

Prepare Your Tastebuds!

For those who want to "taste and see" how amazing Doug's Tamale Pie is (see chapter 8, "The Marriage Supper"), here you go. And since there will be no death and therefore no meat dishes in heaven (Isa. 11:7; 65:25) here is a chance to start practicing a plant-based diet with a recipe that will send your taste buds into overdrive. *Because of the growing popularity of books and movies like **Forks Over Knives** and **In Defense of Food,** we know there will be variations with real/imitation meat and real/imitation cheese.

"Uncle Doug's Tamale Pie" by Doug Strawn

2 cans fat-free Hormel *Vegetarian Chili
1 can black olives, chopped
1 can chopped chilies
1 can tomato paste
3 cups shredded sharp cheddar *cheese
1 tsp. chili powder
Layers of 3 corn tortillas (about 30 tortillas)
3/4 can of *Vegeburger
1 8 oz. jar salsa

In a large mixing bowl mix all ingredients EXCEPT tortillas and *cheese

In crock pot put a bit of olive oil in the bottom and layer 3 tortillas then chili mixture. Then *cheese.

Repeat (keep layering) until to the top or ingredients run out (about 12-15 layers). Top with *cheese and cook on low for 4 hours.

Prepare your taste buds!

*based on diet preference of meat, vegetarian or vegan, use substitutes

For more great recipes, visit:

ForksOverKnives.com/recipes
MinimalistBaker.com

To find great plant-based restaurants
in your area, download the app:

Happy Cow

PREVIEW: BEFORE THE REAPING

The following is an excerpt from the closing chapter of Martin's forthcoming prequel on final events: ***Before the Reaping***.

"Behold, the Lord maketh the earth empty, and maketh it waste, and turneth it upside down, and scattereth abroad the inhabitants thereof...The earth mourneth and fadeth away, the world languisheth and fadeth away, the haughty people of the earth do languish."

-ISAIAH 24:1,4

"And it shall come to pass in that day, saith the Lord God, that I will cause the sun to go down at noon, and I will darken the earth in the clear day."

-AMOS 8:9

"And there was a great earthquake, such as was not since men were upon the earth, so mighty an earthquake, and so great...and every island fled away, and the mountains were not found."

-REVELATION 16:18,20

"And another angel came out of the temple, crying with a loud voice to him that sat on the cloud, Thrust in thy sickle, and reap: for the time is come for thee to reap; for the harvest of the earth is ripe."

-REVELATION 14:15

The ghostly white feathers of the approaching dove starkly contrast the black smoke rising from the distant skyline behind her. As she soars out of the burning seaside metropolis below, you notice a green leaf tucked securely in her beak. The plumes of smoke from the distant city ominously mingle with the gathering storm clouds overhead. You and six others have stopped to catch your breath, some sitting, some kneeling, some bending in exhaustion with hands on knees, transfixed by the apocalyptic scene. The small clearing, just over a jagged ridge in these mountain woods, can only be a brief resting spot. They're not far behind you.

Your heart pounds beneath your soaked shirt. Sweat pours off your face, dripping onto your dusty shoes. You cannot believe this is happening. Sure, you had read about it many times in the Bible but had always placed it far into the future. Events have transpired rapidly over the past two years, though, and now you're running for your lives. Last month the decree was passed that your type should be killed. Scholars had for years been predicting the edict, pointing to the fifteenth verse of Revelation thirteen. Not that long ago, both their dire predictions of social upheaval and lofty descriptions of Heaven seemed like distant fairy tales to you. Something to safely half-joke about and take seriously "someday." So much has changed. How wrong you were. Thankfully, your eyes had been opened in time by a friend among this weary group, who had truly understood you and actually cared. Little had you realized that one day you would be fleeing together, targeted by that fateful decree. Your only hope now is the Second Coming.

As you scan the quake-stricken city below, your eyes finally rest on the distant hillside graveyard outside the city. A loved one of yours was buried there, and you believe with all your heart you are about to see her again. Next, you spot the drab, gray building at the base of the burning skyline. The county jail. Two of your friends have already been captured and are incarcerated there. They also refused the mark. You send up another quick prayer for them as the distant flames continue to rise all around its plain, gray façade.

Your prayers are cut short by the growing, faint barking. Rest time is over. You peek over the edge of the ridge and spot the distant, yelping hounds straining at their leashes, pulling their armed masters up the hillside. Looks like about a quarter mile. They've closed the gap significantly since the last time you checked. You turn to face your onlooking friends and slowly shake your head, raising an eyebrow. There is no plan. Everyone knows it. Prayer is all you've got, but so far, it's proven more than enough.

The snowy dove is settling onto a tree up ahead, leaf still in her beak. Your small band has spent much of your time in these hills on your knees, agonizing with God for deliverance. He has answered prayer after prayer, but almost never in the way you expected. One prayer was for divine guidance through these unfamiliar foothills. Now this dove appears. *What's a dove doing in a place like this? And where'd she find a green leaf during this historic drought?* All eyes are on her as the distant barking grows louder. Someone suggests what you were thinking: There have never been wild doves anywhere near here, so is this another sign? And should you follow her? Is it even possible to follow a bird? You all agree to try, as three of your friends join you on the ridge, peering down at the approaching militia. Time to go.

As you turn to leave, the earth pounds violently beneath you, halting your escape and knocking your little group off your feet. Your body slams hard to the ground, with no time to brace yourself. You roll painfully onto your back and wipe the blood from your elbow, looking around at the others. Everyone seems okay. These aftershocks are hitting more frequently. The very earth you stand on - formerly "terra firma," *solid ground* - even fails you in this trying hour. Or does it? You crawl back to the ridge and see that the temblor that floored your group shook most of the pursuing soldiers back down the much steeper section of the hillside. Far beyond that, your eyes once again fall on the flaming, gray prison where your two friends await execution.

At this very moment, those friends, a young married couple, are pulling themselves back up to their knees behind steel bars. An empty cell separates them. They resume their prayers, claiming Psalm 102:20 but are immediately thrown to the concrete again by the violent aftershocks as the cell lights flicker and fail into blackness. The devastating jolt that knocks out the power, jars open their cell doors as rays of light from the gaping, cracked roof now flood the hallway. The building still rumbles on its foundations, concrete dust falling from every joint overhead as it sways violently.

The woman excitedly declares that it's time to go home as the two rush out of their cells. Her husband grabs her hand and plants a kiss on it before turning to make their escape. The roof is about to collapse, and they know it as they stumble down the crumbling hallway. Guards are flocking to any exit they can find, oblivious to the escaping prisoners.

The pair quickly charge past the collapsing eastern wing, which would have been their closest escape route. The front entry is now the clearest shot as they sprint toward freedom. The whole building rumbles and sways to the left as exposed studs and crumbling plaster pop and spray, giving way to the weight of the heaving structure. Another aftershock knocks the pair to the dusty floor, just inside the front entry, which is miraculously stable amid the shifting, cracking walls on all sides. It is coming down. The man jumps to his feet and pulls his wife up, scrambling for the doorway. The two lunge out of the building, engulfed by a mushroom of smoke and dust that erupts through the door as the building collapses behind them.

The aftershock may have bought you some time with the advancing militia, but the faint sound of helicopters can now be heard in the distance, and you know exactly what they're after. Or rather *who* they're after. Your little band instinctively gathers underneath the broad tree where the dove landed, concealing you from the advancing helicopters for now.

But soon giant circles of white light trail the ground around you. They're still looking. And not just for your little band. You know there are others in these mountains as well, fulfilling Isaiah's prediction that your refuge would be the mountains and "munitions of rocks" (Isa. 33:16). That same passage also told believers that their bread and water would be sure, a promise your group has presented to God repeatedly in these mountains.

As you scan the dark horizon to assess the growing number of armed choppers, dozens of tiny black spots can be seen migrating your way. Drones, for sure. Military drones, to seek out, identify and transmit your precise coordinates. Your stomach churns, blending emotions and hunger. You haven't eaten for several days in your weary flight, but God has maintained you. A young techie in your group suggests what type of drones these probably are, but it's hard to make out their faint profiles against the clashing, black clouds overhead.

As they advance toward your position, you finally realize that these are not drones at all, but ravens. And they have more in their beaks than a solitary green leaf! This is not the first time these birds have visited you, and you know what this means. Just as God sent ravens to feed Elijah when he was fleeing for his life, so now, He has sent these creatures. They drop their morsels on the ground, near the foot of the tree and disappear over the next mountain ridge. Dried out bread pieces and a few figs on stems. No banquet ever looked so delicious to you! You quickly thank God and squat down to scoop up a handful of the figs, passing them up to distribute among the famished group. Another friend steps out from under the tree to gather a few dusty pieces of bread when suddenly the ground spits up a hundred tiny dust clouds, accompanied by the distant crackling of gunfire.

The sound startles the ivory dove, and she quickly takes flight further up the sparsely wooded hillside. David comes to mind when facing Goliath. The three Hebrews come to mind when thrown into the fiery furnace. Esther comes to mind when risking her own life to save God's people. *If God is with us, who can be against us?* (Rom. 8:31) Your courage returns as you think about the power and providence of God. You grab the hand of a friend and pull her out from under the tree, bullets riddling the trunk behind you.

As you scramble up the hillside, your little company ultimately surmounts another small ridge, obscuring you once again from their range of fire for just a moment. Your view of the city inferno below becomes clear again, and you witness the last few seconds of the largest skyscraper plunging into the buildings behind it. In apparent slow-motion it tumbles, like a giant, fallen redwood, sending the smaller high-rises jolting to either side, shaken to their core. Three of them follow suit like gargantuan dominoes as two more teeter and implode straight down into dueling smoke mushrooms. You cannot believe what you are seeing and pray that your two cell-bound friends were protected through that cataclysmic scene. A peace slowly dissipates your concern. Somehow you know they're okay.

You wonder if fatigue is causing delusions now, as the terrain beyond the metropolis rises to form what looks like a giant earth-wave rolling toward the city. The remaining broken towers are lifted violently and strewn against one another in one, giant eruption of flame and smoke. Buildings are launched off their foundations and careen in every direction, leveling everything in sight. The mammoth earth-wave rolls on unhindered. Directly toward your mountain.

The dove is still in sight as it settles into a tree at the top of a sheer cliff above you. *How to follow her now?* Your group quickly looks around, everyone searching for an answer to the unspoken question. But no answer is discovered. And time's up.

You spin around to see the soldiers scrambling over that last ridge, urged on by unseen forces that even they don't understand. Your back is against the towering cliff, too sheer to ascend but the promise flashes inside you: "With God, I can scale a wall" (Ps. 18:29). A teenage girl among you is doubtlessly inspired by similar thoughts as she motions everyone to advance straight up the cliff, following the dove. But the distant cracking of gunfire scatters your group in all directions. You decide to follow the girl.

Slamming your hands onto the jagged cliff rocks, you begin your ascent, briefly exposing yourselves to the clear view of the advancing militia, who take full advantage of your position. Bullets carve a thousand holes into the rocks on all sides, and you could swear some of them are striking the stones directly in front of you as dirt and rock pelt your face.

Your arms are giving out. For the first time, you don't feel your physical strength can do this. The teenager has made it over, and she reaches down, calling for you to take her hand as bullets shred the rocks around you. *Her shouts are barely audible in the chaos. Does this young girl really think she can pull you up over that edge?* But you remember that you two are not alone, and human strength is meaningless now. God's promise echoes in your mind: "My strength is made perfect in weakness" (2 Cor. 12:9), as you let go of your grip on the wall and slap your hand in hers. She strains with all she's got, calling out for divine help as the dogs yelp far beneath you. You look straight up and see the pain on her face, her hair whipping violently in the wind as the lightning flashes angrily overhead and the storm howls like a million angry demons. Sticky blood from your elbow has reached your shoulder as your arm is jarred against the cliff wall. As she pulls, you gaze in disbelief as the cloudy sky above her suddenly turns to night, and then back to stormy daylight again. Everything is out of order.

"The Lord takes the earth and turns it upside down... and causes the sun to go down at noon" (Isa. 24:1; Amos 8:9)

In one, final yell and heave, she drags you up over the edge of the cliff and the two of you tumble onto the ground, safely out of range of the soldiers below. However, the sound of the growing storm had masked the roar of what was awaiting you just beyond the cliff.

The ridge you just surmounted has stranded the two of you at a section of the mountain that only provides a clearing of a few hundred feet and then ends at the base of another, much higher cliff. The dove now settles into plain sight on a nearby branch as three of the helicopters hover ominously above the peak. They've obviously spotted you. A separate group of soldiers appears from among the trees on the right, blocking your only viable route to freedom. One of the helicopters starts to descend. For the first time since you've been on the run, there is no apparent escape. Like the children of Israel, trapped with the Red Sea on one side and the sheer mountain on the other, you are destined to either be destroyed or witness a historical miracle of deliverance, which is what it would take to save you now.

The thunderous firmament is again turned to night, confusing the deranged soldiers and shielding you from their view. Gunfire pops randomly in your general direction, then stops. You know they have no target in sight. Suddenly light from above explodes all around you, and you look up, eager to witness divine deliverance. This is not your deliverance. The source is the circling helicopter, brightly exposing your position to gunfire. The distant soldiers now have a clear view, aiming directly at the two of you. You instinctively close your eyes in prayer and brace for the impact. No gunfire ensues. The soldiers frantically examine and pound their rifles amid the incessant barking. Several of them toss their guns to the ground, quickly brandishing their knives. Even worse.

Moses' famous line to the Israelites at the Red Sea plays loudly in your mind: "Stand still, and see the salvation of the Lord!" (Exodus 14:13). Looking back, it seemed easy to have faith; you knew how that story ended. But what would God do now? The ocean is more than a mile out. The barrier entrapping you is a mountain of solid granite, with soldiers closing in via your one trail out. The night sky again turns to day, and with seconds to spare, you glance up to the mountain range to the west, witnessing something that no human has ever seen: "And every island fled away, and the mountains were not found" (Rev. 16:20). The peaks themselves are slowly disappearing before your eyes, some sinking directly into the ground and others sheering off and sliding to the base, just as the prophecy said.

As dozens of demon-inspired warriors close in, knives drawn, another promise flashes into your mind. "If ye have faith, and doubt not...if ye shall say unto this mountain, Be thou removed, and be thou cast into the sea; it shall be done" (Matt. 21:21) and "Before they call, I will answer" (Isa. 65:24). *God is answering your prayer right now, before you even ask it.* Your friend bravely turns to face the onslaught, placing her fate in God's hands. By all human accounts it appears that you will now pay for your loyalty to God with your lives. You eye the great pinnacle overhead and the ocean to the east.

With hands clasped, you bow your head, and before the words come out of your mouth, the rolling aftershocks move upon the monolith ahead as the roar of tons of tearing rocks crushing one another rolls out into the valley all around. The massive peak of the mountain sheers off directly in front of you and begins to slide toward the sea, opening a way of escape for you. Some soldiers are frozen in their tracks as the top of the entire eastern peak of the mountain range tumbles away. Possessed and confused, many flee in all directions to escape the onslaught of landslides, spawned by the sheared mountain peak. Others, like Pharaoh and his army, continue their pursuit.

The newly-formed passageway has opened a way of escape not just for you and your friend, but dozens of others who had sought refuge in these mountains; they quickly emerge from the trees and crevasses to take advantage of the open chasm. Helicopters are closing in from behind, unhindered by the churning ground below.

Several of the faithful ones together recite another promise of God as they march through the rocky ravine:

"God is our refuge and strength, a very present help in trouble. Therefore will not we fear, though the earth be removed, and though the mountains be carried into the midst of the sea" (Ps. 46:1-2).

As the ground trembles all around you in the newly-formed valley, you see the trees to the west are mysteriously being pulverized. Snapping, collapsing, flattened to the ground as if attacked by a giant weed whacker. Your attention shifts to a thousand pounding thuds all around as you realize what is causing the destruction. Giant hailstones are smashing into the ground (Rev. 16:21), pulverizing everything in sight, but you and your friend remain untouched (Ps. 91:10). The three helicopters are pummeled overhead, and start to smoke and turn, plunging out of the sky. The ground beneath you swells as the earth shakes once again, in a destructive blow that knocks everyone to the ground. It is the churning of the final "great earthquake, such as not was since men were upon the earth" (Rev. 16:18).

Helicopter parts, branches, and giant hailstones rain down all around you. Debris is pelting you on all sides, but the hailstones never touch you. There is no hiding place now. All shelter is gone, save the protective hand of God. Running from the hailstones would be a fool's errand, and all the elements are now out of place. You lie face down amid the chaos, hands wrapped over your head, still secure from the devastation that surrounds you. Waiting for the deliverance you know is coming.

As the broken ground begins to settle from that last, giant quake, the destructive hailstones gradually taper off and cease. There is just a moment of stillness, settling over the completely devastated earth. It has an eerie feel to it, as this pause seems strangely like the quiet after the storm, but before something even bigger. Black clouds still roll and collide overhead, but otherwise there is a surreal stillness.

Emerging from the rubble, scattered war-torn believers stumble over the broken ground and again find one another. They gather into small companies of five or six and immediately commence to earnestly pray. Two friends from your previous group reunite with you and the teenage girl, as well as an elderly woman who's been on this ridge weeks longer than any of you, also sustained by God's promises. As you kneel and clasp hands, you notice the dove, landing nearby, green leaf still in her beak. A peace settles over your mind as you close your eyes in prayer.

As your praying group lifts your petitions to the Lord, a supernatural band of light encircles you. Angels are all around you, and though you don't see them, you can sense it, as did Elisha in his time of need (2 Kings 6:15-17). You know they are ministering spirits that have been protecting you in love. Little do you realize how soon you will be meeting them, particularly your own guardian.

In the distance, you notice a few surviving soldiers, scattered and clearly unsure what to do next. They may yet try to harm you, or they could simply try to survive. It is no longer a concern of yours. Despite the evil agencies pressing them forward, they realize that the battle is over. Perhaps the inevitability of that fact had given them their nothing-to-lose mindset. Or perhaps they had lost their sense of reason long ago, like crazed dictators and their legions of followers in every oppressive age. Whatever the case, it's a tragedy, and you pity them. One day they will see, in panoramic view, just where they went off track (Eccl. 12:14; Matt. 12:36; 2 Cor. 5:10; Rev. 20:12). They'll recall each time the Holy Spirit impressed them with a gentle, "This is the way, walk ye in it," and the tender warning, "If ye will hear His voice, harden not your hearts" (Is. 30:21; Heb. 3:15). Even with these hardened warriors, God can declare "What more could I have done?" (Isa. 5:4), since He's "not willing that any should perish, but that all should come to repentance" (2 Pet. 3:9). The Cross demonstrated all of this like nothing else ever could. God's way really is best, because God is Love.

Now, there is no more running. No more hiding. And you fully believe, no more waiting. The end-time prophecies have now all been fulfilled, save one: the appearing of the King. God has sustained you, His strength was made perfect in your weakness, and you are about to go home. "He that shall endure unto to the end, the same shall be saved" (Matt. 24:13). Life on this old earth is over. Today will be Moving Day. As your little circle squeezes hands in prayer, a peace that passes understanding rests upon you. Although you see very little good in your life, you see the perfect life of Christ covering you. And by God's grace, the life of "Christ in you" has fought a good fight, finished the course, and kept the faith (Col. 1:27; 2 Tim. 4:7). Your little group will close your time on earth in this very spot, watching and praying.

You know what you're watching for: "The sign of the Son of Man... coming in the clouds of heaven, with power and great glory" to take you home (Matt. 24:30). The strange, white dove that has appeared so many times now settles right beside your praying group. A beacon of peace amid the destruction. As your prayers continually ascend, your heart races in anticipation of seeing that cloud in the sky. Your petitions are suddenly interrupted by the cry of a friend. "Look, look!" he shouts. You immediately open your eyes and lift them to the eastern sky. Chills tingle your spine as you see it in the farthest edges of the firmament, beyond the angry, black clouds. It appears dark and tiny at first, but gradually grows larger and brighter as it slowly moves toward earth...

...To be Continued in *Heaven, Think On These Things*

WHEN WE ALL GET TO HEAVEN

By E.E. Hewitt

Sing the wondrous love of Jesus,
Sing His mercy and His grace;
In the mansions bright and blessed
He'll prepare for us a place.

> Refrain:
> When we all get to heaven,
> What a day of rejoicing that will be!
> When we all see Jesus,
> We'll sing and shout the victory!

While we walk the pilgrim pathway,
Clouds will overspread the sky;
But when trav'ling days are over,
Not a shadow, not a sigh.

Let us then be true and faithful,
Trusting, serving every day;
Just one glimpse of Him in glory
Will the toils of life repay.

Onward to the prize before us!
Soon His beauty we'll behold;
Soon the pearly gates will open;
We shall tread the streets of gold.

Sheet music and accompanying audio
available free at Hymnary.org

ABOUT THE AUTHOR

Carl Martin is an optimist, thanks to the promises of God. But this was not always so. Immediately after his high school graduation, he took a prodigal journey away from both his hometown and his spiritual life. He moved to Southern California in pursuit of a career in Hollywood, where he studied acting and screenwriting and soon landed an agent. But through a providential series of events, his eyes were opened, and he dedicated his life and abilities to serving Christ and spreading the gospel. Professionally, he has trained hundreds of managers and employees in EEOC and government compliance, leadership, time management, goal-setting, and interpersonal development in corporate America. Carl has spoken at universities, churches, camp meetings, schools, retreats, and other events across the United States and overseas. He has held speaking tours in Jinotega, Nicaragua and in eight cities along the eastern coast of Australia in 2016. He currently lives near Chattanooga, Tennessee with his wife Coleen and their daughter Darby. His son Daltry now lives in Los Angeles. For speaking schedule and inquiries visit HeavenThinkOnTheseThings. com.

Made in the USA
Columbia, SC
16 January 2021